高等学校"十二五"规划教材·科技英语系列

新编科技英语写作教程

主 编 姜珊 严宁 徐蕾

哈尔滨工业大学出版社

内 容 简 介

本书与《新编科技英语翻译教程》和《新编科技英语写作教程》相配套书中内容。本书侧重于提高作者的科技英语写作能力,实用性较强。从实用性角度出发,从语法、学术论文写作一直到实用文体写作,由浅入深,层层推进。

本书可作为大学本科高年级学生及研究生教材,也可供专业教师及广大科技工作者使用。

图书在版编目(CIP)数据

新编科技英语写作教程/姜珊,严宁,徐蕾主编. —哈尔滨:
哈尔滨工业大学出版社,2012.12
ISBN 978-7-5603-3757-9

Ⅰ.①新… Ⅱ.①姜… ②严… ③徐… Ⅲ.①科学技术-英语-写作-高等学校—教材
Ⅳ.①H315

中国版本图书馆 CIP 数据核字(2012)第 186145 号

策划编辑　郝庆多
责任编辑　王桂芝　段余男
出版发行　哈尔滨工业大学出版社
社　　址　哈尔滨市南岗区复华四道街10号　邮编150006
传　　真　0451-86414749
网　　址　http://hitpress.hit.edu.cn
印　　刷　哈尔滨工业大学印刷厂
开　　本　787mm×960mm　1/16　印张 18.5　字数 430 千字
版　　次　2012年12月第1版　2012年12月第1次印刷
书　　号　ISBN 978-7-5603-3757-9
定　　价　40.00元

(如因印装质量问题影响阅读,我社负责调换)

前　言

信息化和全球化促使国际之间的交流日趋频繁,对于从事科学研究的学者来说。有了更多的机会把自己的科研成果展现给世界。近年来,我国越来越多的科研人员、高校教师、硕士生和博士生有机会在国际学术会议上宣读论文、在国际学术期刊上发表论文,这就要求除了具备高水平的科研能力外,还需要有高水平的英语科技论文写作能力,而这也正是本书编写的初衷。

本书由三部分构成,第一篇是科技英语语法,由黑龙江科技学院的姜珊编写,共14.5万字,该部分选取科技英语写作中出现率较高的语法现象,包括词法、时态、语态、非谓语动词,从句及虚拟语气等。第二篇是科技英语学术论文写作,由哈尔滨工程大学的严宁编写,共14万字,该部分包括撰写论文前的准备工作、题目和署名、摘要、正文、致谢和参考文献,并对这几方面对学术论文写作进行了比较全面的讲解,为读者提供了一个较为全面的论文写作模式。第三篇实用科技应用文写作,由哈尔滨理工大学的徐蕾编写,共14.5万字,该篇以国际通用的书写规范为标准,详细讲述书信、报告、项目申请、问卷等应用文体的写作构成、特点、标准及流程,配有丰富的实例和讲解,具有很强的应用及参考价值。相信对于科技工作者来说,必将起到积极的引导作用。

本书内容丰富,涵盖面广,涉及计算机、通信、生物技术、数学、物理、化学等领域。编写过程中引用了最新的科研成果,参考和引用了有关论著、文章及其他文字资料,文中未能一一注明,在此向有关作者表示感谢。由于编者水平有限,疏漏或不当之处在所难免,敬请同行专家及广大读者提出宝贵意见。

编者

2012年6月

目 录

第一篇 语 法 篇

第一章 词 法 1
  第一节 冠 词 1
  第二节 名 词 7
  第三节 形容词、副词 17
  第四节 动 词 24
  第五节 连 词 28
  第六节 介 词 30
  第七节 与数字有关的表达 35

第二章 时态和语态 43
  第一节 时 态 43
  第二节 被动语态和主动语态 50

第三章 非谓语动词 58
  第一节 动词不定式 58
  第二节 分 词 61
  第三节 动名词 65

第四章 从 句 69
  第一节 定语从句 69
  第二节 状语从句 75
  第三节 同位语从句 79
  第四节 名词性从句 80

第五章 虚拟语气 86
练习答案 88

第二篇　学术论文写作

- 第六章　撰写论文前的准备工作 ... 101
- 第七章　科技英语论文的题目和署名 ... 116
- 第八章　科技英语论文摘要的撰写 ... 125
- 第九章　论文正文的撰写 ... 141
- 第十章　论文致谢和参考文献的撰写 ... 174

第三篇　实用科技写作

- 第十一章　实用文体写作前的准备 ... 186
- 第十二章　简　历 ... 191
  - 第一节　标准简历 ... 191
  - 第二节　电子简历 ... 196
  - 第三节　功能简历 ... 197
- 第十三章　书　信 ... 202
  - 第一节　正式书信的基本原则 ... 202
  - 第二节　书写的分类 ... 203
  - 第三节　一般书信的格式 ... 203
  - 第四节　信封的写法 ... 210
  - 第五节　书信的特殊形式 ... 211
  - 第六节　传　真 ... 218
  - 第七节　其他各种类型的书信 ... 220
- 第十四章　报　告 ... 242
  - 第一节　报告的定义 ... 242
  - 第二节　报告的分类 ... 242
  - 第三节　报告的组成 ... 242
  - 第四节　各类报告的具体分析 ... 251
- 第十五章　项目申请 ... 269
- 第十六章　问　卷 ... 285
- 参考文献 ... 288

第一篇　语法篇

第一章　词　法

第一节　冠　词

英语中的冠词有两类，不定冠词与定冠词，形式有三种：a，an 和 the。作为一种虚词，冠词本身不能独立使用，只能附着在一个名词上帮助说明这个名词的含义。

1. 不定冠词 a，an

（1）一般情况，单数的可数名词前一定要用冠词，当泛指时用不定冠词。

An equation is **a** statement of the equality between two equal numbers or number symbols.

等式是关于两个数或数的符号相等的一种陈述。

The platforms extend to **a** depth of over 100 feet under the sea.

平台深入海底 100 英尺。

Every processor comes with **a** unique set of operations such as ADD, STORE, or LOAD that represent the processor's instruction set.

每一个处理器都具有一个专门的操作集，例如："加"、"存储"或"下载"等，代表着这个处理器的指令集。

The lathe should be set on **a** firm base.

车床应安装在坚实的底座上。

Such a ring of conductors is called **an** electric circuit.

导体的这样一个环路称为电路。

（2）使用 a 或 an 的原则是根据其后所跟名词的第一个音素的读音，若为辅音，则用 a；若为元音，则用 an，并不是以第一个字母拼写为准。

a computer　　　　　　　　　　**an** orange

a university　　　　　　　　　　**an** hour

注意　对于专业术语的缩写词，也应按照上述原则，即以词首字母的发音来判断，如：

an FMC(flexible manufacturing cell)柔性制造单元

an LWR(light water reactor)轻水反应堆

an SRAM(static random access memory)静态随机存取存储器

然而,有一些缩写专有名词,如 ROM,RAM,laser,radar 等,由于拼读发音原则,即把这些缩写词当成一个词来读,这时,不定冠词就要使用 a 而不是 an 了。

(3)说明类属关系时,在表语或同位语的名词前加不定冠词。

Collagen, **a** fibrous protein found in connective tissue, bone and cartilage, basically holds the body together.

胶原蛋白是存在于结缔组织、骨质和软骨中的纤维蛋白质,它的基本作用是将人体各组织结合在一起。

A shaft is **a** rotating or stationary member, usually of circular cross section.

轴是一个转动或静止的杆件,其横截面通常是圆形。

A processor is **a** functional unit that interprets and carries out instructions.

处理器是一个翻译和执行指令的控制单元。

(4)当形容词修饰一单数的可数名词时,如果该形容词又被 so, as how, however, too 等修饰时,不定冠词要置于这一形容词之后;遇到 quite 和 rather 时,多半置于其后;遇到 such, many 和感叹句中的 what 时,也只能置于其后。

Quantum is such **a** successful theory that it supplies methods of accurately calculatiy the results of diverse experiments.

量子学是一种成功的理论,它提供了多种方法精确地计算不同实验的结果。

However difficult **a** problem was, he tried his best to solve it.

无论问题有多难,他都尽全力去解决。

2. 定冠词 the

(1)主要和一个名词连用,表示某个特定的人或事物。

①上文中已经提到过的或同一句中第二次提到的。

The function of mechanism is to transmit or transform motion from one rigid body to another as part of the action of a machine.

机械结构是机械运动的一个部分,它的功能是把运动从一个刚体传递或转换到另一个刚体。

An SRAM is an array of addressable flip-flops. **The** array can be configured as such that the data comes out in single bit, 4 bit, 8 bit, and etc.

SRAM 是可寻址的触发器列阵。该列阵可配置成 1 位、4 位、8 位等数据格式。

②带有后置修饰语的前面,一般用定冠词。

Various speeds may be obtained by **the** use of large and small pullers.

利用大小皮带轮可以获得不同的转速。

③世界上独一无二的。

The sea covers nearly three-quarters of the world's surface.

海洋几乎覆盖地球表面的四分之三。

(2)形容词和副词的最高级前要有定冠词。

The Hammer is **the** most economical type of equipment for generating load and energy necessary to carry out a forging process, provided that the material being forged can support high deformation velocities.

如果锻造材料能够承受很高的变形速度,锻锤就是生成锻造工艺所必需的载荷和能量的最经济的设备。

Perhaps **the** most influential of the early computerlike devices were the Electronic Numberical Integrator and Computer, or ENIAC.

也许早期最具影响力的类似计算机的装置应该是电子积分计算机,或简称 ENIAC。

(3)序数词前要用定冠词。

The second step in the kinematic analysis of mechanisms is to determine the number of degree of freedom of the mechanism.

机械结构运动分析的第二步是确定机械结构的自由度数。

Although invented in 1948, **the** first all-transistor computer did not become available until 1959.

虽然发明于1948年,但生产第一台全晶体管计算机直到1959年才成为现实。

(4)专有名词前加定冠词的特殊情况。

通常来说,专有名词前不加冠词。

人名:Liu Xiang, Mrs. Wang, Einstein, Edison

地名:Hongkong, Germany

其他:February, Tuesday

但是,如果这个专有名词是由普通名词和另外一些词构成的,其前多数要加定冠词。

①某些国名。

the People's Republic of China 中华人民共和国

the United States of America 美利坚合众国

the United Kingdom 联合王国

②某些机构组织。

the United Nations 联合国

the Ministry of Education 教育部

the State Department 美国国务院

③报纸、会议、条约等的名称。

the Washington Post 华盛顿邮报

the Atlantic Pact 大西洋公约

④大洋、海、河、山脉前。

the Yangtze River 长江

the Himalayas Mountain 喜马拉雅山
the Pacific Ocean 太平洋
注意 五大洲前不加定冠词 如:Asia,America,Europe
　　　 湖名前一般不加定冠词:如 Lake Baikal,Lake Success
(5)人体器官、组织和解剖部位名称前一般要加定冠词。

the small intestine 小肠　　　　　**the** stomach 胃
the esophagus 食管　　　　　　 **the** left atrium 左心房
the cerebellum 小脑

(6)表示某个参数的单位时一般要用定冠词。

the Unit of resistance is the ohm. 电阻的单位为欧姆。
the Unit of length is the meter. 长度的单位是米。

3. 省略或不加冠词的情况
(1)不可数名词,表示一般概念的物质名词及抽象名词前,通常不加冠词。
Hydrogen is lighter than oxygen. 氢气比氧气轻。
Water boils at 100 ℃. 水在一百摄氏度沸腾。
We can't live without air. 没有空气我们就不能活。
Knowledge begins with practice. 认识从实践开始。
(2)可数名词复数表示一类的时候,通常不加冠词。
Lions will give birth to tigers in an experiment that could revolutionize the preservation of endangered species.
狮子要生老虎的这项实验可能会使濒危物种保护发生革命性的变革。
Contact sensors may be further subdivided into tactile sensors and force-torque sensors.
接触式传感器可进一步分为触觉传感器、力和扭矩传感器。
(3)书籍、论文的标题前冠词可以省略,如果标题是可数名词,通常用复数形式,也可用定冠词加单数名词。
(An)Introduction to Data Structure. 数据结构介绍。
(The)Research on Low-pass Filters. 低通滤波器的研究。
(A)Comparison of DSP and VSP. 数字信号处理和模拟信号处理的比较。
(A)Study of Carbon Nanotubes. 对碳纳米管的研究。
Microprocessors 微处理器
The Railroad Track 铁路轨道
(4)图示说明文字中一般可省略冠词。
Figure 3(The)complex function of(an)RC low-pass filter. 低波过滤器复函数。
Figure 13-3(The)overall design flow for RTL synthesis-based design.

基于 RTL 综合设计的整个设计流程。

Figure 6-2(The) development phase of(the) software life cycle. 软件生命周期的开发阶段。

(5)方程、表达式、公式、图表、章节、页码等后跟数字表示"第……"时，其前面不得加冠词。

It is possible to buy a single integrated circuit containing, say, four identical gates, as shown in Figure 13-1.

我们可以买到一片如图 13-1 所示的集成电路，它包含四个完全一样的门电路。

The principle properties are given in Table 3-2, where a, b, and c are any elements of a Boolean algebra.

主要特性由表 3-2 给出，其中 a, b 和 c 是布尔代数中的任意元素。

The key to Exercise 7 is on Page 56.

练习 7 的答案在 56 页。

This question was described in Section 4.3.

这个问题在第 4.3 节已经讲过了。

This point will be discussed in Chapter 4.

这个问题将在第 4 章加以讨论。

(6)表示职位的名词或者独一无二的人之前一般不用冠词。

Steve Riggio, vice chairman of Barns and Noble, can see a time in the near future when there will be an electronic version of virtually every book in print.

巴尼斯和诺布尔公司副主席斯蒂夫里吉奥能够预见到，在不久的将来的某个时候，几乎每本印刷的图书都将有一个电子版本。

如果不是独一无二的，则必须加上冠词。

The first president of Stevens was Henry Morton, a distinguished scientist and linguist.

史蒂文斯的首任校长是亨利莫顿，一位杰出的科学家和语言学家。

Exercise

练习一

把下列词组译为英语。

左权将军　　　　　　　　古希腊
东南亚　　　　　　　　　远东
西印度群岛　　　　　　　昆仑山脉
联合王国　　　　　　　　美利坚合众国
日内瓦协定

练习二

在下列句子的空白处填上适合的冠词。

1. _____ typical room has _____ height of 2 or 3 meters.
2. _____ Volume 1 can be used as a text for undergraduate course. _____ Volume 2 can be used as a text for graduate.
3. There are 60 minutes in _____ hour.
4. _____ Electricity is widely used in industry and agriculture.
5. _____ journal bearing, in its simplest form, is _____ cylindrical bushing made of _____ suitable material and containing properly machined inside and outside diameters.
6. Of _____ voltage is applied across _____ terminals of _____ closed circuit, _____ electric current will flow in _____ circuit.
7. _____ resistance of _____ given section of _____ electric circuit is equal to _____ ration of its voltage to _____ current through this section of _____ circuit.
8. _____ Europe and _____ America are separated by _____ Atlantic Ocean.
9. _____ Pearl River flows into _____ South China Sea.
10. _____ two islands lying to _____ west of _____ continent of _____ Europe are called _____ British Isles. _____ larger of the two, consisting of _____ England, _____ Scotland and _____ Wales, is known as _____ Great Britain, _____ smaller, _____ Ireland.
11. In _____ opinion of _____ Capitain Brown the shortest way to _____ Philippines would be through _____ Panama Canal.
12. One of _____ most crucial stages in _____ exposition of any subject in _____ physics is _____ choice of nation.
13. This book is _____ product of teaching classical mechanics on both _____ undergraduate and _____ graduate levels intermittently over _____ past 20 years.
14. __1__ Electricity is generated at __2__ large power stations by __3__ big machined known as __4__ generators. They are, in fact, __5__ large dynamos, and are driven by __6__ powerful engines which get its power from __7__ water or __8__ steam. __9__ electricity which gets its power from __10__ water is known as __11__ hydro-electricity. __12__ flow of __13__ electricity along __14__ wire may be compared to __15__ flow of __16__ water along __17__ pipe, and consequently it is known as __18__ current.
15. If you consider _____ water flowing along _____ pipe, _____ volume of _____ water passing _____ certain point in _____ given time is similar to _____ electric cur-

rent. _____ Electric current is measured in _____ amperes.

16. _____ pressure of _____ water in _____ pipe may be compared to _____ electric potential. _____ Potential is measured in volts.

17. _____ resistance of _____ wall of _____ pipe to _____ water current may be compared to _____ resistance of _____ wire to _____ electric current; i. e. _____ narrow pipe offers more resistance than _____ wide pipe, and similarly, _____ thin wire offers more resistance than _____ thick wire of _____ same metal. _____ Resistance is measured in _____ ohms.

练习三

翻译下列句子。

1. 计算机系统是由计算机和一些外部设备构成的。
2. 化学家们在天平上计量质量。
3. 这是一个 n 值的函数。
4. 该晶体管的集电极必须连接到电源的正极。
5. 系统控制是一门跨学科的科目。
6. 信息就是知识。
7. 空气是物质。
8. 基尔霍夫定律(Kirchhoff's rules)对分析网络很有帮助。
9. 图6.3画出了数字计算机的方框图。
10. 这一点将在第五章加以讨论。
11. 数学是科学上非常有用的工具。

第二节 名 词

科技英语的特点要求作者用最准确、最简练的语言来表述自己的思想,传达大量的真实、客观的信息。而名词和由其构成的一系列名词化结构正是科技英语中最主要的信息载体。科技英语中大量名词和名词化结构的使用,是其区别于普通英语的标志之一。

1. 名词的数

(1) 不规则的复数。

英语中有少量名词存在不规则的复数形式,通常是一些拉丁词源或外来词源。下面列举一些科技英语中名词的不规则复数变化。

单数	复数	单数	复数
antenna	antennae	index	indexes, indices（数学）
apparatus	apparatus, apparatuses	locus	loci
appendix	appendixes, appendices	matrix	matrices, matrixes（用于媒体）
axis	axes	maximum	maximums, maxima
bacterium	bacteria	medium	mediums, media
basis	bases	millennium	millennia
corpus	corpora	minimum	minimums, minima
criterion	criteria, criterions	mitochondrion	mitochondria
datum	data	phenomenon	phenomena, phenomenons
diagnosis	diagnoses	prognosis	prognoses
erratum	errata	species	species
focus	focuses, foci	schema	schemata
formula	formulas, formulae	spectrum	spectra, spectrums
fungus	fungi, funguses	stratum	strata
genus	genera	symposium	symposia, symposiums
hypothesis	hypotheses	taxon	taxa

（2）作前置修饰语的名词的数。

①名词作名词的前置修饰语时,常用其单数形式。

machine language 机器语言　　　　tooth malocclusion 牙齿错位咬合

a cigarette light 打火机　　　　　　computer monitor 计算机显示屏

②数词－名词的前置修饰语中,名词用单数形式,这种前置修饰语中的名词一般多为度量、衡量等单位。

20-mile track 20 英里长的铁路　　　an eight-year-old boy　八岁大的男孩

15-second countdown　15 秒倒数　　10-million-electron-volt energy level 10 MeV 的能级

③数词＋名词的前置修饰语中,因为没有连字符,名词多用复数形式。

15 seconds countdown　15 秒倒数

10 million electron volts energy level 10 MeV 的能级

（3）几种特殊的名词复数形式。

①缩略词的复数。

如果缩略词为小写字母,为避免造成误解,其复数形式要用 's 来表示,若是大写字母,其复数形式用 's 或 s 表示。

This two emf's/EMF's/EMFs are equal.　　这两个电动势是相等的。

Manufacturers provide a large variety of IC's/ICs designed to effect proper interfacing.

制造商提供了用于实施适当接口的各种各样的集成电路。

②字母及数字的复数。

a. 字母及数字的复数多用 s 表示。

Special resonant component can have Q's as high as several thousand.

特殊的谐振部件的 Q 值可以高达几千。

The computer can interpret the same binary configuration of 0's and 1's as data or as an instruction.

计算机能把 0 和 1 的同样的二进制排列翻译成数据或一条指令。

b. 当数字小于 1 时，所修饰的名词需用复数形式。

In this case, both the resistor and the source absorb 0 watts.

在这种情况下，电阻器和电源吸收的功率均为零瓦特。

The odometer of a car has a resolution of 0.1 miles.

汽车里程表的分辨率为 0.1 英里。

③缩略词的复数形式应置于点之前。

Figs(1-2) and (1-3) show this process. 图(1-2)和图(1-3)说明了这一过程。

The answer to all these exercises are given on pp. 11 to 14. （注：page 这个词的缩略形式为 p. 但其复数形式不是 ps., 而应该是 pp.）

所有这些习题的答案都列在第 11~14 页上。

2. 名词的格

特殊的所有格形式。对于所有者共有的所有格形式是只在最后一个姓氏后加上 's 而构成，如：

Bush and Marshall's result Chang and Li's research

3. 合成名词

所谓合成名词（又称名词串）可以定义为两个或更多的名词（还可以另加必需的前置和后置修饰词），共同构成一个概念，即一起表示"一个名词"的概念。这种合成词也可称为名词性词组，在科技英语中主要充当句子的主语、宾语和补语。它用一种简单的结构来传递大量的信息，这正符合科技英语的要求，因此科技英语中合成名词占有很大的比例。合成名词分为基本合成名词和扩展合成名词。

（1）基本合成名词。

基本合成名词一般由两个名词构成一个新名词，核心词是第二个词，第一个名词是限定词。两个词在逻辑上可以为主谓关系，也可以为动宾关系，还可以起到充当补语和状语的作用。

主谓关系：

sound vibration 声震动　　　　　water flow 水流
laser testing 激光焊接　　　　　electron bunching 电子聚束
search engine 搜索引擎　　　　　clamp device 紧固装置
interlocking device 连锁系统　　charging resistor 充电电阻器

动宾关系：
load increase 负载增加
word processing 文字处理
phase inverter 倒相器
mounting screw 安装螺丝
break jack 切断塞孔

impulse test 冲击试验
air conditioning 空调
marker selector 标志选择器
reducing elbow 缩接弯头
drive pulse 驱动脉冲

充当补语的作用：
coupling coil 耦合线圈
drop method 滴入法

focusing circuit 聚焦电路
search key 检索关键字

充当状语的作用：
end shielding 末端屏蔽
random sampling 随机采样
push-pull detector 推拉式铲运机
field study 现场研究

parallel feeding 并联馈电
emergency wiring 紧急备用线路
night indication 夜间显示
digit drive 数字驱动

（2）扩展合成名词。

扩展合成名词是多重名词合成名词或多重形容词与名词的合成，在两个名词合成为一个新词的基础上扩展，可以是三个或更多的词合成为一个新词，来表达一个完整的概念。

①前置修饰语。

前置是指在基本合成名词前加上形容词或名词，在形容词前加上副词或形容词。

optimal basic feasible solution 最优基本可行解
plane analytic geometry 平面解析几何
membrane proximal region 病毒包膜临近区

atomic force microscope 原子力显微镜
cellular base station 蜂窝状基站

对于两个或两个以上形容词共同修饰名词的情况，应该格外注意的是修饰词的排序问题。一般来说，排序原则是关系越紧密、限制性越直接的修饰语，应该越靠近核心词。可以记一个形容词排列顺序口诀，即：

"大哥限描大，二哥形龄颜，小弟籍物类，同站名词前。"

分别解释为：

限：限定词。the, my, a, this…

描：描绘性形容词。brave, beautiful, lovely, nice…

大：大小、高低、长短等形容词。big, large, small…

形：形状。round, square…

龄：年龄大小、新旧、年代等。young, old, new…

颜：颜色。red, blue, green…

籍：国籍、地区、出处。Chinese, America, Japanese…

物：物质材料的形容词。golden, wooden, wax…
类：表示类别、用途。medical, chemical, writing…

a pretty little square old black Japanese wooden writing desk
一个旧的很漂亮的黑色的日本式的方形木制小写字桌

a beautiful short new red Chinese woolen coat
一件漂亮的中式新的短装红羊毛外套

需要指出的是，这种方法在使用上有局限性。用作修饰语的名词（组合）必须能说明主导名词所固有的技术属性，所构成的词组可以看成是一个技术术语。如果不属于这种情况，应该避免使用一串名词，不能随意堆积。因为这样一长串的名词组合表达力较弱，语言节奏也弱，往往会令读者费解。而此时，就应考虑后置修饰语的使用。

②后置修饰语。

后置修饰语往往是采用适当的介词，把某一部分关系不紧密的前置修饰语变成后置修饰语，以加强表达力。

the Buriat people of Siberia　　西伯利亚的布里亚特人
arrays of nanomechanical devices　　纳米力学器件阵列
differential equation of first order　　一阶微分方程
elimination by addition or subtraction　　加减消元
American National Standard Code for Information Interchange 美国信息交换标准代码
PCI extensions for Instrumentation　　面向仪器系统的 PCI 扩展
Complex organisms with renewable tissues　　具有可再生组织的复杂生物
Regulations on Safety and Protection of Radioisotopes and Radiation-emitting Devices
放射性同位素与射线装置安全和防护条例
Supervision and administration system on the safety and security of radioactive sources
放射源安全与保安监管体制

4. 名词的修饰语

前面提到过，科技英语中谓语较短，而主语和宾语较长，因此句子中的名词或合成名词往往要在其前后加上修饰语来起到修饰限定的作用。名词+修饰语的搭配一般有以下几种形式。

（1）名词+动词不定式（短语）。

There are a large number of problems, since the ability to systematically solve a wide variety of problems is one of the goals of a course in mechanics.

书中有大量的练习题，因为系统地求解各类习题的能力是力学课程的目的之一。

Forming techniques, Fig. 4, use a shaping device and pressure to cause material to take on a new size and shape.

成形工艺，如图4所示，采用成型设备和压力使材料获得新的尺寸和形状。

The first book **to treat** transient stresses at all fully was *stress waves in solids* by H. Kolsky,1953.

第一本全面阐述瞬态应力的专著是 Kolsky 于 1953 年出版的《固体中的应力波》。

Separating removes excess material **to produce** the desired size, shape, feature, and surface finish.

切削工艺去除多余的材料,可获得预期的尺寸、形状、特征和表面光洁度。

From the beams in our homes to the wings of an airplane, there must be an appropriate melding of materials, dimensions, and fastenings **to produce** structures that will perform their functions reliably for a reasonable cost over a reasonable lifetime.

从家里的房梁到飞机的机翼,我们必须用合适的材料、尺寸和连接件来组成这些构件,以使其可靠地完成相应功能,而且价格合理,寿命长久。

Geotechnical specialists perform soil experiments **to determine** if the earth can bear the weight of the project.

岩土专家进行土工试验来判断地层是否能承受工程项目的重量。

(2)名词+分词(短语)。

The force **acting on** the cutting plane as defined above usually also has component in the direction of the plane itself(i.e. lying in the plane). This component is called the shearing force.

在上述定义下的作用于截面上的力,通常在平面本身所在方向(即在平面内)也有分量。这一分量称为剪切力。

A material **having** the same elastic properties at all points within the material is said to be homogeneous. A material **having** different elastic properties at different points within it is nonhomogeneous.

若某种材料在其上所有点皆具有相同的弹性,则称为是均匀的。若某种材料在其上不同的点具有不同的弹性,则称为是非均匀的。

Civil engineers **working** in this specialty build facilities to ensure safe and efficient movement of both people and goods.

这个专业的土木工程师建造能够安全有效地运送人和货物的设施。

The user's voice, **consisting of** sound waves, is converted into digital form by digital signal processing circuits that are usually on a separate board added to the computer.

用户的语音是由声波构成的,声波被数字信号处理线路转换成数字形式,这种线路通常制作在单独的板上加插到计算机里。

The TDM slots **shown** in Figure 11.2 are part of complex framing hierarchy.

图 11.2 所示的 TDM 时隙只是一个复杂租帧结构的局部。

Another striking example of fracturing **caused** by release waves was the slitting down the middle of a flat plate **following** the simultaneous detonation of two layers of explosive between which it had been sandwiched.

另外一个惊人的拉伸波引起断裂的例子是:一块平钢板夹在两层炸药中间,两层炸药同时起爆,结果在平板的中心层产生断裂。

The direction **indicated** are the positive directions for these stresses; i. e., as usual, tension is taken to be positive and compression negative.

所标的方向是这些应力的正向,即通常以拉应力为正,以压应力为负。

The number of surgical procedures **needed** for the flexion-controlled device has been reduced.

调节控制膝盖弯曲装置所需外科手术的次数相应减少。

Compared to vacuum tubes, transistors are much smaller, faster, and cheaper to manufacture.

和真空管相比,晶体管的尺寸小得多,切换速度快得多,生产成本低得多。

By asserting these internal and external control signals in the proper sequence, the control unit causes the CPU and the rest of the computer to perform the operations **needed** to correctly process instructions.

控制单元通过以正确的顺序激发这些内部或外部控制信号,使 CPU 和计算机的其余部分完成正确处理指令所需要的操作。

(3)名词 + 介词短语。

Due to the small number of channels, users often had to wait a long time before getting a dial tone.

由于信道数量很少,用户往往得等待很长时间才能听到拨号音。

CDMA is typically used **for** wireless systems **with** a fixed base station and many mobile stations at varying distance from it.

CDMA 通常在无线通信系统中,有一个固定的基站和许多与基站距离随时变化的移动站。

With this assumption, the law of transformation between inertial frames arises naturally and contains only one undetermined parameter.

在这一假设的基础上,惯性参考系之间的转换定律就很自然地出现,并且只含有一个尚未确定的参数。

There is a distinct difference **between** the statement of the need **and** the identification of the problem which follows this statement.

接下来就要确定满足这种需要所要解决的问题,这与叙述这种需要完全不同。

Such systems are **referred to** as speaker dependent because each person who wants to use the systems has to train it on his or her voice. **With** lager vocabulary systems of up to 50,000 words, training on individual words is not practical.

这一类系统称为依赖口述人的,因为每一个使用该系统的人都要训练,使它认识自己的语音。对于应用词汇高达 50 000 单词的系统来说,上述训练方法并不可行。

(4)名词 + 形容词(短语)。

Three projects **relevant to** structure research are discussed.

讨论了有关结构研究的三个课题。

The left hemisphere provides the analytical map that takes us from one point to another, while the right hemisphere provides the geometrical vision necessary to see the goal and landmarks along the way.

左半脑提供解析的地图,使我们能从一个地方到达另一个地方,而右半脑提供所需的直观视野,让我们看到沿路的路标和路牌。

The component of this force **perpendicular to** the plane is called the normal component or normal force.

该力垂直于平面的分量称为法向分量或法向力。

Every beam of light reflects off the interface at an angle **equal to** its angle of incidence.

每一束光线在界面上反射的角度和其入射角度是相同的。

For transmission to occur, the sending device must be equipped with a light source and the receiving device with a photodiode **capable of** translating the received light into current usable by a computer.

为了使传播发生,发送仪器必须配有光源,而接收仪器要配有光电二极管来保证接收到的光能够转化成电流,可为计算机使用。

形容词短语作后置修饰语,有时用逗号与所修饰的名词隔开。这时,它的作用相当于一个非限定性定语从句,当然可以换成非限定定语从句。

The research machine called Blue Gene/L will have the capability to process data at a rate of on terabit per second, **equivalent to the data transmitted by ten thousand satellites**.

这个称为 Blue Gene/L 的研究机器具有每秒 1 太比特处理数据的能力,等于一万个气象卫星传播的数据。

(5)名词 + 定语从句。

定语从句作名词的后置修饰语,在科技文章中出现的频率要比前几种情况都多,所传达的信息量也大。

The human brain contains two hemispheres **whose** characters have been shown to be different but complementary. In most individual, the right hemisphere, **which** is associated directly with the left hand, the left field of vision and so forth, is superior in handling geometrical concepts, and the left hemisphere, **which** is associated directly with right hand, the right field of vision and so forth, is superior in handling formal analytical concepts.

人的大脑由两个半球构成,它们的特征各不相同但又互补。对大多数人来说,右半脑直接与左手、左视场等相联系,它擅长处理几何(直观)的概念,而左半脑直接与右手、右视场等相联系,它擅长处理严谨的解析(抽象)概念。

To read data from memory, the microprocessor performs the same sequence of operations (**that**) it uses to fetch an instruction from memory.

微处理器从存储器读取数据所执行的操作程序,同从存储器中取一条指令是一样的。

Some time during this cycle, memory writes the data on the data bus to the memory location **whose** address is on the address bus.

在这个周期的某个时刻,存储器将数据总线上的数据写入地址总线指示的存储单元内。

Crystalline quartz consists of an extended structure **in which** each oxygen atom is bonded tetrahedral to four oxygen atoms, and each oxygen atom is bonded to two silicon atoms.

石英晶体由(向空间)延展的结构构成,在此结构中每个硅原子以正四面体的结构结合四个氧原子,而每个氧原子结合两个硅原子。

(6)同位语。

Many of AMPS' fundamental properties have been directly inherited by its **digital successor, D-AMPS**, in order to achieve backward compatibility.

为了实现向下兼容,AMPS 系统的许多基本特性都由其后来的继承者 D-AMPS 继承下来。

Everything that a computer does is overseen by **central processing unit (CPU), the microprocessor brain of the computer system.**

监管着计算机所做的一切的部件叫做中央处理单元,是计算机系统的微处理器"大脑"。

Qinghailake, the largest inland body of salt water in China, lies 3,198 meters above sea-level.

青海湖是我国最大的内陆咸水湖,海拔 3 198 m。

One, Haixipi Island, has an area of 0.46 km^2. and the other, Bird Island, measures 0.11 km^2.

一个叫海西皮岛,面积 0.46 km^2,另一个叫鸟岛,面积 0.11 km^2。

Male homosexual AIDS patients also show an increased incidence of certain tumors, most commonly **Kaposi's sarcoma, a rare cancer characterized by a rash of dark blue or reddish brown spots on the skin and by internal tumors.**

某些肿瘤在男性同性恋艾滋病患者中发生率上升,最常见的是卡波西氏肉瘤,这是一种少见的癌症,其特点为皮肤上出现大量深蓝色或红褐色的斑点,以及内脏发生肿瘤。

Future Ian Pearson sees **a convergence between intelligent computers and biotechnology, the advent of implanted chips and enhanced intelligence.**

未来学家伊恩皮尔逊看到了智能计算机和生物技术之间的一个会聚点——计算机植入晶片和增强智能技术的出现。

Exercise

练习一

写出下列单词的复数形式。

basis   antenna
axis   formula
index   maximum
minimum   schema
stratum   symposium

练习二

翻译下列句子。

1. 机械工程师不断地发明机器来生产商品,不断地开发精确性和复杂性越来越高的机械工具来生产机器。
2. 保险公司可能使用一台主计算机处理全公司的客户数据。
3. 需要一番思索和努力才能把它表达成一个需要解决的问题。
4. 连接件是一个通用术语,它包括这样一些有很大区别的、多种多样的部件。
5. 在20世纪80年代早期引入的工作站,是昂贵的、能力强的桌面计算机。
6. 机械工程师有四个通用于上述所有领域的作用。
7. 使用最紧密,同时又与原子的电子结构联系最紧密的是长氏周期表。
8. 微处理器和使它工作的其他必备部件一起,被安装在一个称为主板或系统板的主线路板上。
9. 机械工程是工程学的一个分支,它研究机械和动力的产生,尤其是力和运动。
10. 第三个作用是生产产品和动力,包括计划、运作和维护。
11. 为了尽量减少混乱,启用新数字似乎更为合理,且可能得到国际认可。
12. 我们将列出新编号,以使你能够理解这两套元素族的命名。
13. 超级计算机的费用在数十万美元至数百万美元之间。
14. 内存常称为主存或随机存取存储器,是临时的工作存储器。
15. 旧式的电话网络,为传递人类声音而建立的模拟系统,仍然存在。
16. 尽管有这样的名字,这种内存也不能记忆。

第三节　形容词、副词

一、形容词

1. 作定语

Plenty of companies were eager to accept the aluminum and glass as **raw** materials for **new** products.

很多公司都愿意收购铝和玻璃废旧制品,利用它们作为新产品的原料。

Asteroids are **bigger** versions of meteoroids that race across the night sky.

小行星比掠过夜空的流星大一号。

In the past, making structures quake-resistant meant **firm** yet **flexible** materials.

过去,要保证建筑物的抗震性能就是依靠坚固而有弹性的建筑材料。

有时形容词作定语时需要后置

The particles of matter do attract one another to different degrees depending on the type of matter **involved**.

物质的微粒是不同程度相互吸引的,吸引的程度取决于所涉及的物质的种类。

In modern markets, success **overseas** often helps support domestic business efforts.

在当今的市场,成功的海外业务有助于商业活动。

Promotions often follow or accompany an assignment **abroad**.

紧跟或伴随驻外任务的往往是升职。

The book contains something **new**.

这本书里有些新内容。

GenBank is a public database **available** through the Internet.

GenBank 是一个可以通过互联网看到的公共数据库。

2. 作表语

In the cream, the bacteria are **free** to grow throughout the mixture.

细菌在奶油混合物中可以自由地繁殖。

When the trapped electrons are **far** apart, they do not interact strongly.

当被约束电子相距较远时,它们的相互作用力不大。

The source of this interference remains **unconfirmed**.

干扰的来源尚未得到证实。

3. 复合宾语的一部分

They found theory of relativities quite **difficult**.

他们发现相对论很难。

Sleeping 15 minutes to two hours in the early afternoon can reduce stress and make us **refreshed**.

在下午早些时候睡 15 分钟到 2 小时就能减轻压力,使人精神饱满。

4. 形容词作状语

This coal was coarse powder, **clean and brilliant**.

这种煤呈粗糙的粉末状,干净又有光泽。

Afraid of difficulties, they prefer to take the easy road.

他们由于害怕困难,宁愿走容易的道路。

Every object, **large or small**, possesses gravitation.

每个物体,不论大小,都具有万有引力。

There are many problems, **both technological and financial**, that remain to be solved.

有很多问题有待于解决,既包括技术问题又包括财政问题。

5. 形容词短语

(1) 作后置定语。

Doctors tailor therapies to the exact form of disease in each person and select the drugs **likely to work best**, with the mildest side effect, in those individuals.

医生根据每位患者的确切疾病类型进行针对性治疗,选择可能最好而副作用最小的药物。

Investigators are proposing that the galactic clouds are the places where the prebiological evolution of compounds **necessary to life occurred**.

研究者提出银河系星云是某些化合物发生前生物进化的地点,而这些化合物是生命的形式所必需的。

It was discovered early on that many of the major hallucinogens have a molecular structure **similar to that of serotonin**.

许多主要的致幻剂都有与复合胺相似的分子结构,这点很早就发现了。

(2) 作状语。

The generic code of a human being is nothing but the letters A, T, C and G, repeated over and over in varying order, **long enough to fill more than 200 telephone books**.

人类遗传密码就是只有字母 A,T,C 和 G 以不同的顺序反复不断的重复,长度可占满 200 多本电话号码簿。

In this case, the ball flies off **tangent to its original circular path**.

在这种情况下,该球朝正切于其原来的圆形路径的方向飞离过去。

Contrary to common belief, Mr. Smith was not the first to use the ideas.

与通常的观念相反,史密斯先生并不是第一个使用该概念的人。

Most asteroids orbit the sun **far from Earth**.

大多数小行星远离地球运行。

二、副词

1. 副词的主要作用是作状语,它们可以用来修饰动词、形容词、副词,也有的时候修饰整个句子。使用时要注意副词的位置。

(1)副词在句首修饰整个句子。

Typically the queen honeybee is mother to all the bees in a hive.

一般来说蜂王是一个蜂群中所有蜜蜂的母亲。

Unfortunately it is not feasible to use conventional techniques to mesoscale fields.

不幸的是,使用传统的技术检测中强度洋流是不可行的。

Similarly, determining the color, physical state, or boiling point of an element or compound does not change it into a different element or compound.

同理,确定一种元素或化合物的颜色、物理状态或沸点不会将其变成另一种不同的元素或化合物。

(2)不及物动词后加介词或形容词后加介词时,副词通常位于这两个词中间。

Analyzing the physics of dance can add **fundamentally** to a dancer's skill.

分析舞蹈的原理能从根本上增加一个舞者的技巧。

In most individuals, the right hemisphere, which is associated **directly** with the left hand, the left field of vision, is superior in handling geometrical concepts.

对大多数人来说,右半脑直接与左手、左视场相联系,它擅长处理几何的概念。

In chapter 8, an investigation of quantities that might be conserved in a collision leads **naturally** to the momentum conservation laws of Newtonian and relativistic mechanics.

第 8 章通过探讨碰撞过程中有可能守恒的物理量,很自然就导出了牛顿力学和相对论力学的动量守恒定律。

(3)被动语态中,副词的位置则要根据句式的需要来确定。

A solid has a definite volume and a definite shape. Its particles are held together so **tightly** that their motion is **highly** restricted.

固体具有固定的体积和固定的形状。构成固体的颗粒相互间结合得非常紧密,难以运动。

Homogeneous matter can also consist of two or more substances mixed together so **completely** and **uniformly** that the resulting mixture cannot be distinguished **visibly** from pure elements and compounds.

均相物质也可以是由两种或多种物质混合而成,混合必须彻底搅拌均匀,达到与纯物质和纯化合物无法明显区分的程度。

The subject is arranged in such a way that additional material can be inserted **easily** and **naturally**.

主题是以这样一种方式编排的,使得补充教材可以很容易很自然地穿插进来。

(4)表示频率的副词通常放在动词前。

The influence of the biological component of an ecosystem is **often** greater in fresh waters than in marine or terrestrial system.

生态系统中生物元素的影响在淡水中比在海洋中或陆地上大。

The loss would **generally** outweigh the gain.

这样做往往得不偿失。

In the following discussion we **usually** assume the emf of a source to be constant.

在下面的讨论中我们通常假定电源电动势是恒定的。

(5)在主系表结构中,副词一般位于系动词之后。

The two claws of the mature American lobster are **decidedly** different from each other.

发育成熟的美国龙虾的两鳌彼此明显不同。

While it is true that living organisms are profoundly affected by their environment, it is **equally** important to remember that many organisms are also capable of altering their habitat significantly.

生物体确实深受环境影响,但同样重要的是很多生物体也能有效地改变其生存环境,有时这种改变也能限制其自身成长。

A chemical is **simply** one of the millions of different types of matter found in the world.

一种化学物质只是世界上千百万不同种类物质中的一种。

(6)修饰不定式的副词位置比较灵活。

To measure them **properly**, monitoring equipment would have to be laid out on a grid at intervals of at most 50 kilometers with sensors at each grid point lowered deep in the ocean and kept there for many months.

要正确地检测,必须至少50公里作为一个间隔在网络上设置监控设备,网上的传感器需放入海洋深处达数月之久。

There are a large number of problems, since the ability to **systematically** solve a wide variety of problem is one of the goals of a course in mechanics.

书中有大量的习题,因为系统地求解各类习题是力学课程的目的之一。

2. 副词作定语的情况

(1)地点副词作定语。

The table **below** lists resistivity of some substances.

下面的表格列出了一些物质的电阻率。

Molecules at the hot end of a rod vibrate faster as the temperature **there** increases.

金属棒热端的分子随着那里的温度的增加而震动得越来越快。

The capacitance of a capacitor depends on the size of the plates and their distance **apart**.

电容器的电容取决于平板的大小及其分开的距离。

（2）时间副词作定语。

The problem **now** is to determine the magnitude of the force.

现在的问题是要确定力的大小。

The difficult **then** was the measurement of that parameter.

那时的困难是测量那个参数。

Scientists **today** will solve the problems tomorrow.

今天的科学家将解决未来的问题。

三、形容词和副词的比较级

1. 比较级前可以有一个表示程度的状语

Predators are statistically **much** more likely to dream than prey, which are in turn much more likely to experience sleep.

从统计上看，食肉动物比被捕食动物有更多的有梦睡眠，而被捕食动物有更多的无梦睡眠。

Injuries and death were **relatively** less in Los Angeles because the quake occurred on a holiday.

洛杉矶地震损失和伤亡不太严重的原因是地震发生在假期。

An outside force can be used to compress or push them together into a **much** smaller volume.

可以用外力将气体压缩到更小的容器里。

The new smart structures would save many lives and would be **much** less likely to be damaged during earthquakes.

这种新型智能楼房在地震时会拯救众多生命，减少地震的破坏。

2. 表示"和……一样地"，"不及……"和"达……"这类概念时可以用 as…as 结构

From about 3.2 billion years ago onward, things were relatively quiet for Earth **as well as** the Moon.

从大约32亿年前开始，对于地球和月球来说一切都变得十分平静。

Some small craters were formed **as recently as** 2 million years ago.

另外一些火山口则是在最近200万年前形成的。

3. 表示"越来越……"

The life span of humans in industrial countries becomes **longer and longer** and many would like to maintain full activity with good health throughout their lives.

在工业化国家，人们的寿命变得越来越长，许多人想在自己的整个生命中保持良好的健康和充沛的活力。

More and more salt formed, **less and less** water existed, until there was a totally dry salt flat.

盐越来越多,水就越来越少,最终形成完全干燥的盐层。

4. 表示"越……越……"

The bigger the person, **the less** harmful the bite is likely to be, which is why children suffer far more seriously from snake bites than adults.

越重的人被蛇咬,其被伤害的程度就越小,这也就是为什么小孩子被蛇咬后的情况比成年人更严重的原因。

The matter is made up of tiny particles that are always in rapid motion and that **the higher** the temperature of a sample of matter, **the greater** the average energy of motion of its particles.

物质是由始终处于快速运动中的微粒组成的,物质的温度越高,其微粒运动的平均能量就越大。

The more soluble the component is in water, **the greater** the possibility for uptake.

某成分越易溶于水,吸入人体的可能性就越大。

5. "of + 复数名词"来表示最高级的比较范围

Of all the uncombined elements, nitrogen is the most abundant element accessible to man.

在所有未化合元素中,氮是人类可接触的最丰富的元素。

Of all man's recent interventions in the cycles of nature the industrial fixation of nitrogen is by far the most extensive.

在人类干预的自然循环中,唯有工业固氮到目前为止是最广泛的。

Exercise

练习一

翻译下列句子,注意形容词的用法。
1. 它的外特性是一条平行于 x 坐标轴的直线。
2. 靠近核子的电子相互间贴着要比外层轨道上的电子更紧。
3. 这个遥控扫描公司能在肉眼察觉不到农作物问题的时候就可以做出判断。
4. 这个物体与存在的其他物体相互作用。
5. 这种情况下不会发生任何转动。
6. 这些是所能获得的最小微粒。
7. 甚至在这种情况下,也存在两种可能的方向。
8. 现在卫星通信没什么神秘的了。
9. 所有的电子设备都将数字化。

10. 人体由无数个大大小小的结构组成。
11. 这个幂的规则适用于一切有理数,包括正的和负的。

练习二

翻译下列句子,注意副词的使用。
1. 当前,有关使用这类物品的规定,由各个航空公司决定。
2. 我们必须彻底改变对睡眠的态度。
3. 很显然,我们生来就该午睡。
4. 通常这些参数中有一些是已知的。
5. 习惯上把流向器件的电流指定为正。
6. 该设备主要由五部分组成。
7. 这些参数容易测得。
8. 较长的垂直线走势对应于正极。
9. 在第7章中广泛地适用了这种方法。
10. 在下面的讨论中我们通常假定电源电动势是恒定的。

练习三

翻译下列句子,注意形容词和副词比较级的使用。
1. 左右脑连接的越好,他们就配合得越默契。
2. 睡眠越深入,脑电波就越缓慢。
3. 这样的原油储量为低黏度原油储量的几倍。
4. 这种设备变得越来越复杂了。
5. 这块钢板薄达零点几厘米。
6. 该终端距计算中心远达三公里。
7. 当水蒸发时,较轻的分子蒸发得要略快一点。
8. 太阳看起来比其他星星亮得多。
9. 在天上的所有行星中,太阳看起来最大。
10. 在这里的所有机器中,这台性能最佳。

第四节 动 词

1. 系动词 be

(1) 主语 + be + 表语的结构非常简单,而且由于 be 不带有任何感情色彩,客观性强,因此在科技英语中使用得十分广泛。这种结构常用来描述主语的属性,如年龄、颜色、物质、性能、价格、质量、大小等。

Engineering **is** one of the oldest occupations in history.
工程是历史上最古老的职业之一。
Ice is solid. Water **is** liquid. Steam is gaseous. Steam and water are fluids.
冰是固体。水是液体。蒸汽是气体。蒸汽和水为流体。
A coin **is** circular in shape.
硬币是圆形的。
The sphere **is** 200 mm diameter.
球的直径是 200 mm。
A processor **is** a functional unit that interprets and carries out instructions.
处理器是一个翻译和执行指令的控制单元。
Pregnant woman **are** particularly vulnerable to malaria.
孕妇特别容易感染疟疾。
The building **is** approximately 50 meters high.
这栋大楼大概有 50 m 高。

(2) be + of + 名词。

这种结构可用来说明句子主语在度量、大小、颜色、类别等方面的特征。of 后一般跟表示"物质"、"材料"、"形状"、"设计"、"用途"等意义的名词。

Coins may **be of** different sizes, weights, shapes, and of different metals.
货币可能在大小、重量、形状和铸造的金属方面都有所不同。
These pens **are of** many different colors.
这些笔有许多不同的颜色。
The two rooms **are of** a size / of the same size.
这两个房间大小一样。
Ball and roller bearings **can be of** the self-aligning type.
滚珠和滚珠轴承可以是自定位型。
He **is of** the same weight as his brother.
他和他弟弟一样重。
The book **will be of** great value to students of biology.

这本书对学生物的学生将很有用。

The discovery **is of** great importance.

这个发现很重要。

This medicine **is of** no use.

这种药无效。

This matter **is of** no significance.

这件事无关紧要。

(3) 系动词 be 可以把某些结构,如合成名词、介词短语、名词短语、名词化结构、分词子句和不定式子句等连接起来构成句子。由于其无感情色彩的特点,更容易实现语言的客观叙事功能。

The sphere **is** above all the other solids. The sphere **is** over the upright cone. The upright cone **is** on the cylinder. The upright cone **is** under the sphere and the cylinder **is** under the upright cone. The rectangular solid **is** behind the cylinder. The invented cone **is** beyond/behind the cube. The cylinder **is** in front of the rectangular solid. The cube **is** in front of the inverted cone. The cube **is** beyond the rectangular solid. The sphere **is** at the end of the line.

球体位于所有其他物体的上方。球体在圆锥体的正上方。圆锥体在圆柱体的上面。圆锥体在球体的下方,圆柱体在圆锥体的下方。长方体位于圆柱体的后面。倒圆锥体在立方体的后面。圆柱体位于长方体的前方。立方体在倒圆锥体的前面。立方体位于长方体更远的一边。球体位于垂线体的末端。

Engineering **is** one of the oldest occupations in history. Without the skills included in the broad field of engineering, our present-day civilization never could have evolved. The first tool makers who chipped arrows and spears from rock **were** the forerunners of modern mechanical engineers. The craftsmen who discovered metals in the earth and found ways to refine and use them **were** the ancestors of mining and metallurgical engineers. And the skilled technicians who devised irrigation system and erected the marvelous buildings of the ancient **were** the civil engineers of their time. One of the earliest names that has come down to us in history **is** that of Imhotep, the designer of the stepped pyramid at Sakkara in Egypt about 3,000 BC.

工程是历史上最古老的职业之一。如果没有广阔的工程领域里所拥有的各种技术,就不可能有我们今天的文明。那些用石头削切箭头和枪矛的早期工具制造者,是现代机械工程师的先驱。那些在地球上发现了金属柄找到了精炼和使用金属的方法的工匠,是采矿和冶金工程师的鼻祖。而设计灌溉系统并建造古代神奇建筑物的熟练技术员,则是当时的土木工程师。从历史上流传下来的最古老的名字之一是伊穆霍泰普,他是大约公元前 3 000 年的古埃及撒喀拉梯形金字塔的设计者。

2. 一些表示状态、持续、表象、感官、变化、终止含义的动词也可以作为特殊的系动词来使用。这类词包括 keep, remain, stay, seem, appear, look, feel, sound, become, grow, turn, prove 等。

The evidence **seemed** inescapable that light consisted of electromagnetic waves of extremely short wavelength.

这个证据似乎说明了光是由极短波长的电磁波组成的。

The speed of propagation of the waves could be computed from purely electrical and magnetic measurement, and it **turned out** to be very nearly 3×10^8 m·s^{-1}.

结果证明,电磁波的速度非常接近 3×10^8 m·s^{-1}。

The theory of evolution **remains** a lightening rod for school boards, politicians and television preachers.

对学术界、政客和电视传媒而言,进化理论仍然是争论的焦点。

Some chromosomes that start prophase as minute threads **appear** quite bulky before its conclusion.

有些染色体在前期开始时仅仅为微丝,而在这一阶段结束前看起来却相当大。

If a flexible membrane surrounds the cell, it **becomes** visibly elongated.

如果有一个弹性细胞膜包围这个细胞,它会显著地被拉长。

Its result **proves** correct.

其结果证明是正确的。

We have mentioned that rotary forces must have **grown** important during the late stages of condensation.

旋转力在冷凝的最后阶段必定更重要,这一点我们已经提到。

3. 表示因果的动词

科技文章的逻辑性决定了在科技英语中能够准确表达因果逻辑关系也是十分重要的,这里列举出一部分表达逻辑关系的动词(词组)。

主语表示原因:account for, allow, allow for, amount to, arise form, bring to, bring about, cause, contribute to, enable, give rise to, involve, lead to, offer, permit, reduce to 等。

主语表示结果:ascribe to, arise through, result from, lead from, depend on, attribute to 等。

An earthquake warning system **is in use to** warn all shores likely to be reached by the waves. But this only enables people to leave the threatened shores for higher ground.

地震警报系统用来警告所有海浪有可能到来的海滨。但是这个只能让人们离开危险的海滨去更高的地方。

Reversals of the field **give rise to** a series of magnetic strips running parallel to the axis of the rift.

磁场的逆转形成一系列与断层轴线平行的条形磁区。

These three requirements have **led to** the evolution of complex control system.

这三个要求促进了复杂的控制系统的发展。

These functions attempt to bring about the changes necessary to meet present and future needs.
这些功能试图进行必要的改变以满足当前和将来的需要。

Exercise

练习一

翻译下列句子。

1. 能源、矿物和金属构成我们现今社会技术的三大支柱。
2. 1微米等于千分之一毫米。
3. 针头直径大约1毫米。
4. 这些因素并不能解释这个有趣的问题。
5. 早在19世纪20年代初人们就意识到这一现象是非常有用的。
6. 生产力处于非常低的水平。
7. 连接件的种类有很多种。
8. 龙卷风中心的气压通常是13磅/平方英寸。
9. 这一点在食肉动物的幼兽身上表现特别明显。
10. 这些水底下的地震有时会抬高地震海浪。
11. 大多数石英是一种紫水晶,高温使其变为棕色。
12. 导致海洋的盐度变化的基本过程有三个。
13. 细胞只能在一定的温度范围内存活。
14. 随着时间的推移,人们对这种差异的描述越来越精确和有意义。
15. 这种分类并不恰当。
16. 这似乎违背了热力学原理。
17. 蜗杆被制成沙漏形状,使承载力进一步提高。

练习二

翻译下面的段落,注意系动词 be 的使用。

鼠标是可以在桌面上滚动以使指针在计算机显示屏上定位的一种装置。指针是一个符号,通常是一个箭头,用来选择屏幕上列表中的项目或确定光标的位置。光标,也称为插入点,是屏幕上的一个标记,用来显示下一次输入数据的位置,例如某个文档的文本。

第五节 连 词

连词也是一种虚词,它不能独立担任句子成分,而只起连接词与词、短语与短语及句与句的作用。连词主要可分为两类:并列连词和从属连词。并列连词:用来连接平行的词、词组和分句。科技英语写作中要注意并列连词特别是 and 的用法。而从属连词是用来引起从句的,关于从句我们将在后面的章节中详细讲解。本章主要介绍并列连词,特别是 and 的使用。

1. 如果两个事物并列,其间要有并列连词(两个分句并列同样如此,不过此时也可以用分号来表示 and 的含义);如果有几个事物并列,则在最后两个事物之间用一个并列连词。

What information technology products had the greatest impact on our lives **and** business over this century?
在这个世纪中,什么信息技术产品对我们的生活和商业有过最大的影响?

What mechanisms control handedness **and** keep left-handedness rare?
是什么样的机制控制着旋转的方向,并使左旋的比例稀少呢?

Now the World Wide Web has become telephone, loudspeaker, radio, television, camera, phonograph, doctor **and** lover.
现在,万维网已经变成了电话、扩音器、无线电、电视、照相机、唱片机、大夫和爱人。

Some of the earliest efforts of mechanical engineers were aimed at controlling man's environment by pumping water to drain or irrigate **and** by ventilating mines.
机械工程师的一些最初的努力是通过抽水排涝或灌溉土地,以及给矿井通风,来控制人类的环境。

Here, q is the amount of heat absorbed in joules, and m is the mass of the substance in grams.
这里,q 是吸收的热量,单位为焦耳,m 是物质的质量,单位为克。

In forming sodium chloride, sodium atoms give up an electron (thereby becoming positively charged) **and** chlorine atoms gain an electron (thereby becoming negatively charged).
在氯化钠的形成过程中,钠原子失去一个电子从而带正电,而氯原子得到一个电子带了负电。

2. 如果几个从句并列,除第一个从句外,其他从句前的引导词都不能省略。

For such reasons, we can assume **that** there must be an important random factor in neural development **and** in particular, **that** errors must and do occur in the development of all normal brains.
由于这些原因,我们可以假设,在神经发育过程中必然会存在着某种重要的随机因素,尤其是在所有正常大脑的发育过程中,误差必定会产生,并确实在发生。

Some physical quantities require only a magnitude and a unit to be completely specified. Thus it is sufficient to say **that** the mass of a man is 85 kg, **that** the area of a farm is 160 acres, **that** the frequency of a sound wave is 660 hertz, **and that** a light bulb consumes electrical energy at the rate of

100 watts.

有些物理量只需要一个数值和一个单位就可以完全确定,因此我们只要说出以下内容就足够了:一个人的质量为 85 千克,一个农场的面积为 160 英亩,一个声波的频率为 660 赫兹,一个灯泡消耗电能的功率为 100 瓦。

One of the outstanding developments of 20th century physics has been the discovery **that** all matter is endowed with wave properties **and that** a beam of electrons, for example, is reflected by a crystal in much the same way as is a beam of X-rays.

20 世纪物理学的突出成就之一是人们发现了一切物质均被赋予了波的特质,以一束电子为例,它像一束 X 射线那样被晶体所反射。

3. 以 therefore, hence, thus, however 等副词开头的并列分句前一般应该加 and,或者用分号隔开,或者把分句改写成一个单独的句子。

Fever would make it more difficult for an infecting bacterium to acquire iron **and thus** to multiply.

发烧使细菌难以得到铁,也就难以繁殖。

In this case, the pressure at the base of each component is the same **and therefore** the system is in equilibrium.

在这种情况下,每个部件底部的压力是相同的,所以该系统处于平衡状态。

Exercise

练习一

翻译下列句子。
1. 电路的基本元件是电源、能量转换器及它们之间的连接导线。
2. 土木工程师设计并建造房屋、铁路、道路、桥梁、隧道、港口、给水和污水系统,以及其他公共设备。
3. 这台设备大而复杂。
4. 这台机器的优点是结构简单,性能好。
5. 为了定性地解释该电路的工作情况,我们假设 R 是无限大的,二极管是理想的。
6. 这个方法的优点是相位标度是线性的,相位移的大小是没有争议的。
7. 图 3-5 说明了另一种可采用的,有时更为方便的观点。

第六节 介 词

介词是英语中最活跃的词类之一,特别是一些常用介词,搭配能力极强,可用来表示不同的意思。介词不能在句中独立充当一个成分,而需和一个名词或与之相当的动词构成介词短语,来在句中充当一个成分。介词短语在句中的主要作用有:

1. 状语

You are involved **with** chemicals and chemical reactions every instant of your life.
你生活的每一瞬间都涉及化学物质和化学反应。
All chemicals can be classified **as** either elements or compounds.
所有的化学物质都可以分成元素或化合物。
This is the first time that a structural difference has been found **between** the brains of women and men.
这是首次发现在女性和男性大脑间有结构上的差异。

2. 定语

In science, a theory is a reasonable explanation **of** observed events that are related.
在科学中,理论是对所观察到的相关事件的合理解释。
The resulting force exerted **on a** given surface area of the container is called pressure or force per unit area.
作用于容器给定表面积上的合力被称为压力或单位面积上的压强。
This is an example **of a** scientific law.
这是科学定律的一个示例。
The idea **of** the "atom" has a long history.
原子的由来有很长的历史。
The difference **between** a liquid **and** a gas is obvious under the conditions of temperature commonly found at the surface of the Earth.
在地球的表面,在相同的温度和压强下,液体和气体是有明显区别的。

3. 表语

This book will be **of** help in exposing computer scientists to the latest technology.
本书将有助于计算机专家们了解最新的技术。
This view is **out of** date.
这个观点已经过时了。
Albert Einstein won the Nobel Prize when he was **in** his forties.
爱因斯坦四十多岁时获得了诺贝尔奖。
This difference is **in** a part of the brain that is used in most complex intellectual process.

这个差别存在于大脑的一部分,这部分被用在大多数复杂的智力过程。

几个常见介词的用法

1. of

These pens are **of** many different colors.

这些笔有许多不同的颜色。

Of solids metals conduct heat most quickly.

在所有固体中金属传热最快。

The preservation **of** embryos and juveniles is a rate occurrence in the fossil record.

胚胎与幼体被保存下来在化石记录中是少见的事情。

The concept **of** "atomic weight" or "mean relative atomic mass" is fundamental to the development of chemistry.

"原子量"或"平均相对原子质量"的概念是化学发展的基础。

There are wide differences in the ability **of** various substances to conduct heat.

各种物质的导热能力差异很大。

2. with

AC can be changed into DC **with** great ease.

交流电可以极其容易地被转变成直流电。

The boat's speed decreases **with** the increase in water resistance.

船速随着水的阻力的增大而减小。

With rockets, things are different.

对于火箭来说,情况就不同了。

Power can be measured **with** a wattmeter.

功率可以用瓦特计来测量。

Many elements combine **with** hydrogen to form combustible liquids.

许多元素可以与氢化合形成各种易燃的气体。

This is a function **with** two variables.

这是具有两个变量的函数。

With resistance present, a part of power has been lost as heat.

由于存在阻力,一部分功率以热能形式被损失掉了。

With time-invariant currents and voltages, the magnetic and electric fields of the associated electric plant are also time-invariant.

对于时不变的电流和电压,与电气设备相联系的电场和磁场也是时不变的。

3. by

By Hook's law, one can find out the force.

根据胡克定律便可求出该力。

The two halves of the brain are linked **by** a trunk line of between 200 and 300 million nerves.

大脑的两个半脑是由一个2亿到3亿神经的干线来连接的。

By analyzing the parameters of the device, we can understand its features.

通过分析该设备的参数,我们就能了解它的特点。

We can overcome the difficulty **by** this method.

我们可以用这种方法来克服困难。

That laboratory is a room 4 **by** 12 m.

那个实验室是一间 4 m×12 m 的房间。

4. for

Consider **for** a moment the number at the top which is called the atomic number of the element represented in that block.

考虑一下顶端的数字,我们称之为该板块中所代表的元素的原子符号。

For $x > 1$, this equation does not hold.

若 $x > 1$,则该式不成立。

In this case, Eq. (2 – 1) will be solved **for** the unknown.

在这种情况下,要解方程(2 – 1)以求出未知数。

The methods **for** solving this problem are many.

解决这个问题的方法有很多种。

These solutions are **for** reference only.

这些解决方案仅供参考。

For this reason, Faraday was unable to calculate the velocity of the propagation of electromagnetic waves.

由于此原因,法拉第未能计算出电磁波的传播速度。

It takes about 8 minutes **for** sunlight to reach the earth.

太阳光到达地球大约需要8分钟。

5. on

On being compressed, a substance will be reduced in volume.

物质一经挤压其体积就会缩小。

The influence of temperature **on** pressure should be taken into account.

温度对压力的影响应该考虑进去。

On the second half cycle, Q1 is off while Q2 is on.

在第二个半周,Q1 截止而 Q2 导通。

6. in

Here t is measured **in** seconds.

这里 t 的度量单位为秒。

They represent two relations **in** these two unknowns.

它们代表了用这两个未知数表示的两个关系式。

Sound waves travel **in** all directions.

声波是朝四面八方传播的。

States 1 and 2 differ **in** pressure, volume, and temperature by a definite amount.

两个状态的压力、体积和温度相差一定的量。

In our discussion of differential equations, we shall restrict our attention to equations of the first degree.

我们在讨论微分方程的时候,应把注意力集中在一次方程上。

7. over

This balloon can fly **over** 100 kilometers.

这个气球能够飞越 100 公里。

This new method has many advantages **over** the original one.

这种新的方法与原来的相比有许多优点。

It is easy for us to determine the car's average velocity **over** this distance.

我们很容易确定该汽车在这段距离上的平均速度。

Turning this knob gives the control **over** the brightness of the light spot.

转动这个旋钮就能控制光电的亮度。

This line is **over** six times as long as that one is.

这根线的长度是那根的 6 倍多。

There is a bridge **over** the river.

这条河上有一座桥。

Exercise

练习一

翻译下列句子,注意介词的使用。
1. 此次测量非常精确。
2. 所有这些仪表中,这一台最贵。
3. 化学这门科学在当今世界非常有用。
4. 把金子从矿石中提炼出来并不容易。
5. 这个级数能够迅速地收敛。
6. 半导体的导电率随温度的变化而变化。
7. 有了雷达,我们可以看到远方的物体。
8. 我们能够用这种磁铁来制作电铃。
9. 这根线与 x 轴平行。
10. 波长各不相同的电波以相同的速度传播。
11. 典型的噪声裕度通常比保证值大约高 75 毫伏。
12. 根据式(3),我们可以得到下面这个表达式。
13. 这是克服这个缺点的唯一方法。
14. 这个设备的尺寸是 12 × 18 × 6 英寸。
15. 该温度可保持长时间不变。
16. 这本书对于初学者来说太难了。
17. 我们必须解这个方程式求出 x。
18. 这是一本电气工程师手册。
19. 这货物太重,那台起重机吊不起来。
20. 经简化后其结果如下所示。
21. 这些是有关该材料机械性能的资料。
22. 这个国际会议将于周日举行。
23. 我们用牛顿来度量力。
24. 直流电只朝一个方向流动。
25. 这些练习的难度很不相同。
26. 我们能够测量出压力的微弱变化。
27. 将它传送到远方会损耗一些能量。
28. 这个温度与前面提到的 150 ℃ 相比有了明显的下降。

29. 电压在很宽的频率范围内是十分稳定的。
30. 桥式起重机从我们的头顶开过。

第七节　与数字有关的表达

1. 分数的表示法

(1)分数词是以基数词和序数词合成的,基数词代表分子,序数词代表分母,除了分子是"1"的情况外,序数词都要用复数。

四分之一　one-fourth　　　　　　　九分之五　five-ninths

二又七分之三　two and three-sevenths

三分之二　two-thirds　　　　　　　此外还有一些表示法

二分之一　a(one)half　　　　　　　四分之一　a(one)quarter

四分之三　three quarters

对于比较复杂的分数词读法如下:

55/123　fifty five over one hundred and twenty three

23/8　twenty three over eight

(2)表示"零点几(十分之几)"、"零点零几(百分之几)"等。

零点几　a few tenths　　　　　　　零点零几　a few hundredths

零点零零几　a few thousandths

其后如果有单位,就要在后面 + of + 单位

零点零几克　a few hundredths of a gram

(3)表示"千分之……"、"万分之……"、"百万分之……"等分母较大的数时,有两种方式。

a. 分子:基数词 + parts(基数词为1时用单数形式)

分母:per(= in a) + 数词 或 in + 阿拉伯数字

百万分之七　　seven parts per million(= in a million)

或:seven parts in 10^6

千分之三　　three parts per thousand(= in a thousand)

或:three parts in 10^3

b. 分子:a + 序数词 + part

分母:per(= in a) + 数词 或 in + 阿拉伯数字

百万分之七　　a seven part per million(= in a million)

千分之三　　a three part per thousand(= in a thousand)

2. 数量的增减与倍数的表示

在科技写作中常常会出现数量增加减少或表达倍数的句子,英语中表达倍数有很多种概念。下面列举一些表达方式:

(1)数字 + 比较级 + than。

Output value was 59 **percent higher** than in 1986.

产量比 1986 年增长了百分之五十九。

(2)表增减的词 + to/by + 百分数或数字。

The output of cotton was **increased by** 20 **percent**.

棉花产量增长了 20%。(增加到 120%)

The output of cotton **increased to** 120% of the last year.

棉花产量增长到去年的 120%。

比较上面两个句子,我们可以注意到,当和"to"搭配时表示的意思是增加到或减少到多少,而和"by"搭配时,则表示净增加和减少了多少。

(3)times + 形容词比较级 + than。

The new method was over **ten times more** efficient than the traditional one.

新方法比传统方法效率提高 10 倍以上。

The substance reacts **four times slower** than the other one.

这种物质反应速度是另一种物质的 1/4。

Output of chemical fertilizer was **more than** 2.5 **times greater**.

化纤产量增长了 1.5 倍。

Mercury weights **about** 13 **times** more than water.

水银的重量约比水重 13 倍。

(4)times + as + 形容词/副词 + as。

Its total output value of industry last year was 83 **times as high as** that of 1949.

去年它的工业总产值是 1949 年的 83 倍。

The pinion rotates **five times as fast as** the gear.

小齿轮的转速为齿轮的 5 倍。

The education budget of 1938 was 30 **times as small as** that of 1959.

1938 年的教育预算是 1959 年的 1/30。

A yard is **three times as long as** a foot.

一码是一英尺的 3 倍长。

(5)times + 名词。

The volume of the sun is about 1,300,000 **times that of the earth.** (that of = the volume of)

太阳的体积约为地球体积的 1 300 000 倍。

Aluminum has nearly 5 **times the thermal conductivity** of cast iron.

铝的导热率几乎是铸铁的 5 倍。

The earth is 49 **times the size** of moon.

地球的大小是月球的 49 倍。

(6) x-fold + increase/ decrease.

During this period its territory **increased ten-fold**.

这时期它的领土扩大了 9 倍。

They produced two million computers this year, **a fourfold increase** over last year.

他们今年生产了 200 万台计算机, 是去年的 4 倍。

(7) by a factor of…

The sample has been magnified by **a factor of** 11.

该样品被放大了 10 倍。

Every time a binary number is shifted one place to the left, the number increases by **a factor of two**.

二进制每向左移 1 位, 该倍数扩大 1 倍。

(8) as much/many/fast/long + again + as 表示多/快/长 1 倍。

Wheel A turns **as fast again as** wheel B.

A 轮转动比 B 轮快一倍。

The bridge is **as long again as** that one.

这座桥比那座桥长 1 倍。

(9) 由 twice 构成的结构。

The diameter of a circle is **twice** its radius.

圆的直径是其半径的两倍。

"Concorde" can fly at **twice** the speed of sound.

协和式飞机能以两倍于音速的速度飞行。

Britain now produces more than **twice** as much nuclear power as the United States.

英国现在生产的核电能是美国的两倍多。

This isotope of hydrogen weights **twice** as much as ordinary hydrogen.

氢的这种同位素比普通的氢重 1 倍。

(10) double, treble 等。

If you **double** the distance between two objects, the gravitational attraction gets four times weaker.

如果两个物体之间的距离增加了1倍,这两个物体之间的引力将减小到原来的1/4。

The commercial value of the looms was **trebled** overnight.

纺织机的商业价值一夜提高了两倍。

3. 数字的使用规则

由于科技文献的属性不一样,对数字使用规则的要求也不同,下面列举一些使用中的一般规则。

(1)科技论文中,十以下的整数通常应该用词表示,如 one, two, three 等。

In a **three**-dimensional rectangular block of very small size is considered to be removed from a body subject to external loads, there will be **one** normal stress and **two** shearing stresses on each of its **six** faces.

There are four classes of macromolecules in living things.

但若在同一个句子或段落中出现两个以上有比较性质的数字,则数字的表达形式应一致,而且表达形式通常以最大数字的形式为准。

There are **44** autosomes and **2** sex chromosomes in the human genome, for a total of **46**.

(2)不要用阿拉伯数字作为句子的开端。若句子必须以数字开始,则要使用英文数字;否则需须改写句子,使阿拉伯数字处在除句首之外的其他位置。

Fifteen cases are shown who have suffered growth arrest after implantation.

Approximately **20** million years ago, central and east Africa was densely forested.

There are **12** physicians at the meeting.

不要写成:12 physicians are at the meeting.

(3)叙述文字中如果数字超过百万,要用阿拉伯数字和数字组合来表示。There is a chain-of-existence extending from your cells back to the earliest cells, over 3.5 **billion** years ago.

(4)带有计量单位的数字,为了精确起见,采用科学计数法,即系数乘以10的方幂的形式。

The speed of propagation of light is 3×10^8 **m/s**.

光的传播速度是 3×10^8 m/s。

(5)通常阿拉伯数字是每三位一节用逗号分隔。

5,654   18,600   1,366,455   1,234,567,789

当数字后带有公制单位的量时,对于只有四位数字的百位与千位之间,不使用逗号,也不留空格。但是,如果表格中,同列的其他数字有超过四位且采用了逗号或留有空格时,为了对齐数位,则该四位数的数字也应使用逗号或留出空格。

对于超过四位数且很长又无法用方幂表达的数字,数位应当按照不同期刊的各自要求分组。常见的有两种方式:

三位一组,以逗号隔开(不包括小数部分)例如:

8018 12,345.67089 1,234,567

三位一组(包括整数与小数部分),空一小格。例如:

8 018.007 2

31 415.926 535

(6)年份、门牌号、电话号码、邮编、页码不用三位分隔法。

2009(年份)

Serial No. 14896 - AN

1111 Wall Street(门牌号)

Page 1234

Evansville, IN 47701 - 1957(邮编)

(805)555 - 6132(电话号码)

(7)阿拉伯数字可用于表示时间、金额、计量值、及小数或百分比。

8:25 am $ 5.6   3 kg   5.78   35 % 或 35 percent

但注意,在 o'clock 前只能加字母,比如说:9 o'clock

(8)论文中大于十的序数词可以缩写,小于十的序数词不能缩写。

first   second   third   21st   22nd   77th

(9)小于一的分数必须用词表示。

one half   two-thirds

(10)书籍中章节和页码通常用阿拉伯数字书写。文章中的图号和表号也常用阿拉伯数字书写。

Chapter 5   Page 11   Figure 3

(11)在表示单位的符号或缩写之前的数字应用阿拉伯数字,且在阿拉伯数字与符号或缩写之间通常需要一个空格。

Tertiary filtration of wastewaters containing **20 ~ 30 mg/L** suspended solids following biological treatment can be reduced to less than 5 mg/L by direction filtration.

生物处理之后对含有悬浮固体达 **20 ~ 30 mg/L** 的废水采用直接过滤进行三级处理可使悬浮固体减少到 **5 mg/L**。

(12)使用阿拉伯数字书写日期时,只能是基数形式,虽然日期必须读成序数。

Oct. 21, 1995   Sep. 7, 2008

(13)在列表中,同一列的所有数据应该采用相同计量单位。

(14)除非隐含有精确度不确定的原因,在时间及计量单位前采用小数,而不是分数。

2.5 h(而不是 2 1/2 h)   3.25 g(而不是 3 1/4 g)

(15)在表达只有两个数值的项目之间,使用"and"。但是在两个引文的文献之间却采用逗号。

Figure 1 and 2   Compound A and B Woodward(4,5)reported

在表达数值范围或者超过三个数值的系列时采用短破折号。

pp 124 – 129   temperature 100 ~ 105 ℃

The X – ray structures of 4a – 4d were resolved and are reported.

当由 from…to… 或者 between…and… 表述数值范围时,不要用短破折号。

Those with a pH between 7 and 1 are considered basic.

当数值范围上下限之一或两者均为负数,或者含有修饰该数字的符号,包括方幂时,不要用短破折号。

-78 ℃ to 20 ℃   2.5 to 100 mL

1.02×10^{-5} to 4.5×10^{-5} 或写成 $(1.02-4.5) \times 10^{-5}$

4. 计量单位

(1)采用国际计量单位。

国际单位制的基本单位

物理量	单位名称	符号
length	meter	m
mass	kilogram	kg
time	second	s
electric current	ampere	A
temperature	kelvin	K
amount of substance	mole	mol
luminous	candela	cd

国际单位制的辅助单位

物理量	单位名称	符号
plane angle	radian	rad
solid angle	steradian	sr

具有特殊名称和符号的导出单位

物理量	单位名称	符号	导出形式	对应的基本单位形式
energy work	joule	J	$m^2 \cdot kg \cdot s^{-2}$	$N \cdot m$
force	newton	N	$m \cdot kg \cdot s^{-2}$	$J \cdot m^{-1}$
pressure stress	pascal	Pa	$m^{-1} \cdot kg \cdot s^{-2}$	$N \cdot m^2$
power	watt	W	$m^2 \cdot kg \cdot s^{-3}$	$J \cdot s^{-1}$
electric charge	coulomb	C	$s \cdot A$	$s \cdot A$
electric potential	volt	V	$m^2 \cdot kg \cdot s^{-3} \cdot A^2$	$W \cdot A^{-1}$
electric resistance	ohm	Ω	$m^2 \cdot kg^{-1} \cdot s^{-3} \cdot A^2$	$V \cdot A^{-1}$

物理量	单位名称	符号	导出形式	对应的基本单位形式
electric conductance	siemens	S	$m^2 \cdot kg^{-1} \cdot s^3 \cdot A^2$	$A \cdot V^{-1}$
electric capacitance	farad	F	$m^{-2} \cdot kg^{-1} \cdot s^4 \cdot A^2$	$C \cdot V^{-1}$
magnetic flux	weber	Wb	$m^2 \cdot kg \cdot s^{-2} \cdot A^{-1}$	$V \cdot s$
magnetic flux density	tesla	T	$kg \cdot s^{-2} \cdot A^{-1}$	$Wb \cdot m^{-2}$
inductance	henry	H	$m^2 \cdot kg \cdot s^{-2} \cdot A^{-2}$	$Wb \cdot A^{-1}$
luminous flux	lumen	lm	$m^2 \cdot m^{-2} \cdot cd = cd$	$cd \cdot sr$
illuminance	lux	lx	$m^2 \cdot m^{-4} \cdot cd = m^{-2} \cdot cd$	$lm \cdot m^{-2}$
frequency	hertz	Hz	s^{-1}	s^{-1}
activity of radionuclides	becquerel	Bq	s^{-1}	s^{-1}
absorbed does	gray	Gy	$m^2 \cdot s^{-2}$	$J \cdot kg^{-1}$

采用国际计量单位的缩写，与其前面的数字应空出一格。

数字与百分比符号(%)，角度单位(°)，分(')，秒(")不要空格。

(2)如果数字作为单位的修饰单元，那么中间加以连字符。但是数字与浓度或温度单位构成的单元中，却只留空格，不加连字符。

10 ℃ interval　　　0.2 N H_2SO_4　　　2 M increment

在正文中，除了用于温度单位的 K 之外，不要单独使用不带数据的计量单位缩写。而应该写成

We measured volume in milliliters.

Time was recorded in picoseconds.

Temperature was measured in ℃.

温度中℃之间没有空格，但与前面的数字之间空出一格。

无论数字是单数还是复数，单位缩写不改变形式。

(3)非数字后面的单位要采用拼写形式。这是对于具有单复数形式的单位，又要区分单数或复数。

a few grams　　　　　　　　　milligrams per liter

但也有例外：

在表格与图示坐标轴上，即使前面没有数字，也要采用计量单位的缩写。

被用于单位的人名不要大写。

但是 Celsius 和 Fahrenheit 却总是大写，因为它们已不再是单位，而是温度度量的名称。

(4)在复合计量单位拼写形式中，不要用/，而采用词 per。

They cut the amount of organic process wastes generated from 4,300 tons per year to only 300 tons per year.

(5)不要混合使用单位的缩写形式与拼写形式。

10 kilometers per second 而不是 10 km per second.

(6)在以一个词开头的计量单位及复合的表达式中,缩写单位之前采用/,而不是 per。

A mean dosage of 6.8 mg of each drug/kg body weight was successful in immobilizing polar bears older than one year.

The sample was found to have n M = 1,000 kg/mol and radioactivity of 6×10^3 counts/(s·g).

(7)文章及各章节标题中的缩写计量单位,如果原来是小写的,就不要大写。

Synthesis of 2-μm Molecular Wires.

Exercise

练习一

翻译下列句子。

1. 在所有恶性交通事故中,有五分之一是因超速行驶引发的。
2. 农用柴油机的产量增加了一倍多。
3. 这时期它的领土扩大了九倍。
4. 化纤产量比 1975 年增加了两倍。
5. 化肥产量增长了 1.5 倍。
6. 输入是输出的 100 倍。
7. 其速度为光速的 3/10。
8. 这只箱子比那只重 5 倍。
9. 这个音符的波长比在空气中同一音符长了两倍多。
10. 它的粮食产量比 1976 年增长了百分之十六点五。

第二章 时态和语态

第一节 时态

作为谓语的动词用来表示动作发生的时间的各种形式称为时态。和汉语不同,英语在不同时间发生的动作,要用不同形式的动词来表示。因此,每表述一句话都要考虑时态问题。英语中共有十六个时态。而科技英语中涉及的时态,要比其他文学类文体少得多。在科技文体中常用的时态有一般现在时、一般过去时、一般将来时和现在完成时。在行文中使用恰当的时态来传达准确的信息也是很重要的一环。

1. 一般现在时

一般现在时在科技英语中使用频率最高,也是最常见的一种时态形式。用来表述某些现象或某个研究领域的普遍事实,这些事实不受时间的影响。此时,句子的时态应采用一般现在时。

下面一段文字摘自论文的引言的开头部分,主要是介绍了这篇论文所研究的领域,叙述了该领域的一般信息,引出了将要讨论的问题。由于这些信息都是客观存在且不受时间影响的普遍事实,行文中采用了一般现在时。

Due to the infinite dimension of their Hilbert space, continuous-variable CV systems allow one, in principle, to store an infinite amount of entanglement. Even in realistic settings, the entanglement of two-mode squeezed states generated in parametric amplification processes with present technology can be much more than one ebit, thereby largely exceeding the maximum amount of entanglement between a pair of qubits. Nonetheless, discrete variable systems—and, most notably, qubits—are naturally privileged for the implementation of many quantum-information tasks, with the prominent example of quantum computation. In this respect, it is of interest to investigate the efficiency at which entanglement can be transferred from continuous-to discrete-variable systems by realistic coherent interactions and to envisage strategies to improve such efficiency. This is relevant in view of the relative ease with which highly entangled CV states can be currently generated. With efficient transfer procedures, such entanglement could be distributed to separate discrete-variable systems and employed for general quantum-information processing purposes.

下面是对理论模型分析的一段文字,属于有关数学逻辑关系的文字,不受时间的影响,通常也采用一般现在时。

The difference between fuzzy and non-fuzzy partitions becomes clearer if we consider how many rules can be generated from a single training pattern(i. e., how many rules can be activated by a single training pattern). In the case of the crisp partition in Fig. 6(b), only a single non-fuzzy if-then rule can be generated from a single training pattern. That is, the non-fuzzy if-then rule in the shaded area including the training pattern is generated. This is because there is no overlap between neighboring subspaces(i. e. ,no overlap between neighboring crisp intervals on each axis). On the other hand, if we use the fuzzy partition in Fig. 6(a), four fuzzy if-then rules in the shaded area can be generated from the single training pattern. The generated four rules cover the larger square region denoted by dashed lines. In general, 2n fuzzy if-then rules can be generated from a single training pattern for an n-dimensional pattern classification problem when we use a fuzzy partition such as Fig. 6(a).

这是出现在结果部分的一段文字,虽然文字中所描述的图表在时间上属于过去的概念,但就其科学真理性而言,这个结果的得出是不受时间所影响的,具有普遍意义的,因此,使用的也是一般现在时态。

Comparative Raman spectra of the composites are shown in Fig. 4; the peaks associated with the carbon materials are much stronger than those of the matrix, due to resonance and absorbance effects. The two typical graphitic peaks can clearly be seen, the so-called G-peak, at ~ 1,585 cm^{-1}, arising from the in-plane vibrations, and the D-peak, at 1,350 cm^{-1}, originating from disorder in the graphitic structure. The D/G intensity ratio is frequently used to assess the degree of crystallinity in carbon samples; a lower ratio indicates fewer defects in the crystal structure. The Raman data clearly reveal the differences in crystallinity between the various nanomaterials used. As might be expected, the arc-grown sample has the highest crystallinity, whilst the aCGNTs are significantly higher quality than the other catalytically-grown materials. A number of polymer peaks are clearly visible and identifiable by comparison with the pure polymer spectrum. They appear unaffected by the presence of the different nanofillers, although their intensity is low, and hence any subtle changes would be hard to identify.

2. 一般过去时

相对于一般现在时而言,一般过去时在涉及科技史,或强调某一结论基于在此之前的某一事实的发生时经常出现。

By the middle of the seventeenth century, while most workers in the field of optics accepted the corpuscular theory, the idea had begun to develop that light might be a wave motion of some sort. Christian Huygens, in 1678, showed that the laws of reflection and refraction could be explained on the basis of a wave theory and that such a theory furnished a simple explanation of the recently discovered phenomenon of double refraction. The wave theory did not find immediate acceptance, however. For one thing, the objection was raised that if light were a wave motion, one should be able to see around corners, since waves can bend around obstacles in their path. We now know that the bending, while it does actually take place, is so small that it is not ordinary observed. As a matter of fact, the bending of a light wave around the edges of an object, a phenomenon known as diffraction, was noted by Grimaldi in a book published in 1665, but the significance was not understood at the time.

上面一段文字是属于科技历史的范围,在描述光的本质的发展历程,因此采用了一般过去时态。

The arc-grown nanotubes(AGNT), aligned catalytically-grown nanotubes(aCGNT), and entangled catalytically-grown nanotubes(eCGNT)were produced using previously reported techniques. The catalytically-grown nanofibres(CNF) were purchased from Applied Sciences Inc., USA, grade PR-19-PS. The average outer diameters of the nanomaterials were 15,43,10 and 155 nm, respectively. All materials were multi-walled and used as produced. All of the catalytically-grown materials were essentially pure except for the presence of the catalytic transition metal. The AGNT sample contained significant graphitic and nanoparticulate impurities, with a total nanotube weight content around 40%. The matrix material was a polyamide-12, VESTAMID L1,700, from Degussa. Linear aliphatic polyamides are semicrystalline polymers that usually exhibit a relatively high modulus, toughness and strength, low creep and good temperature resistance. They are used widely as engineering materials and fibres. Most commonly, polyamide-6 and 6,6 are used for commercial production of fibres for textile and engineering applications. Polyamide-12 fibres only represent a small fraction of the polyamide fibre market but exhibit an excellent strength/toughness balance.

The polymer pellets and carbon powders were weighed and dried, and then blended in a DSM twin-screw microextruder, operating at 220 ℃ at 80 rpm. The extrudate was roughly chopped and fed into a Rheometrics Scientific capillary rheometer also operating at 220 ℃. A single strand was spun from a 1 mm diameter die, and wound up at around 0.5 m/s to produce a final fibre diameter targeted at 125 mm. Nanocomposites with a range of loading fractions up to 15 wt% were produced, depending on the availability of the nanofillers. Specifically, the following filler weight fractions were realised:5, 10 and 15 wt% CNF,1.25,2.5 and 5 wt% a CGCNT, 1.25,2.5 and 10 wt% AGNT,and 1.25,2.5, 5 and 10 wt% eCGNT.

Thermal gravimetric analysis(TGA)was carried out using a Mettler TG50 thermal analysis unit. 10 mg of the PA12 nanocomposite fibres were placed into an aluminium oxide crucible and heated up in air(heating rate of 10 ℃/min from 25 to 1,000 ℃ under a constant air flow of 20 l/min). The samples were held initially at 100 ℃ for 1 hour, in order to remove any water present. Composite samples were fractured under liquid nitrogen and mounted for observation in a JEOL 6430F FEG SEM, operating at 10 kV, after coating with chromium. 2D wide angle X-ray scattering(WAXS)fibre diffraction patterns were collected using Ni-filtered Cu Kα radiation on a Photonics CCD system and were calibrated using silicon powder. 1D X-ray diffraction data was collected on a Bruker(Siemens) D500 in transmission mode, using similar radiation. Individual fibre tensile testing was performed on a TA Instruments 2,980 Dynamic Mechanical Analyzer applying a constant force ramp of 0.1 N/min, at 30 ℃, with a gauge length of 5.5 mm, held between thin film clamps. At least 3 fibres were tested for each filler type and loading fraction, with the diameters measured for each sample. The maximum elongation that was achievable using this equipment was about 400%. Differential scanning calorimetry (DSC) was performed using a TA Instruments DSC 2920 operating at either 10 ℃/min or 30 ℃/min, between room temperature and 210 ℃. Prior to the cooling runs, the samples were held isothermally at 210 ℃ for 5 minutes to erase the thermal history. Raman spectra were collected on a Renishaw micro-Raman system using a 50£ lens and a 25 mW argon laser(514 nm), with both the incident and back-scattered light polarised parallel to the fibre axis.

上文是一篇论文中的实验环节部分,可以看到,由于实验程序是作者过去的研究活动,因此,这部分时态采用的是一般过去时。

A range of multi-wall carbon nanotubes and carbon nanofibres were mixed with a polyamide-12 matrix using a twin-screw microextruder, and the resulting blends spun to produce a series of reinforced polymer fibres. The aim was to compare the dispersion and resulting mechanical properties achieved for nanotubes produced by the electric arc and a variety of chemical vapour deposition techniques. A high quality of dispersion was achieved for all the catalytically-grown materials and the greatest improvements in stiffness were observed using aligned, substrate-grown, carbon nanotubes. The use of entangled multi-wall carbon nanotubes led to the most pronounced increase in yield stress, most likely as result of increased constraint of the polymer matrix due to their relatively high surface area. The degrees of polymer and nanofiller alignment and the morphology of the polymer matrix were assessed using X-ray diffraction and differential scanning calorimetry. The carbon nanotubes were found to act as nucleation sites under slow cooling conditions, the effect scaling with effective surface area. Nevertheless, no significant variations in polymer morphology as a function of nanoscale filler type and loading fraction were observed under the melt spinning conditions applied. A simple rule-of-mixture evaluation of the nanocomposite stiffness revealed a higher effective modulus for the multi-wall carbon nanotubes compared to the carbon nanofibres, as a result of improved graphitic crystallinity. In addition, this approach allowed a general comparison of the effective nanotube modulus with those of nanoclays as well as common short glass and carbon fibre fillers in melt-blended polyamide composites. The experimental results further highlight the fact that the intrinsic crystalline quality, as well as the straightness of the embedded nanotubes, are significant factors influencing the reinforcement capability.

上文是一篇论文的摘要部分,主要是对实验和调查结果的描述,作者把研究活动作为了摘要的重点来描述,表达的是已经过去的意思,因此采用了一般过去时态。

3. 现在完成时

现在完成时在科技英语中出现的频率不高,通常用于强调一个动作持续一定时间,并且对现状有影响。

下面几段文字都出现在论文的开始部分,都是作者在介绍相关领域已经取得的成果,说明这一成果已经带来的影响,这既是一种背景资料的介绍,也为下文引出作者所要研究的范围做了必要的铺垫。而现在完成时在此也就比较活跃。

On the other hand, the set – valued (alias multivalued) integration has shown to be a useful tool for modeling a lot of situations in several fields ranging from Mathematical Economics to Optimization and Optimal Control. Recently, special attention has been paid to the Pettis integral of multifunctions (alias, set-valuedmaps, multivalued maps, correspondences, etc.). For example, let us mention the recent contributions of Amrani, Castaing, Amrani and Castaing, Amrani, Castaing and Valadier, and Ziat, which deal with the Pettis integral of bounded, especially weakly compact, convex – valued multifunctions.

Since their discovery, carbon nanotubes (CNTs) have been at the core of many studies because of their unique properties. With the understanding of some of the basic transport mechanisms involved in the electronic transport through CNTs, today studies become more and more oriented toward measurements on individual CNT. To achieve such an ambitious aim, we need to sharpen the tools that have been set up. Both deposition and connection of CNTs needs to be reviewed and enhanced. CNTs are generally deposited on the substrate by random deposition. Once in a suspension, the CNTs are deposited by the mean of a droplet, sometimes followed by ultrasonic pulse. This deposition presents the advantage of being easy to handle, however it lacks control of the direction of the CNTs on the substrate.

Internal levels of atoms coherently interacting with bosonic light fields are natural candidates as discrete-variablereceivers of CV entanglement. In fact, the entanglement transfer between two radiation modes and a pair of two-level atoms through coherent interactions has already been investigated 3 ~ 5. Also, the state transfer between macroscopic atomic clouds and light has been theoretically considered recently 6 and important steps have been made towards its experimental demonstration 7, relying on measurements and coherent interactions. In the limit of a macroscopic number of polarized atoms, the atomic component of such systems behaves as a CV system, so that the entanglement transfer relates, actually, two CV systems of different nature. For a resonant Jaynes-Cummings coupling 8, the interaction reduces to the action of a beam splitter between the two systems, allowing, in principle, perfect state and thus entanglement transfer. However, if the receiving system is really a discrete variable one, like a small number of atoms i. e. , a "microscopic" cloud would be then the transfer is no longer perfect. Some questions of fundamental and practical interest arise in this instance: How many atoms are actually needed in order to realize an "essentially perfect" transfer, thus exhausting the resources of the CV system? How does the transition between microscopic and macroscopic entanglement transfers behave?

4. 一般将来时

一般将来时在科技文章中通常在涉及到设想或计划时使用,此外在引言部分也会用一般将来时来描述将在论文中谈到的内容。

The purpose of this paper is twofold. On the one hand, we aim to study the entanglement transfer from two light modes to a pair of atomic ensembles made up of a small number of two-level atoms or, equivalently, to systems with Hilbert spaces of small dimension d 2. We will show that, for two-mode squeezed states realistically achievable in laboratories, all the entanglement can be extracted by a few atoms, in an essentially microscopic regime. Moreover, we will shed further light on the transition from the finite-dimensional regime to the CV behavior displayed by macroscopic ensembles, explicitly elucidating the algebraic reasons lying behind this transition and the physical conditions allowing one to treat macroscopic ensembles as CV systems. On the other hand, we propose a method to increase the entanglement transfer to a pair of two-level atoms qubits by letting further pairs interact successively with the same entangled light field and then by postselecting the local measurements on such pairs. We will show that, following this route, the entanglement transferred to the first pair of qubits increases considerably with respect to the strategy pursued in Refs. Remarkably, we demonstrate that such an "extraction" procedure, aiming at achieving a Bell state of the first two atoms, can be made "arbitrarily perfect" by repeated iterations of the probabilistic protocol.

Exercise

练习一

阅读下列段落,指出所使用的时态及原因。

Para A

The book in Fig. 8-1 shows only stresses acting on planes parallel to the xy, xz, and yz planes. In addition, normal and shearing stresses act on all other planes within the block, at all orientations-with one exception: On one set of mutually perpendicular planes, the shearing stresses are zero. Those planes are called the principal planes, and the normal stresses on those planes are called the principal stresses. Among the principal stresses are the greatest and smallest normal stresses occurring on all possible planes through a point.

Para B

Light is a form of electromagnetic energy. It travels at its fastest in a vacuum: 300,000 kilometers/second (approximately 186,000 miles/second). The speed of light depends on the density of the medium through which it is traveling (the higher the density, the slower the speed).

Para C

The human brain contains two hemispheres whose characters have been shown to be different but complementary. In most individuals, the right hemisphere, which is associated directly with the left hand, the left field of vision and so forth, is superior in handling geometrical concepts, and the left hemispheres, which is associated directly with right hand, the right field of vision and so forth, is superior in handling formal analytical concepts.

Para D

During the 1950s, most computers were similar in one respect. They had a main memory, a central processing unit (CPU), and peripherals. The memory and CPU were central to the system. Since then a new generation of computing has emerged in which computing and data storage need not be centralized. A user may retrieve a program from one place, run it on any of a variety of processors, and send the result to a third location.

Para E

Hopkinson as early as 1914 observed that an explosively loaded plate often spalled off the side opposite from that on which the explosive was denoted….

While repeating certain Hoplinsons experiments, we noted some surprising result. For example, denoting layers of various thickness of explosive in contact with plates of varying thickness, thin layers of explosive produced at times thicker spalls than thick layers and vice versa….

Multiple spalling occurred most commonly when the stress level was high and especially of long duration. Extensive experiment in which the shape and duration of the wave were related to the positions and thickness of the multiple spalls established the mode of generation:

The first spall fracture surface immediatedly at its abrupt inception placed in effect a free surface in front of that portion of the wave which had not yet passed. This newly created surface began at once to reflect the trailing portion and if that portion was still intense enough, another spall formed.

The process repeated itself until the intensity of the rear portion of the wave was less than the critical normal fracture strength of the material. It was most surprising to us that these new fracture surfaces opened quickly enough to reflect rear portion of the wave.

Para F

There have been many approaches to modeling "the waters above". A review of most of these may be found in Dillow. Some have considered liquid water canopies, cloud canopies, solid ice canopies, ice crystal canopies, ice rings, charged water ions, and water vapor. All but a few have considered such canopies to be in contact with the atmosphere. A recent, popular treatment by Humohreys suggests that "the waters above" are actually a cosmic canopy which was originally near earth but is now far out in space. This paper will address the traditional "vapor canopy theory" which is believed to have been present from Creation to the Flood and likely contributed to the heavy rain of the Flood.

Para G

  This article will explore some of the current attitudes and implications to using the Bible as a source of information to "do" science. The consequences of Christian scientists restricting themselves to non-Biblical sources of information will be discussed and an appeal made to take the Bible more seriously in formulating research questions and interpreting scientific data. A case will be made that the Bible can be used to develop a worldview of earth history which is superior to a naturalistic worldview. Although, the Bible obviously does not contain a great deal of scientific detail, it does provide a framework which should direct our scientific thinking. After all, if the Bible is God's Word and it reveals Truth, then the closer we get to the Truth in our presuppositions, the faster we will discover the Truth in the details.

练习二

翻译下列句子。
1. 本文提出了一种新的编码系统。
2. 光速以直线的形式通过密度为常数的纤芯传播，直到它抵达纤芯与包层的界面。
3. 这在第二章已经讨论过了。
4. 在大脑与内脏的神经细胞以及肠胃细胞中发现了许多不同的大分子，这些肠胃细胞的行为就好像激素分泌细胞一样。
5. 从三小时前反应开始时，温度就不断上升。
6. 从那时起，国际空间站将是人类文明向地球以外扩展的一个永久性窗口。
7. 将来，我们就不需要用老式的工具来工作了，机器将为我们做所有的事情，他们甚至会和我们交谈以及玩游戏。人们会有大量的空余时间。但是人们会怎样来打发这些时间呢？
8. 前一节，我们介绍了力的概念。
9. 20世纪40年代他们设计出了第一代电子计算机。
10. 到现在为止，我们一直在讨论平移运动。

第二节 被动语态和主动语态

  英语动词的语态有两种，主动语态和被动语态。科技英语一个突出的语言特点就是被动语态的大量使用,大约占整个谓语动词使用的三分之一,由于科技英语描述的重点在于行为和状态本身,也就是说,更加强调行为的承受者而非行为的执行者,这时,使用被动语态即能突出描述的重点,又显得更加客观和严谨。然而,如果一味地使用被动语态,行文就可能会显得复杂、繁琐。而主动语态简洁、流畅、一目了然的优势就会体现出来。因此,在科技英语中合理地选用主动语态与被动语态也是必须要注意的。

1. 主动语态和被动语态选用的一般规则

(1)当不必说出或无法说出行为的执行者时采用被动语态。

Water is a natural resource that, within limitations, **is continuously renewed**.

水是一种自然资源,它在一定限度内被不断更新。

For a long time aluminum **has been thought as** an effective material for preventing metal corrosion.

长期以来,铝被当作一种有效防止金属腐蚀的材料。

Events in a circuit **can be defined** in terms of voltage and current.

电路的工作情况可用电压和电流来描述。

(2)当强调行为的承受者而非行为的执行者时使用被动语态。

Volume 1 **can be used** as a text for undergraduate course. Volume 2 can be used as a text for graduate course.

第一卷可以作为本科生的教科书。第二卷可以作为研究生的教科书。

The breadth and detail of the coverage is such that the book **can also be used** by students wanting to learn mechanics on their own, or by instructors wanting to direct students through self-paced programs.

教材的深度和广度是这样考虑安排的,既可以为打算自学力学的学生提供教材,又可以为希望通过自己设定的教学提纲来指导学生的老师使用。

Three machines **can be controlled** by a single operation.

三台机器能由一个操作者操纵。

(3)为了句子结构的连贯,有时需要使用被动语态。

较好:They are going to build an apartment house here next year. It is going to **be built** right besides the Office building.

他们明年要在这里修建一座住宅楼,就修在办公楼旁边。

较差:They are going to build an apartment house here next year. They are going to build it right besides the Office building. (如果两句都用"they"作为主语就会显得呆板)

较好:This heating phenomenon **is caused** by microwaves, which are the electromagnetic waves arising as radiation from electrical disturbances at high frequencies.

这种加热现象由微波引起。所谓微波是电磁波,它产生于高频电干扰辐射。

较差:Microwaves, which are the electromagnetic waves arising as radiation from electrical disturbances at high frequencies, causes his heating phenomenon. (如果将主语改成主动语态, 那么整个句子就会前重后轻, 显得不平衡)

较好: Several misinterpretation of the experimental data **were found** in the report, but the report was still published by the journal.

这篇文章有几处对实验数据解释不当的地方, 但是期刊还是刊载了。

较差: Several misinterpretation of the experimental data were found in the report, but the journal still published the report. (这是一个复合句中, 子句中更换了谓语状态, 容易造成阅读的不便甚至误解)

(4) 主动语态常常比被动语态语气自然有力。如果采用主动语态比采用被动语态使句子较为简洁或直截了当, 则采用主动语态。

较好: The use of microprocessor **requires** a working knowledge of binary, decimal, and hexadecimal numbering systems.

使用微处理器需要掌握二进制、十进制和十六进制数制系统的基本知识。

较差: A working knowledge of binary, decimal, and hexadecimal numbering systems is required in the use of microprocessor. (句子结构显得繁琐, 失去平衡)

较好: This section **provides** a background for those who are unfamiliar with number systems.
本节为那些不熟悉系统的读者提供这方面的背景知识。

较差: A background for those who are unfamiliar with number systems is provided in this section. (弱化了要强调的对象 section)

较好: Our work in this area **demonstrates** that such processes are under strict stereo electronic control.

我们在这个领域的工作, 说明了这样的过程是在严格的立体电子的控制下进行的。

较差: The fact that such processes are under strict stereoelectronic control is demonstrated by our work in this area. (句子显得不流畅)

2. 被动语态在科技文章中的频繁使用

被动语态的句子常出现在科技论文中, 尤其是当作者描述某种方法、过程或因果关系时。

A range of multi-wall carbon nanotubes and carbon nanofibres **were mixed** with a polyamide-12 matrix using a twin-screw microextruder, and the resulting blends spun to produce a series of reinforced polymer fibres. The aim was to compare the dispersion and resulting mechanical properties achieved for nanotubes produced by the electric arc and a variety of chemical vapour deposition techniques. A high quality of dispersion **was achieved** for all the catalytically-grown materials and the greatest improvements in stiffness **were observed** using aligned, substrate-grown, carbon nanotubes. The use of entangled multi-wall carbon nanotubes led to the most pronounced increase in yield stress, most likely as result of increased constraint of the polymer matrix due to their relatively high surface area. The degrees of polymer and nanofiller alignment and the morphology of the polymer matrix **were**

assessed using X-ray diffraction and differential scanning calorimetry. The carbon **nanotubes were found** to act as nucleation sites under slow cooling conditions, the effect scaling with effective surface area. Nevertheless, no significant variations in polymer morphology as a function of nanoscale filler type and loading fraction **were observed** under the melt spinning conditions applied. A simple rule-of-mixture evaluation of the nanocomposite stiffness revealed a higher effective modulus for the multi-wall carbon nanotubes compared to the carbon nanofibres, as a result of improved graphitic crystallinity. In addition, this approach allowed a general comparison of the effective nanotube modulus with those of nanoclays as well as common short glass and carbon fibre fillers in melt-blended polyamide composites. The experimental results further highlight the fact that the intrinsic crystalline quality, as well as the straightness of the embedded nanotubes, is significant factors influencing the reinforcement capability.

在这个段落中一共出现6处使用被动语态的地方,其中,第2处的was achieved被动语态是基于上一句中所指出的研究目的所达到的一个结果,强调的是一种状态,故而使用被动语态显得更加的简明客观,而其他5处被动语态的使用都是省略了行为的执行者,从这些句子中可以看出,行为的承受方才是文章关注的焦点,因此要使用被动语态。而且不论mix,observe,assess还是find,这些动作的执行者一定应该是撰写这篇文章的研究人员,没有必要提及。

Prenatal detection of chromosomal abnormalities **is accomplished** chiefly by amniocentesis. A thin needle **is inserted** into the amniotic fluid surrounding the fetus(a term applied to an unborn baby after the first trimester). Cells withdrawn **have been sloughed** off by the fetus, yet they are still fetal cells and **can be used** to determine the state of the fetal chromosomes, such as Down's syndrome and the sex of the baby after a karyotype **has been made**.

在这段讲述如何判断染色体异常的段落中使用了5处被动语态,第1处中by引导的是途径,这里无法提出行为的执行者,故而使用了被动语态。第2处动作的执行者对于这段描述没有必要说明,第3处中强调的是"cells withdrawn"而不是"fetus",并且为了使行文更加流畅,第3处和第4处同时都使用了被动语态。而第5处中的用法和第1处类似,都是无法指出行为的执行者。

The relationship between microtubular dynamics, dismantling of pericentriolar components and induction of apoptosis **was analyzed** after exposure of H460 non-small lung cancer cells to anti-mitotic drugs. The microtubule destabilizing agent, combretastatin – A4(CA – 4)led to microtubular array disorganization, arrest in mitosis and abnormal metaphases, accompanied by the presence of numerous centrosome-independent "star-like" structures containing tubulin and aggregates of pericentrosomal matrix components like c-tubulin, pericentrin and ninein, whereas the structural integrity of centrioles **was not affected** by treatment. On the contrary, in condition of prolonged exposure or high concentrations of CA – 4 such aggregates never formed. Treatment with 7.5 nm CA – 4, which produced a high frequency "star-like" aggregates, **was accompanied** by mitotic catastrophe commitment characterized by translocation of the proapoptotic Bim protein to mitochondria activation of caspases-3/9 and DNA fragmentation as a result of either prolonged metaphase arrest or attempt of cells to divide. Drug concentrations which fail to block cells at mitosis were also unable to activate apotosis. A detailed time-course analysis of cell cycle arrest and apoptosis indicated that after CA-4 washout the number of metaphases with "star-like" structures decreased as a function of time and arrested cells proceeded in anaphase. After 4 h, the multiple α – and γ – tubulin aggregates coalesced into two well-defined spindles in a bipolar mitotic spindle organization. Overall, our findings suggest that the maintenance of microtubular integrity plays a relevant role in stabilising the pericentriolar matrix, whose dismantling **can be associated** with apoptosis after exposure to microtubule depolymerising agents.

本段中第1处的动作执行者是研究人员,没有必要列出,使用被动语态让句子结构更加简洁,避免出现理解错误。第2处和第3处都是强调行为过程,而最后1处使用被动语态则是出于上下文连接的需要。

3. 人称的使用
(1) 人称的使用。

在科技英语中,如果第一人称使用过多,会造成主观臆断的印象,使文章失去它的客观性和普遍性,因此要慎用第一人称,如果使用第一人称的句子能够使表达更清晰,以及表达一个目的、作出一个决定及发表一个声明,或者以示对事实及声明负责时,就可以采用第一人称。

The effect of Rashba spin-orbit(SO) interaction on the whole states in a quantum dot is studied in the presence of an external magnetic field. **We demonstrate** here that the Rashba SO coupling has a profound effect on the energy spectrum of the holes revealing level repulsions between the states with the same total momentum. **We also show** that the resulting spin-orbit gap is much larger than the corresponding one for the electron energy levels in a quantum dot. Inter-hole interactions only marginally reduce the spin-orbit gap. This enhanced Rashba effect would manifest itself in the tunneling current which depends on the spin-orbit coupling strength.

上文中 demonstrate 与 show 都是在表达作者的声明,因此使用第一人称更加清晰且有力度。

但是像 we believe, we feel, we concluded, we can see 这种有强烈主观色彩的动词就要尽量避免和第一人称搭配使用。

值得注意的是,在数学文章中,用 we 作主语的句子特别多。

①We will begin by reviewing, very briefly, the fundamental notions of control theory as they apply to finite dimensional linear constant coefficient system in Hilbert spaces.

②We note that A(x) is still continuously differentiable and B(x) is still continuous.

③We consider the system…

④We suppose that, after the transformation indicated above, this result in(3.12)being replaced by…

⑤When the boundary condition(3.12)is replaced by(3.13)we again obtain a generalized solution…

⑥We remark here that H1([0,1]; En) refers to the Sobolev space of N-demensional vector functions defined on [0,1] whose derivatives, defined in the sense permitted in the theory of distributions, are square integrable.

⑦We will use the following notations.

⑧We collect in the following proposition some known facts about Triebel spaces.

除了第一人称的使用,有时第二人称 you 也会出现在科技文章中,具有一定的指导意义,让读者在读到文字信息的时候,可以感受到这种意义的气氛。

Currently 94% of Web users either Internet Explorer or Netscape Navigator, but recently some new browsers have been developed that are beginning to attract attention. The browser Opera is becoming very popular because of its speed—it is currently the world's fastest browser—and because it is much smaller than existing browsers (it can fit on a single diskette). It can also remember the last Web page you visited, so the next time you surf, **you** can start where **you** left off. And like the big two, **you** can get it for free; the catch is that **you** have to watch blinking ads in one corner, or pay 40 $ for the ad-free version of Opera.

Specific words and phase: This can be anything. The firewall will sniff each packet of information for an exact match of the text listed in the filter. For example, **you** would instruct the firewall to block any packet with the word "X-rated" in it. The key here is that it has to be an exact match. The "X-rated" filter would not catch "X-rated" (no hyphen). But **you** can include as many words, phases and variations of them as you need.

上面两段文字里都出现了 you 这一人称,使读者能产生身临其境的感受,较有说服力且句子更加流畅。

(2)动词的拟人化。

在英语和汉语科技文章中,一些无生命的事物搭配主动语态的及物动词,可以拟人化为具有主动行为的能力并带有宾语。

表达"范围、范畴"或"领域、状态相关"等的及物动词以及及物短语动词本来就可以用在无生命主语句中作为主动谓语,下面列举一些常见的动词:to allow, to compose, to comprise, to conjugate, to consist of, to constitute, to contain, to entail, to forbid, to incorporate, to inhibit, to involve, to lead, to permit, to prohibit.

It is very easy to **set up** a memory system that consists of a single chip.

A base 8(octal) number **contains** 8 digits: 0 through 7.

A classic application of a stack **involves** the execution of a program involving procedures as found in our pseudocode.

而现在表达"行为和动作"的动词或者动词短语,比用于无生命主语句中的主动语态谓语的数量要多得多,而且越是常见的动词,这样的使用也越多。这些句子隐去了行为的真正原动力,即人,而把非生命的动作承受者转化成了一个动作的主题。即语义不合逻辑的"无生命事物进行主动行为并带有动作的承受者"的拟人化使用现在变得越来越多。在化学和计算机文献中应用广泛。

to abrogate	to draw	to accelerate	to enable
to activate	to enhance	to affect	to exceed
to afford	to fail	to agree	to favor
to assume	to focus	to attract	to follow
to begin	to give	to call	to handle
to carry	to have	to commence	to illustrate
to complete	to imply	to concur	to improve
to continue	to indicate	to convert	to initiate
to deactivate	to inspire	to deal with	to interpret
to demonstrate	to interrupt	to depict	to involve
to describe	to lead	to discuss	to lose
to display	to make	to maximize	to represent
to minimize	to require	to open	to result
to optimize	to reveal	to outline	to revert
to play	to serve	to point out	to show
to present	to proceed	to produce	to promote
to prove	to provide	to rationalize	to receive
to reflect	to rely on	to render	to stimulate
to slow down	to spawn	to suffer	to suggest
to support	to terminate	to undergo	to yield

The linear organization **will require** a 12 to 4,096 decoder, the size of which is proportional to the number of outputs.

Data structures **provide** a more understandable way to look at data; thus, they **offer** a level of abstraction in solving problems.

Static resources allocation is simple to implement, however, it could **lead to** suboptimal utilization because the allocation is made on the basis of perceived needs of a program, rather than its actual needs.

The challenges **have attracted** large numbers of chemists and spawned a whole are of inquiry within chemistry.

The result **points out** a limitation of one-dimensional separation of complex protein samples: many components comigrate in a single band.

When the chromosome condensation **initiates** in G2 phase reaches the point at which individual condensed chromosomes first become visible with the light microscope, the first stage of mitosis, prophase, has begun.

The review **gives** a brief account on the current status of enediyne biosynthesis and the prospective of applying combinational biosynthesis methods to the enediyne system for novel analog production.

This article **discussed** some possible roles for self-access pathways, particularly in cultures which have no tradition of self-study.

但是,要注意习惯上并非所有的及物动词都可以这样使用,现在习惯上公认能够这样使用的动词,还只是及物动词中的一部分。至于哪个动词或者短语可以使用,还是需要靠大量的阅读科技英语文献来积累,且不可生造。当然,以上的使用针对的是科技论文,对于科普类的文章,这类的句子就非常常见了。

语言文字都是在发展变化的,现在不可以使用的,不代表将来就一定不能使用。但是,如果是撰写科技论文,要尽量体现出客观和准确性,因此,要尽量少用这类拟人化的句子。

Exercise

练习一

翻译下列句子,注意被动语态的使用。
1. 其他问题也可被预见到。
2. 石油生产技术可以分成三个等级。
3. 定稿的图样常常画在描图纸、布或聚酯薄膜上。
4. 这项实验现在仍被引用作为证明。
5. 这种效应解释了那些为经典化学法则所不允许的化学反应。
6. 尽管人们知道肾上腺激素能够调节记忆存储,但它并不是通过血液进入脑细胞的。
7. 实验表明,通过从群落中驱逐一条已有的小丑鱼来造成空缺。

练习二
1. 风速较慢或天气潮湿时,很多风媒植物不释放花粉。
2. 导线能用作天线。
3. 今年移动通讯会议将于何时举行?
4. 调查显示在同一时期,二氧化碳含量也随温度变化而变化。
5. 乙醇和甲醇具有优于其他碳基替代燃料的重要优势。
6. 负载电阻 R 形成了一个消耗能量的概念。
7. 本文全面研讨了现行的化石燃料的脱硫问题。

第三章 非谓语动词

第一节 动词不定式

大部分动词的不定式形式由 to 加动词短语构成,不定式在句子中可以充当主语、表语、宾语、定语、同位语、状语和补语等。

1. 作主语

To make the existence of such relationships clear and to emphasize the usefulness of the periodic table, in the remainder of this chapter we shall discuss some of the clearer trends in the properties of the elements and of some of their common compounds.

为了弄清这些关系的存在,并强调周期表的实用性,我们将在本章的后面几节中讨论元素性质及元素的几种常见化合物的性质中一些较为清楚的倾向。

以 it 作形式主语,动词不定式作主语。

It is important **to note** that the first letter of every chemical symbols is capitalized.

有一点非常重要:每个化学元素的首字母必须大写。

It is most important **to begin** to learn the names of 43 of the most common chemical elements along with the chemical symbols for them.

在开始学习常用化学元素中的 43 种元素名称时,学会它们的化学符号是极其重要的。

It is advisable **to write** or print a small letter differently from the capitalized form of the same letter.

书写或印刷时应使用一个小写字母,以区别于大写字母。

It will not be necessary **to calculate** the component of the velocity perpendicular to the magnetic field.

不必计算垂直于磁场的速度分量。

It takes only dozens of seconds for a computer **to solve** this problem.

用计算机解这道题只需几十秒钟。

Since that time, however, it has been possible **to determine** phylogeny from comparisons of molecules.

然而,从那时起,通过分子比较确定进化史有了可能。

As microevolution continues, a population may become so different that it is no longer **to reproduce with** members of other populations.

小进化积累后,一个种群变得与其他种群明显不同,这个种群内的个体不再能与其他种群的个体繁殖后代。

It is not always easy **to tell** the difference between a physical and chemical change.

区分物理变化和化学变化并不总是一件容易的事。

It's both more meaningful and more useful **to express** the components of a vector A with respect to a frame S' as Ai' rather than A'i.

要表示矢量 A 相对参考坐标系 S' 的分量,使用符号 Ai' 比 A'i 意义更清晰也更有益。

2. 作表语

As phase continues, a second group of microtubules appears **to grow** from the poles of the cell toward the centromeres.

随着前期的继续,第二微管团出现,并从细胞的两级向着丝点方向生长。

The purpose of this chapter is **to introduce** to you the nature of chemistry: the branch of science that deals with matter and energy in the natural world.

本章的目的在于引导读者走进化学世界并懂得:化学是研究自然界中物质与能量的一门科学。

The contribution of the model is **to show** that the winds of an El Nino, which raise sea level in the east, simultaneously send a signal to the west lowering sea level.

此模型的贡献在于显示了厄尔尼诺现象中的风使东海平面升高,同时也向西部低海平面区发送一个信号。

3. 作宾语

In animal cells, the two centriole pairs formed during G2 phase begin **to move** apart early in prophase, forming between them an axis of microtubules referred to as spindle fibers.

在动物细胞中,在有丝分裂前期的初期,在 G2 期形成的两个配对的中心粒开始分别向两级移动,在它们之间形成一个叫做纺锤丝的微管轴。

Many wind-pollinated species fail **to release** pollen when wind speeds are low or when humid conditions prevail.

风速较慢或天气潮湿时,很多风媒植物不释放花粉。

Some scientists have precipitously ventured hypotheses that attempt **to explain** the development, from these larger molecules, of the earliest self-duplicating organisms.

一些科学家仍迫不及待地提出了假说,试图解释最早的那些自我繁殖的生物体是如何从这些较大分子发展而来的。

4. 作定语

Robert Hooke, one of the first scientists **to use** a microscope to examine pond water, cork and other things, referred to the cavities he saw in cork as "cells", Latin for chambers.

罗伯特虎克是最早使用显微镜来检测池塘水、软木和其他东西的科学家之一,他把在软木中所见到的腔称为"细胞",在拉丁语中"细胞"表示小室的意思。

One view of life is that it is a struggle **to acquire** energy form sunlight, inorganic chemicals, or another organism, and release it in the process of forming ATP, that is adenosine triphosphate.

关于生命的一个理论是尽力从太阳光、无机化合物或其他有机体中获得能量,再在形成ATP(三磷酸腺苷)的过程中释放出来。

The voyage would provide Darwin a unique opportunity **to study** adaptation and gather a great deal of proof he would later incorporate into his theory of evolution.

这次航海旅行给达尔文提供了独一无二的机会,来研究生物适应性及收集大量的证据,后来这些证据成为他的进化论的一部分。

As an effort **to reduce** confusion, the new numbers seem logical and may receive worldwide approval.

为了尽量减少混乱,启用新数字似乎更为合理,且可能得到国际认可。

The nonmetals are electrical insulators: The ability **to conduct** electricity is either extremely small or undetectable.

非金属是电绝缘体:其电导率要么非常小,要么检测不到。

The first book **to treat** transient stresses at all fully was *stress waves in solids* by H. Kolsky.

第一本全面阐述瞬态应力的专著是Kolsky于1953年出版的《固体中的应力波》。

5. 作状语

Much material is covered, but no attempt has been made **to write** an encyclopedic text on classical mechanics.

尽管收录了众多的材料,但作者并不打算写一本百科全书式的经典力学教科书。

These proteins function as gateways that will, in exchange for a price, allow certain molecules **to cross** into and out of the cell.

这些蛋白质有通道的功能和交换作用,允许特定的分子进出细胞。

Very recently the American Chemical Society has recommended that the use of Roman numerals **to indicate** columns in the periodic table be discontinued.

就在最近,美国化学学会提出建议,要求终止使用罗马数字来表示周期表的列。

It enables the student **to appreciate** salient aspects, **to acquire** some skill in dealing with transient stresses, and **to solve** some very special problems before encountering the complexities that develop when such concepts as elastic-plastic behavior are introduced.

这能使学生欣赏到其突出的方面,学到处理瞬态应力所需的一些技巧,还能解决一些非常实际的问题,无需引入弹塑性波概念而使问题复杂化。

The success of limb-sparing surgery has also stimulated technological developments in designing and manufacturing endoprostheses **to restore** function to the damage limb.

这项旨在挽救肢体的外科手术方案的成功,也激励了恢复受损肢体功能的内修补器材设计和制造的技术开发。

6. 作补语

These branches make it easier **to study** chemistry.

这些分支使化学的研究变得容易了许多。

The version easiest **to use** and most clearly related to the electronic structures of the atom is the so-called long-form shown in Table 2.1.

使用最方便,同时又与原子的电子结构联系最紧密的是表 2.1 所示的长式周期表。

The chapters are short **to make** assimilation easier and to aid in the addition, deletion or rearrangement of material.

每一章不宜太长,以便于内容的消化吸收,同时也有利于教材的增、删和重新编排。

The human brain contains two hemispheres whose characters have been shown **to be** different but complementary.

人的大脑由两个半球构成,它们的特征各不相同但又互补。

第二节 分 词

分词作为动词的另一种非限定形式,主要起形容词和副词的作用。分词有两种,现在分词和过去分词,这两种分词在句子中能担任的成分大体相同,主要是在意思上有主动被动之分,现在分词一般有主动的意思,过去分词一般有被动的意思。分词在句子中可作定语、状语、表语和补语等。

1. 作定语

分词作定语,一般遵循"单分在前,分短在后"的原则,即单个分词作定语时一般置于被修饰词之前,而分词短语作定语时一定要置于被修饰词之后。

There is a **growing** interest among theoretical and **applied** researchers alike in the structural properties of these materials.

这些材料的结构特性引起了理论和实际工作者的浓厚兴趣。

Scientists think that 99.9 percent of your genes perfectly match those of the person **sitting beside you**. But **remaining** 0.1 percent of your genes vary and it is these variation that most interest drug companies.

科学家认为你的基因与坐在你旁边的人 99.9% 一致,但仍有 0.1% 不一样,而正是这点差异令制药公司大感兴趣。

Carefully **designed** DNA arrays could announce the precise cause of infection in a patient whose flulike symptoms do not point to one clear culprit.

如果不能确诊流感样症状患者的真正病因,精心设计的 DNA 微列阵就能揭示出其感染的准确原因。

If you collect the carbon dioxide gas in a **closed** container and heat the compound to a high temperature, it can be broken into carbon and oxygen, the element from which it was made.

如果将二氧化碳气体收集于一封闭的容器中并加热至高温,二氧化碳将分解成其组成元素:碳和氧。

The intensive work of materials scientists and solidstate physicists has given rise to a class of solids **known** as amorphous metallic alloys or glassy metals.

材料科学家和固体物理科学家的集中工作已经研制出了某一种类型的固体:称为非晶体金属合金或玻璃金属。

Blood **collected** from umbilical cords and placentas—which are usually thrown away following birth— contains stem cells that can rebuild the blood and immune systems of people with leukemia and other cancers.

从分娩后通常被丢掉的脐带和胎盘采集的血中含有干细胞,这些干细胞能够重建白血病和其他癌症患者的血液和免疫系统。

2. 作状语

现在分词短语作状语时,通常都表示主语正在进行的另一动作,来对谓语表示的主要动作加以修饰或作为陪衬。过去分词作状语说明动作发生的背景和情况,也可表示原因,时间,条件等。

Beginning with blood and sperm cells, the team separated out the 23 pairs of chromosomes that hold human genes.

研究小组首先从血液细胞核精液细胞开始,分离出了携带有人类基因的 23 对染色体。

The emphasis is on computational power, **using** algorithms to sequence the data. The advantage is efficiency and speed.

重点是依靠计算机的计算能力,使用算法对数据进行排序。其优势在于效率和速度。

The letters stand for the DNA chemicals that make up all your genes, **influencing** the way you walk, talk, think and sleep.

这些字母代表了组成你的全部基因的 DNA 化学物质,它们影响着你走路,讲话,思考和睡觉的方式。

For the better part of a century, **following** the 1859 publication of Charles Darwin's on the Origin of Species, a parade of scientists speculated on life's chemical origins.

从 1859 年查尔斯达尔文的《物种起源》发表以来的大半个世纪中,许多科学家都在推究生命的化学起源说。

Recognizing the apparent advantages of umbilical cord blood transplantation, a number of medical centers have established banks so that mothers can donate her baby's cord blood by a stranger in need.

认识到脐带血所具有的这些明显优点,一些医疗中心已建立了脐带血库,以便让母亲能将其婴儿的脐带血捐赠出来供陌生人在急需时使用。

First **introduced** commercially in 1996, DNA microarrays are now mainstays of drug discovery, and more than 20 companies sell them or the instruments or software needed to interpret the information they provide.

DNA 微阵列 1996 年首次进入商业领域,现在是药物开发研究的主流方向,美国有 20 多家公司销售 DNA 微阵列,或者销售破译 DNA 微阵列提供的信息所需的仪器或软件。

从上面的例子可以看出,在分词短语作状语时,分词的逻辑主语一般应该就是句子的主语,可根据分词与句子的主被动关系来确定到底用现在分词还是用过去分词。

Microwaves are the name given to the electromagnetic waves **arising** as radiation from electrical disturbances at high frequencies.

微波是高频电干扰辐射产生的电磁波的名称。

Building directly on these 2 – D technologies, we have made 3 – D circuits by coating standard silicon wafers with many successive layers of polysilicon polishing the surface flat after each step.

我们直接利用这些二维技术来制作三维电路,其方法是把许多晶硅一层接一层地覆盖在标准的硅片上,每覆盖一层就将其表面抛光。

Silver is the best conductor, **followed** by copper.

银是最好的导体,其次是铜。

Given current and resistance, we can find out voltage.

若已知电流和电阻,我们就能求出电压。

It(DNA microarray) enabled a team of researchers from the National Institutes of Health, Stanford University and elsewhere to distinguish between known long- and short-term survivors **based on** differences in the overall pattern of activity exhibited by hundreds of genes in their malignant cells at the time of diagnosis.

来自美国国立卫生研究院、斯坦福大学等单位的研究人员组成的一个科学小组在诊断时利用了 DNA 微阵列,并基于恶性细胞的数百种基因所展现出来的总体活动图谱的差异,分辨出了已知的长期幸存者和短期幸存者。

In April a brash young company called Celera Genomics in Rockville, Md., beat the public consortium to the punch, **announcing** its own rough draft of the human genome.

4 月,位于马里兰州罗克维尔一家充满活力的新公司 Celera 基因组学公司在 4 月份给予了人类基因组计划猛然一击,声称自己已有了自己的人类基因组草图。

They are often used to replace chains or gears, **reducing** noise and avoiding the lubrication bath or oiling system requirement.

它们经常用于替代链条或齿轮,可以减少噪音又不需要润滑槽或润滑系统。

Timing belts, **known** also as synchronous or cogged belts, require the least tension of all belt drives and are among the most efficient.

同步齿形皮带也叫做同步的或楔形齿皮带,在所有带式传动中需要的张力最少而效率最高。

在用分词作状语时,它逻辑上的主语一般必须与句子的主语一致。但有时它也可以有自己独立的逻辑上的主语,这种结构称为独立结构。是典型的书面表达。

The voltage **remaining** constant, the current varies indirectly with the resistance.

当电压保持不变时,电流与电阻成反比。

A power reactor **having** no need of air, we can build it underground.

由于电力反应堆不需要空气,所以我们可以把它建在地下。

That **done**, the process reaches the end.

完成那些之后,该过程就终止了。

An electron is about as large as a nucleus, its diameter **being** about 10~12 cm.

电子大约与原子核一样大,其直径为 10~12 cm。

There are several basic laws governing these interactions, all of them **discovered** early in the 19th century.

支配这些相互作用的基本定律有好几个,都是在 19 世纪初发现的。

3. with 结构

with + 名词 + 分词(短语)/ 介词短语/ 形容词短语/ 副词/ 不定式短语/ 名词(短语)

其否定形式可用 without 或 with + no/neither/ none 来表示,这种结构在科技英语写作中广泛使用。

(1)with 结构作状语:处于句首表示条件、时间和原因,处于句尾表示附加说明、方式、条件。

在句首的情况

With its base voltage 0, transistor Q1 will be cut off.

在基极(电压)为零时,晶体管 Q1 就会截止。

With friction present, a part of power has been lost as heat.

由于存在摩擦,所以一部分功率作为热而损耗掉了。

With Q2 on, the voltage fed to the base of Q3 rises.

Q2 导通时,加给 Q3 基极的电压会就上升。

With these definitions in hand, Eq. (6) can be transformed term by term.

有了这些定义后,就可对等式(6)一项一项地进行变换了。

在句尾的情况

Each planet revolves around the sun in an elliptical orbit, **with** the sun at one focus of the ellipse.

每颗行星在椭圆轨道上绕太阳运行,而太阳则处于椭圆的一个焦点上。

A slide projector is to be used **with** its lens 29 ft from a screen.

应该使用一台透镜离屏幕 29 英尺的幻灯机。

Standard screws are all right-handed, **with** left-handed ones employed only for special purpose.

标准螺钉都是右旋的,左螺旋钉只用于特殊目的。

The condition of resonance can be achieved **with** L and C either in series or in parallel.

将 L 和 C 串联或并联均可获得谐振状态。

This parameter shall be measured **with** E grounded.

这个参数应该在 E 接地的情况下加以测量。

(2) with 结构作定语。

Equations **with** radicals in them are normally solved by squaring both sides of the equation.

含有根式的方程通常是通过对方程两边进行平方来解的。

The device **with** buttons on it is a keyboard.

上面带有按键的装置就是键盘。

This is an inequality **with** zero on the right.

这是一个右边为零的不等式。

For this purpose we construct a new set of axes **with** their origin at the Q point.

为此,我们建立原点处于 Q 点的一组新轴。

第三节 动名词

动名词是动词的另一种非限定形式。它在句子中起名词的作用,可单独引起短语用作主语,宾语或介词宾语。

1. 作主语

Recent **findings** suggest that visual signals are fed into at least three separate processing systems in the brain, each with its own distinct function.

最近发现显示视觉信号被传入大脑后,至少要经过三个独立的接收系统,每个过程有不同的机能。

An **understanding** of the functions and capabilities of these three systems can shed light on how artists manipulate materials to create surprising visual effects.

对于这三个系统机能和功能的理解会帮助理解艺术家是如何处理原料来创造奇异的视觉

效果。

Knowing the genome will change the way drug trials are done and kick off a whole new era of individualized medicine.

对基因组的不断了解将改变药物试验的方式,并将开创个性化药物的全新时代。

Receiving a bone marrow transplant from someone who is not a good tissue-type is potentially fatal.

从某个组织配型不好的人那里接收骨髓移植可能是致命的。

Achieving even this nascent step in evolution entailed a sequence of chemical transformation, each of which added a level of structure and complexity to a group of organic molecules.

即使是完成进化历程中这样初始的一步,也需要一系列的化学转变过程。

2. 作宾语

有一类动词只能带动名词作宾语,不能带不定式作宾语。在科技英语写作中常见的这类动词有 avoid, consider, involve, facilitate, require, finish, suggest, practice, resist, cease 等。

This spring Celera announced that it had finished sequencing the rough-draft genome of one anonymous person and that it would sort the data into a map in just six weeks.

今年春天 Celera 公司宣布已经完成一个匿名者的基因组测序草图,而且在 6 个星期内将数据归入图谱。

This involves **calculating** the total energy of the molecules.

这涉及要计算分子的总能量。

Let us consider **doing** a simple experiment.

让我们考虑做一个简单的试验。

We must avoid **using** the symbol.

我们必须避免使用这个符号。

3. 注意正确使用动名词的被动形式

Both types of arrays are already **being investigated** for use in medical care.

这两种基因阵列疗法已处于医疗福利方面的调查研究之中。

Potential energy is capable of **being changed** into kinetic energy.

势能可以转变成动能。

All forms of information must be converted to electromagnetic energy before **being propagated** through an electronic communication system.

在通过电子系统传输之前,各种信息都需先转换成电磁能量。

Enzymes increase the speed of chemical reactions without **being changed** themselves.

酶能够提高化学反应的速度而其本身并不会被改变。

4. 动名词也可以和 about, against, at, before, after, by, besides, for, from, in, on, upon, without 等

介词构成短语,作状语用。

In each case you have carried out a physical change **by changing** the size and shape of a sample of matter, mixing or dissolving two or more substances or changing an element or compound from one physical state to another.

在上述的每一种情况下我们均通过下述方法实现了一种物理变化:改变一种物质的大小和形状,混合或溶解两种以上的物质,或将元素或化合物从一种物理状态转变到另一种状态。

Ethanol and methanol, on the other hand, have important advantages over other carbon-based alternative fuels: they have higher energy content per volume and would require minimal changes in the existing network **for distributing** motor fuel.

从另一个方面来看,乙醇和甲醇具有优于其他碳基替代燃料的重要优势:它们在单位容量下有更高的能量含量,并且只需要在现存的配送燃料的网络中做很小的变更。

The mango system carries information about movement and depth. It is good **at detecting** motion but poor **at scrutinizing** stationary images.

M 系统携带关于运动和深度的信息,它擅长观测运动,细辨静止的形象能力却很弱。

Exercise

练习一

翻译下列句子,注意不定式的使用。
1. 能够确定这个物体的重量。
2. 电路的作用是分配电能和转换能量形式。
3. 电动势能产生一个绕该闭合回路的连续单向电流。
4. 在电路外部,即在负载 R 中,假定电流从端点 a 流向端点 b。
5. 土木工程师建造的住所提供了一个和平而舒适的生活环境。
6. 从那时起,土木工程师这个词用来指建设公共设施的工程师。
7. 他们帮助建造水厂、废水处理厂和垃圾站。
8. 节点的设计是要传递轴向荷载、弯力、弯矩和扭矩。
9. R 是所要测定的电阻。
10. 我发现相对论是很难解释的。
11. 国际电信联盟鼓励经济地提供全方位的电信服务,并融入世界范围的电信系统。
12. 第一个条件是必然的,因为任何系统都只存在于有限的时间内。
13. 构成液体的"微粒"运动相对自由,这是因为它们虽然结合紧密但不牢固。
14. 要对这种最大的海洋生物蓝鲸进行追踪观测是很困难的。

练习二

翻译下列句子,注意分词的使用。

1. 仅含线性元件的电路称为线性电路。
2. 在电路等效图中电源电阻 R',可表示成与负载电阻 R 相串联。
3. 根据 R 和 r 两端电压的相对大小,我们可以推出两种串联电路的变换形式。
4. 世界上的奇迹工程,从金字塔到当今的壳结构都是土木工程发展的结果。
5. 从事环境工程的人们设计系统来净化水和空气。
6. 用于结构的钢材只是一小部分,它需要具备一些优点。
7. 尽管电子通信的基本概念和原理自开创以来并没有多大变化,但实现的方法和电路已有飞速发展。
8. 音乐一般有两种结构:由一串时序的声音组成的旋律和一组同时发出的声音组成的和弦。
9. 在其基极接地的情况下 Q4 是一个很高的抗阻。
10. 在气体中,这些微粒相距很远,其间都是真空。
11. 从下一年度开始,基金会将在全国选定的路面上画人字形线和其他图线。

练习三

翻译下列句子,注意动名词的使用。

1. 随着电流的继续增大,与其电源端电压之比值变了。
2. 施工是一个复杂的过程,它包括安排工作、利用设备和材料以使造价尽可能低。
3. 在这种情况下,钠和氯原子核不再被它们的电子所屏蔽。
4. 压缩气体时其温度会升高。
5. 让我们考虑做一个简单的实验。
6. 通过分析该设备的性能,我们能更好地了解它。
7. 写代数式时,我们经常把某些项归并到一起。

第四章 从 句

第一节 定语从句

定语从句是由关系代词或关系副词引导的从句,其作用是作定语修饰主句的某个名词性成分,被定语从句修饰的名词、代词称为先行词。关系代词有 that,which,who,whom,whose,as 等;关系副词有 where,when,why 等。关系词通常有三个作用:引导定语从句、代替先行词及在定语从句中担当一个成分。

1. 关系代词在从句中作主语

A computer **that** includes cache memory must also have a cache controller to move date between the cache and physical memory.

含有高速缓冲存储器的计算机同时也要有一个高速缓冲控制器,用来在高速缓冲和物理存储器间传输数据。

An equation **which is** true only for certain values of a letter in it, or for certain sets of related values of two or more of its letters, is an equation of condition, or simply an equation.

一个等式若仅仅对其中一个字母的某些值成立,或者对其中两个或多个字母的若干组相关的值成立,则它是一个条件等式,或简称方程。

The real challenge is how to create systems with many components **that** can work together and change, merging the physical world with the digital world.

真正的挑战是如何创建一些带有许多能一起工作并可更换的部件的系统,从而把物质世界与数字世界合二为一。

Back your data. Anyone **who** doesn't have a backup drive is begging for trouble.

备份你的数据。任何没有备份硬盘的人都是在自找麻烦。

2. 关系代词在从句中作宾语

作及物动词宾语时可以省略关系代词

The READ signal is a signal on the control bus (which) the microprocessor asserts when it is ready to read data from memory or an I/O device.

当微处理器准备好可以从存储器或是 I/O 设备读数据时,它就在控制总线上发一个读信号。

The period of light and darkness (which) sun created were the first accepted periods of time.

太阳所产生的光明和黑暗的周期就是人类最早接受的时间周期。

The division of time we use today were developed in ancient Babylonia 4,000 years ago.

我们现在用来划分时间的方法是 4 000 年前的古巴比伦王国发明的。

The meter that we use to measure pressure is known as a pressure gauge.

我们用来测量压力的仪表被称为压力计。

3. 关系代词在从句中作介词宾语

Sets are a means **by which** mathematicians talk of collection of things in an abstract way.

集合是数学家们用抽象的方式来表述一些事物的集体工具。

The speed of light depends on the density of the medium **through which** it is traveling (the higher the density, the lower the speed).

光的速度取决于其传播介质的密度(介质密度越高,速度越慢)。

Another way **in which** cells in one part of the body pass information to distant cells is by the release of chemicals known as hormones.

让身体某一部分的细胞给远距离的细胞传递信息的另外一种方式是通过激素来实现的。

Cohesion is the force **with which** like molecules attract each other.

内聚力就是使同种分子相互吸引的力。

Homeostasis is the maintenance of a dynamic range of conditions **within which** the organism can function.

动态平衡是指有机体可以发挥功能时的动态条件的保持。

When the chromosome condensation initiated in G2 phase reaches the point **at which** individual condensed chromosomes first become visible with the light microscope, the first stage of mitosis, prophase, has begun.

染色体浓缩始于 G2 期,在光学显微镜下可见单个浓缩的染色体时,有丝分裂的第一阶段,前期就已经开始了。

How to live longer is a question **to which** man has tried to find a good answer for hundreds of years.

如何使人活得更长是人类几百年来一直力图寻求满意答案的一个问题。

Another method of locking is the use of a self-locking nut **for which** the top of threads are manufactured at a reduced pitch diameter.

另一个锁紧的方法是使用螺丝帽,制造时在其顶部螺纹处减小其中径。

4. 关系代词在从句中作定语

This machine, called the Electric Discrete Variable Automatic Computer, was the first machine **whose** design included all the characteristics of a computer.

这部机器被称作电子离散变量自动计算机,是第一部包括了计算机所有特征的机器。

The linear organization will require a 12 to 4096 decoder, **the size of which** is proportional to the number of outputs.

这个线组成将需要一个 12-4096 译码器,译码器大小与输出的数量成正比。

The DNA is divided into units known as genes, and each gene carries instructions for the production of one particular protein—most of these proteins are special chemicals called enzymes, **each of which promotes a particular chemical process in the body.**

DNA 分割为一个个基因片段,每个基因都包含着生成特定蛋白质的指令。这些蛋白质大多是叫做酶的特殊化学物质。每一个酶都促使体内一种特别的化学过程的发生。

5. 关系代词在从句中作表语,关系代词可以省略

It is unfortunate that early cancer is painless; otherwise, cancer would not be the problem that it is.

早期癌症没有疼痛感,否则癌症就不会成为现在这样(棘手)的问题了。

The voltage across the resistor R_1 is obtained as the same fraction of the total voltage that R_1 is of the total resistance.

电阻 R_1 上的电压与总电阻的比值等同于 R_1 与总电阻的比值。

The sum of the squares of the deviation of all points from the best line is the least it can be.

各点与最佳线偏离的平方之和是所能获得的最小值。

6. 关系副词在从句中作状语

Although the microwave frequency above is accepted by common usage as the region **where** these specialized techniques are used most frequently, the relationship of size to characteristic wavelength is the true guideline determining when microwave techniques or analysis are applicable to any particular system.

虽然说上面所说的微波频率范围被接受为一般用途的范围,在这个范围里这些特殊技术最为常用,但线路大小与特征波长的关系是决定微波技术与分析是否适用于某个特别系统的真正指导原则。

The ubiquitous refrigerating and air-conditioning plants of the modern age are based on a reversed heat engine, **where** the supply of power pumps heat from the cold region to the warmer exterior.

现代的制冷和空调厂普遍采用反向的热引擎,在这些地方动力把热从冷的地方抽出送到更热的外部。

Carbohydrates have the general formula [CH_2O]n **where** n is a number between 3 and 6.

碳水化合物的通式是[CH_2O]n,这里 n 的取值在 3 至 6 之间

Some scientists believe there is one reason **why** time only moves forward, it is a well-known scientific law: the second law of thermodynamics.

一些科学家相信一个著名的科学定律能够解释时间不可逆原因,这就是热力学第二定律。

The instruction for making the proteins are passed by the DNA in the nucleus to surrounding cytoplasm, **where** the proteins are formed, by means of the nucleic acid "messenger" RNA.

制造蛋白质的指令由细胞中的 DNA 发出给周围的细胞质,通过核酸信使 RNA,蛋白质在细胞质中合成。

7. 先行词为不定代词或被序数词、形容词最高级或 only,no,very,any 等词修饰时不能用

which 而只能用 that

The first basic concept **that** relates one set to another is equality of sets.
谈到两个集合之间的关系,第一个基本的概念就是集合相等。

In any case, any number **that** is raised to its zero power is always 1, or the units position.
在任何情况下,任何数的零次幂总是1,或1个单位。

Unlike an airplane, the space station is flown while it is being built, and each new piece **that** is added may change the way the station behaves in flight.
和飞机不同,空间站在建造时就是浮在空中的,每一个新部分的安装都可能会改变它的飞行。

The most common numbering systems **that** are used with computers are decimal, binary, and hexadecimal.
计算机中最通用的计数制是十进制、二进制、八进制和十六进制。

Computer software problems are also a concern, "Probably the biggest single risk **that** we face on this project", say Stone.
计算机软件问题也值得担忧,"这也许是我们在这个项目上面临的最大的冒险"斯通先生说。

In early human history, the only changes **that** seemed to repeat themselves evenly were the movements of objects in the sky. The most easily seen result those movements were the difference between light and darkness.
在人类早期的历史中,只有天空中的物体似乎是在有规律的反复改变。最容易观察到的就是光明和黑暗的更迭。

In this way the inserted meter will not affect the very thing **that** we wish to measure.
这样一来,接入的仪表就不会影响我们想要测量的参数了。

8. 在 the way, the distance, the direction, the reason, the time, the number of times/units, the amount 等词后可以省略关系副词或"介词 + which",这时也可用关系副词 that 来引导从句

Computers have changed the way we work and play.
计算机已经改变了我们的工作和娱乐方式。

They (human being) counted the number of times the sun appeared between full moons.
人类计算了在两次满月之间太阳出现的次数。

Noon is the time the sun is highest in the sky.
正午是太阳在天空中最高的时候。

Varying the refraction varies the distance each beam travels in a given period of time, resulting in different beams intersecting at regular intervals.
折射率的变化使每束光线在给定时间里所传的距离发生变化,这就造成了在一定距离上不

同的光束会相交。

Reflection come back only from objects in the direction the antenna is pointed.

回波只能从位于天线所指的方向上的物体那里反射回来。

The amount a solid material will expand when heated is measured by its coefficient of linear expansion.

固体受热时膨胀的量由其线性碰着系数来度量。

9. 关系代词作 there be 句型主语时可以省略

The thermometer does not tell us about the amount of heat there is in the liquids.

温度计并不能告诉我们液体中所存在的热量。

The maximum potential difference there can be across the coil of the meter is 0.05 V.

该仪表线圈两端所能存在的最大电位差为 0.05 V。

10. 定语从句修饰 there/here be 句型的主语时，作主语的关系代词可以省略

Here are some ideas will help you to realize how small atoms are.

下面一些概念将有助于你了解原子有多少。

Since the first publication of the periodic law in the 1870s, there have been a large number of forms proposed for the periodic table.

自从 19 世纪 70 年代首次发表元素周期表以来，人们又提出了大量的各种形式的元素周期表。

11. 非限定性定语从句

非限定性定语从句的作用是对所修饰的成分做进一步说明，通常是引导词和先行词之间用逗号隔开，将从句拿掉后其他部分仍可成立。在非限定性定语从句中，用 who, whom 代表人，用 which, whose 代表事物。

(1) which 引导的非限定性定语从句来说明前面整个句子的情况或主句的某一部分。

The CPU reads this signal and continues to output the same address and control signals, **which** causes the buffers to remain enabled.

CPU 读取这一信号，并且继续输出同样的地址信号和控制信号，使缓冲器保持有效。

(2) 当先行词是专有名词或物主代词和指示代词所修饰时，其后的定语从句通常是非限制性的。

The award winners are: Genoa, **which** is a failure-analysis software with unique predictive capabilities, and Remote Agent, which has been used to control NASA's Deep Space 1 mission.

得奖软件为："吉诺亚"，一个具有独特的预报特性的断裂分析软件；"遥控代理者"软件，已用于控制航天局的"深空一号"执行任务。

(3) 非限制性定语从句还能将整个主句作为先行词，对其进行修饰，这时从句谓语动词要用第三人称单数。

Liquid water changes to vapor, **which** is called evaporation.

液态水变为蒸汽,这就叫做蒸发。

(4)有时 as 也可用作关系代词。

①as 引导的修饰整个主句的非限定性定语从句。

As is evident from (8-7), the planes of peak shearing stress are oriented at +45°to the principal planes.

由式(8-7)可以明显看出,剪切应力峰值所在平面与主平面角成正负 45 度角。

Transistors are small and efficient, **as** is well known to us.

晶体管体积小,效率高,这是我们大家所熟知的。

The decibel(dB), **as** its name shows, is just one-tenth of a bel.

顾名思义,分贝就是 0.1 贝尔。

②as 引导的修饰某个名词的限制性定语从句(常与 such 和 the same 连用)。

Such meters **as** we use to measure current are called ammeters.

我们用来测量电流的这类仪表称为电流表。

Such slight nonlinearities **as** are found in vacuum tubes may be neglected in the small-signal cases.

像真空管所呈现的这种微弱的非线性,在小信号情况下可以忽略不计。

③as 引导的一种特殊的定语从句。As 一般位于先行词之后,但也可以位于先行词之前。从句中常见的动词为 call, know, refer to, 从句意为"所说的"、"所称的"、"所谓的"。

These flaws, or "bugs" **as** they are often called, must be found out and corrected.

这些毛病,也就是人们经常说的"虫子",必须要找出来加以纠正。

Unlike "small mail", **as** E-mailers derisively refer to it, a response can shoot back within hours.

不同于电子邮件发送者戏称的"蜗牛邮件",此电子邮件能在几小时内收到回音。

④as + 过去分词、介词短语、副词。

There will only be a short warning of the impact be a meter 30 or 40m in diameter, such **as** happened in the Yunguska event on June 30, 1908, when a meteoritic object is thought to have exploded as a result of friction in the Earth's atmosphere.

对于直径为 30 或 40 m 的流星的撞击只能做一个短期的警告,如 1908 年 6 月 30 日发生的通古斯卡时间,据估计,当时一个陨星穿过大气层时因摩擦生热而发生爆炸。

As pointed out in the previous chapter, forces are not transmitted only by "direct contact".

正如前一节所指出的,力不仅仅是靠直接的接触来传递的。

The method **as** presented here will not work directly for such circus as the Meacham bridge.

这里介绍的方法,不能直接用于像米楔阿姆电桥这样的电路。

12. 表示"……只需要;只能,只"的一种强调形式(all that)

To satisfy this condition, **all** we need to do is shift the path of integration.
为了满足这一条件,我们只需把积分路径移动一下。

All clocks do is cause interrupts at well-defined intervals.
时钟的功能只是在规定好的间隔上产生中断。

This, along with a knowledge of simple power calculations, is **all that** is required for the most of the text.
要学懂本教材的大部分内容,只需了解这一知识的简单的功率计算。

13. 由 than 引导的定语从句及由 since, as, when, while, after, before 等引导的时间状语从句充当修饰名词的状况。

Let us consider the case **when** the torque is zero.
让我们来考虑一下转矩为零的情况。

The final state **after** all temporary phenomena have had their effects is called a steady state.
在所有的暂态现象产生了各自的效应后的最终状态就被称为稳态。

In the 15 years **since** this book was first published, great changes have taken place in electronics.
自本书首次出版以来的这 15 年里,电子学发生了巨大的变化。

第二节 状语从句

由从句表示的状语可以用来修饰谓语,定语状语或整个句子。状语从句的写作要注意正确使用从属连词。

1. 表示时间

An ordinary nut loosens **when** the forces of vibration overcome those of friction.
当振动力克服摩擦力时,普通螺帽就会松开。

When surges in the molten iron occur, magnetic tempests are created.
当熔化的铁流量巨大时,磁暴便产生了。

A hammer and bucking bar are used for heading rivets. The bar is held against the head of the inserted rivet, **while** the hammer heads the other end.
锤子和铆钉顶棒用于导引铆钉。顶棒放在插入铆钉的头上,同时用锤子击打另一端。

While writing this book, I have not had in mind a hypothetical audience, but rather have written as if I were to be the reader.
撰写这本书时,我心中并没有一个设想的读者,只是好像把我自己当成读者来写。

2. 表示地点

Where the production runs are larger, riveting machines are used, exerting pressure on the rivet to head it rather than heading it by hammering.

在较大的流水作业线上,使用铆钉机,在铆钉上施加压力将其铆接,而不是用锤子铆接。

An oil cup is shown attached to one side of the housing, **where** a passageway leads to the oil hole of the bushing.

所示的油杯连接在壳体的一侧,有一通路通向轴瓦的油孔。

The formation of rather complex organic molecules is in the deep cold of outer space, **where** temperature usually reaches only a few degrees Kelvin.

相当复杂的有机分子形成于极度寒冷的外空间,在那里温度常常只有几个开式温度那么高。

3. 表示原因

Since they are so widely used, it is essential that these fasteners attain maximum effectiveness at the lowest possible cost.

由于它们使用广泛,这些连接件基本上可以以最低的成本获得最大的效率。

Since most undergraduate courses do not have the time for such a complete treatment, an introductory abbreviated treatment appears in Chapter 42~44.

由于大部分本科生课程没有时间对这部分内容进行完整阐述,所以在第42章至第44章中做了一个介绍性的简化阐述。

Because they weaken the shaft less, keys with straight or tapered circular cross sections are sometimes used in place of square and rectangular keys.

带有直式或锥形圆截面的键有时用以替代方键或矩形键,因为它们对轴的削弱少些。

Because of the overlapping action of the teeth, helical gears are smoother in action and can operate at higher-Pitch line relocities than spurgears.

由于齿轮的重叠作用,斜齿轮工作比较平稳,运行的节线速度可比直齿轮更高。

Researchers reasons that low-frequency sound waves, **because** they are also well described mathematically and **because** even small perturbations in emitted sound waves can be detected, could be transmitted through the ocean over many different paths.

研究者推断低频声波,因为其非常精确,甚至是对声波的极小干扰亦可被检测到,可以通过不同的通道传输过海洋。

4. 表示目的

In order to achieve line contact and improve the load-carrying capacity of the crossed-axis helical gears, the gear can be made to curve partially around the pinion, in somewhat the same way that a nut develops a screw.

为了使交叉斜齿轮获得线接触和提高承载能力,可以把大齿轮做成沿小齿轮部分弯曲,就像螺母套在螺钉上一样。

Worms are also made in the shape of an hourglass, instead of cylindrical, **so that** they partially envelop the gear.

蜗杆也被制成沙漏形状而不是圆柱形，以使其部分包裹涡轮。

5. 表示结果

Shafting is the machine element that supports a roller and wheel **so that** they can perform their basic functions of rotation.

传动轴是支撑滚轮和轮子使它们能够完成基本转动功能的机械零件。

The longer initial pulse generated by the thicker explosive, while initially producing a thicker spall, will not flatten nearly as rapidly as the shorter pulse produced by the thin layer **so that** at certain distances the thicker explosive eventually generates thinner spalls.

较厚的药层产生的脉冲起初较长，它理应形成较厚的痂片；但是它不如较薄的药层产生的短脉冲那样很快就变平缓了，所以在一定的距离上，较厚的药层最终产生较薄的痂片。

Often an intense impulsive load generates non-planar stress transients, either divergent or convergent **so that** tangential stresses exist along the wave front.

强冲击载荷经常形成不是发散的就是会聚的非平面应力瞬变，所以沿着波阵面就有切向应力存在。

6. 表示条件

If the key is made of steel of the same strength as the shaft and has a width and depth equal to one fourth of the shaft diameter then it will have the same torque capacity as the solid shaft if its length is 1.57 times that of the shaft diameter.

如果键是由与轴一样强度的钢制造的且宽度与深度等于轴径的四分之一，其长度是轴径的1.57倍，那么它就具有与实心轴同样的额定转矩。

If individuals on the edge of a group are more vigilant because they are at a greater risk of being captured, then individuals on average would have to be more vigilant in smaller groups, because the animal on the periphery of a group form a greater proportion of the whole group as the size of the group individuals.

如果处在群体边缘的动物有更高的警惕性是因为它们可能被捕获的危险性更大，那么平均而言，在小群体中的动物应有更高的警惕性，因为随着群体规模的缩小，处在群体周边的动物占整个群体的比例更高。

If intersexual selection operates as theorized, males with more complicated songs should not only attract females readily but should also enjoy greater reproductive success.

如果异性间的选择能够像理论所说的那样起作用，具有较复杂歌声的雄鸟就不但应该更加容易地吸引雌鸟，而且应该拥有更大的繁殖成功率。

If a plane cut through a body subject to external loading, and the portion of the body to one side of the plane is removed, then a free-body diagram of the remaining portion must show a force acting on the cutting plane.

若用一平面去截一个承受外载荷作用的物体,并将平面某一侧的物体去掉,则其剩余部分的分离体图必显示出作用于该截面上的力。

7. 表示让步

Though the extra depth of these keys weakens the shaft considerably, it prevents any tendency of the key to rotate or move axially.

虽然这些键的额外深度相当大地削弱了轴,但它防止了键的轴向转动和移动的倾向。

Though advantageous for established community members, the suspended and staggered maturation of juveniles might seem to pose a danger to the continuity of the community.

尽管对已建立群落的成员来说是有利的,年幼小丑鱼那延缓且踉踉跄跄的发育过程却似乎对其群落的延续性形成了威胁。

Even though bearings are usually lubricated, there is friction and some wear.

即使经常给轴承润滑,还存在摩擦与一些磨损。

Although this results in many of the proofs being a little longer than usual, I feel that it provides a more secure foundation in the subject.

尽管这样一来使得不少证明过程要比通常稍长,但我觉得这么做可为这些题目提供比较可靠的基础。

8. 表示比较

The holding power is greater **than** that of a nail and in many cases they may be backed out with a screw driver.

其保持力大于钉子的保持力,在很多情况下可以使用螺丝刀将其旋出。

Rivets are usually stronger **than** the thread-type fastener and are more economical on a first-cost basis.

铆钉通常比螺纹型连接件结实而且生产成本低。

The influence of the biological component of an ecosystem in fresh waters is often greater **than** in marine or terrestrial systems, because of the small size of many freshwater bodies.

生态系统中生物元素的影响在淡水中比在海洋中或陆地上强,因为淡水系统的水体很小。

J. Krebs has discovered that great blue herons look up more often when in smaller flocks **than** when in larger ones, solely as a consequence of poor feeding conditions.

J. Krebs 发现,大蓝苍鹭在小群体中张望的频率要比在大群体中多,这仅仅是捕食情况较差的象征。

第三节 同位语从句

1. 常用句型

There is evidence that this statement is correct.

有证据表明这一陈述是正确的。

There is no doubt that there is no solution to the equation.

毫无疑问该方程无解。

In this case **there is no guarantee that** the machine functions normally.

在这种情况下不能保证该机器能正常工作。

2. 动宾译法的句型

There is a growing awareness that the exceptional increase in population and living standard is raising formidable problems in pollution of the environment and the exhaustion of natural resources.

人们越来越意识到人口和生活水平的指数增长正在造成可怕的环境污染和自然资源消耗问题。

There is a growing realization that the only effective way to achieve further reduction in vehicle emission is to replace conventional diesel fuel and gasoline with cleaner burning fuels.

人们逐渐意识到实现车尾气排放的更进一步减少的唯一有效方法是用燃烧更洁净的燃料。

They cited new evidence that the underlying igneous rocks on either side of the rift contain significantly different kinds of rare metals.

他们引用了新的证据,即地缝下面的火成岩中含有明显不同的稀有金属种类。

3. 由名词从句转变成的同位语从句

A critical question **whether** the morphological attributes of the female reproductive organs of wind-pollinated species are evolutionary adaptations to wind pollination or are merely fortuitous remains to be answered.

有一亟待回答的问题是风媒传粉给植物雌蕊的形态特征是因为进化适应风媒授粉呢,还是仅仅是偶然的结果。

Although LS9 can produce its bug fuel in laboratory beakers, it has no ideas **whether** it will be able to produce the same results on a nationwide or even global scale.

尽管 LS9 能在实验室的烧杯里生产细菌燃油,但它不知道在全国乃至全球范围内是否能取得同样的结果。

4. 不能直接跟由 that 引导的宾语从句,需要在 that 之前加上 the fact

This second type of design situation is characterized by **the fact that** neither the need nor the problem to be solved has been identified.

第二种设计情况的特点是不论需求本身还是要解决的问题都没有明确地陈述出来。

Terrorists may use radio system in order to damage navigation equipment due to **the fact that** the aircraft may be vulnerable to interference.

恐怖分子或许会利用无线电系统来破坏飞机的导航设备,这是由于飞机容易受电磁场的干扰。

One useful hint about the original function of sleep is to be found in **the fact that** dolphins and whales and aquatic mammals in general seem to sleep very little.

海豚、鲸鱼以及水生哺乳动物睡眠都极少,这一事实可以给睡眠的根本功能提供有用的线索。

5. 短语中的同位语从句

This has exactly the same form as that describing the diode circuit of Sec. 1.3, **with the important difference that** the junction is reverse-biased here.

这个形式与1.3节中描述二极管电路的形式相同,其重要的区别在于结在这里是反向偏置的。

This process is repeated over and over again **with the result that** the hole moves in a random motion throughout the crystal.

这个过程一次又一次地重复着,结果该空穴杂乱地通过了整个晶体

第四节　名词性从句

1. 用it形式主语句的集中搭配

(1) it + 系表结构 + 主语从句。

It is clear that by the separation of this part of the question from the other, which belongs properly to Mechanics, the determination of the motion from dynamical principles will be made much easier than if the two parts were undertaken conjointly.

很明显,把第一部分和本来属于机械学的那一部分分开,从动力学原理来研究运动,这比把两部分合起来考虑容易很多。

It is obvious that a chain with many links will behave differently form one with few.

很明显,具有多连杆的链与连杆少的链在运动上会有差异。

It would seem unlikely that evolution should discriminate against sinistral snails if sinistral and dextral snails are exact mirror images.

如果左旋的和右旋的蜗牛是正确的呈镜像的话,生物进化不可能排斥左旋蜗牛品种。

(2) it + 被动语态 + 主语从句。

It should be carefully noted that Euler based his separation of dynamics into kinematics and kinetics on the assumption that they should deal with rigid bodies.

应注意到的是Euler把动力学分成运动学和动力学是基于它们是研究刚体的假设基础之上的。

It is known that the level of serum iron in animals falls during infection.

大家知道,动物血中铁含量在感染时下降。

It is now established that the Milky Way is far more extended and of much greater mass than was hitherto.

现在已经证实,银河系要比目前为止我们想象中的大得多而且重得多。

It was proposed that tomography be adapted to measuring the physical properties of the ocean in 1979.

1979 年,人们提出采用层面透视法来检测海洋的物理特性。

It has been recognized that mammals and birds differ from other animals in the way they regulate body temperature.

人们早就认识到哺乳动物和鸟类调节体温的方式与其他动物不同。

(3)it + 不及物动词 + 主语从句。

It makes sense that the stupid animals are less frequently immobilized by deep sleep than the smart ones.

愚笨的动物比聪明的动物更少在深度睡眠状态下丧失动作能力。

It turns out that the speed of radio waves us the same as that of light.

结果发现,无线电波的速度与光速相同。

2. 名词性 what 分句

(1)名词性 what 疑问分句,即 what 在这里充当疑问代词,表示"什么,多大,哪个,哪种"

No matter **what** words are used to describe the design function, in engineering it is still a process.

无论用什么词来描述设计的功用,在工程中,设计仍然是指一种过程。

Clearly, geophysicists who seek to explain and forecast changes in the field must understand **what** happens in the outer space.

很明显,试图解释与预测磁场变化的地质学家必须要知道外核的状况。

As few companies could figure out **what** to do with the plastic, much of it is buried in landfills.

由于很少有公司知道怎么去处理,最后都被扔进了垃圾填埋场。

At this stage, it has reached **what** we call the solar surface, and can escape into space without being absorbed further by solar atoms.

在此阶段,能量到达我们所称的太阳表层,并且离散到空间而不再被太阳原子吸收。

What causes a helix in nature to appear with either dextral twist or a sinistral twist is one of the most intriguing puzzles in the science of form.

是什么原因使自然界中的螺旋体现出右旋的转动或左旋的转动是形态科学中最能引人入胜的谜团之一。

(2) 名词性关系分句，表示"……的"。

What is most remarkable about what they are doing is that they are trying to make a product that is interchangeable with oil.

他们所做的事最引人注目之处在于他们力图制造与石油可互换的一种产品。

Seal has produced **what** is probably the greatest population of large carnivorous mammals on Earth.

海豹的数量恐怕是地球上大型食肉哺乳动物中最多的。

(3) 名词性关系分句，表示"所谓的，通常所说的"。

What most people think of when they visualize a computer system consists of the keyboard, screen printer, and the computer or processing device itself.

大多数人想象一个计算机系统时会认为它们是由键盘、显示器、打印机和计算机或处理设备本身所组成的。

In some airline crashes, the strength of the seats is irrelevant because the crash is not **what** the engineers call "survivable".

在一些飞机坠毁事件中，坐椅的强度是无关紧要的，因为这种坠毁不是工程师们所说的那种"可逃生的"。

Women's minds work differently from men's. At least, that is **what** most men are convinced of Psychologists view the subject either as a matter of frustration or a joke.

女性的思想与男性不同。至少，那就是大部分男性所深信的以挫折或玩笑为主题的心理学家的观点。

(4) 表示"现在或原来的样子，状态，情况和数值等"。

From the bacterial point of view, the world is a very different place from **what** it is to humans.

我们所熟知的世界从细菌的角度看完全是另一个样子。

This makes C++ **what** it is today.

这就使得C++成为今天的样子。

Exercise

练习一

使用定语从句翻译下列句子。
1. 有些人相信大多数人是被说服要多睡觉的。
2. 科学地分析运动、时间和各种力的学科叫力学。

3. 指令周期是微处理器完成一条指令处理的步骤。
4. 化学是研究自然界中物质与能量的一门科学。
5. 机械工程师们获得了核能源。它的应用需要有特别高的可靠性和安全性。
6. 没人知道第一个历法是何时出现的。
7. 内存是计算机的工作区域,那里存放着需要立即处理的数据和程序。
8. 这些卓越的信息在今天是一个混合的模型,因此多种系统被连接、操作并且被很多人使用。
9. 在数百万已知的化合物中,至少有 63 000 种我们在天天使用。它包含在我们天天吃的食物中,天天呼吸的空气中,天天饮用的水以及我们所使用的许多产品中。
10. 有件事使数字电路设计师们感到烦恼。
11. 做功的速率被称为功率。
12. 在后面一章我们将看到不同的光源发射出不同类型光谱的原因。
13. 电磁感应是产生几乎是世界上所有电力的方法。
14. 软拷贝输出通常显示在监视器上,这是一个可以在它上面阅读文本和图形的类似电视的屏幕。
15. 功等于力与物体运动距离的乘积。
16. 阻尼振荡取决于开关闭合的时间。
17. 这个图说明了电流随时间变化的情况。
18. 使用者每次打开计算机时可能意识不到它的发生。
19. 人们只需按一下钮。
20. 这是该实验室里最贵的设备。
21. 要做的第一件事是测出该电阻两端的电压。
22. 这是我们能采取的唯一措施。
23. 任何热的物体均辐射热量。
24. 这就是为什么数据/信息一定要以一种相对永久的格式存储在磁盘和磁带上。为了与主存储器相区别,将磁盘和磁带称为辅助存储器。
25. 存储管理包括记录内存哪些部分在使用,哪些是空闲的。它也记录内存被分配给哪些程序使用,并提供了哪个程序能申请更多的内存,或释放内存不再使用的这一机制。

练习二

翻译下列句子,注意定语从句的特殊形式。
1. 如标题所示,本章主要讨论复数的级数。
2. 我们以后将会看到,酸和碱在人体组织的活动中起着十分重要的作用。
3. 如图 2 所示,这种材料是弹性材料。
4. 这个力产生的效应与给定的几个力同时作用产生的效果相同。

5. 余三位的相加可以用本节早些时候讲到的组合式全加起来进行。
6. 这一修正导致了"高速力学"的形成,也就是现在人们所说的"相对论力学"。
7. 如同圆函数的情况那样,我们可以获得上述三种双曲函数的倒数。
8. 将这些数据如图2-6所示的那样画在双对数纸上。
9. 卫星为在其轨道上运行所需要的只是运载火箭给它的初速度。
10. 为了这些访问记录,用户只需要启动浏览器来访问一下网址就行了。
11. 我们要解决各种各样的网络难题,只需要用到这些基本规则。
12. 这种反应堆产生的燃料比它消耗的多。
13. 在输出端提供的能量比在输入端获得的能量大的系统就成为有源系统。
14. 我们必须先求出当c趋于无穷大时的极限值。

练习三

使用状语从句翻译下列句子。

1. 当电能在产生、转换和变幻时,若电路中相关的电流和电压不随时间而变化,我们便称其为直流电路。
2. 只要能量水平的分裂大于热变宽时,量子效应就会出现。
3. 化学传感器已经在制药领域中得到应用,以控制工厂有害排放物的量。
4. 每次打开电话都要输入密码。
5. 因为目前使用的化学传感器仅仅用于检测气体和电化学反应,所以机器人中化学传感器的使用仅限于对某些介质中离子浓度和气体的控制。
6. 在这种情形下,为了降低滤波器的制作难度,需要采用一种多级调制过程。
7. 前面所讲的内容为这个定理做了铺垫,虽然不能作为一种证明。
8. 既然已经了解了什么是计算机,现在让我们来熟悉计算机行业的语言和词汇。
9. 尽管在这些变化中改变了一种或多种物理性质,但却没有生成新的元素或化合物。
10. 讲到电首先要讲讲原子。
11. 虽然一些公司在起飞和降落时,禁止旅客使用这些物品,但是,大部分公司不愿实施全程禁用。
12. 新的设计要给地震多发城市提供更加安全的保障。
13. 在盐壳形成时,偶然的降雨会把淡水浇注在盐壳之上。
14. 晶体有时生长得非常快,以至于它可以在一小滴水的周边形成。

练习四

使用同位语从句翻译下列句子。

1. 这就解释了为什么被捕食动物很少有深度的有梦睡眠。
2. 第五个条件基于一个事实,在现实世界中只能观察到实数值的波形。

3. 飞机容易受电磁场的干扰可能会增加一种危险。
4. 现在人们越来越意识到这些技术在其他一些领域中也是很有价值的。
5. 主要成就之一是人们意识到了材料的性质应包括在分析模型中。
6. 那颗行星上是否有水存在的问题有待讨论。
7. 用户们得不到关于这种机器能使用多久的保证。

练习五

使用名词性从句翻译下列句子。
1. 在每种情况下,均假定负反馈网络中的放大器是单向的。
2. 自来水是由许多溶于水的化合物构成的复杂溶液这一情况并不常见。
3. 显然该方程有两个根。
4. 那个现象如何被发现的仍然是个谜。
5. 大家知道分子是由原子构成的。
6. 应当注意,欧姆定律只适用于金属导体。
7. 由此我们得知一整圈就有 2π 弧度。
8. 我们得到的是一个内阻为零的电源。
9. 我们需要确定在这种情况下铝线必须具有多大的直径。
10. 我们必须懂得函数斜率的含义。
11. 计算机能做人们要求它做的事。
12. 我们需要的是一台示波器。
13. 我们所称的机器实际上是能为人类工作的一种工具。
14. 1895 年,一位德国物理学家发现了现在所说的 X 射线。
15. 这些工厂与原来大不一样了。
16 在这种情况下,磁感应强度为原来的 5 500 倍。

第五章 虚拟语气

虚拟语气所陈述的内容是与事实相反的,不可能实现的或难以实现的,此外还有一些特殊句式的要求。

1. 对现在或将来的虚拟(主句为过去将来时,从句为一般过去式)

If there **were** no plants, we **would have** no animals and no meat.

如果没有植物,我们也就没有肉吃了。

At least this **would be true** if the old water had remained untouched.

如果这种古老的水没有被破坏过,那么这个结论至少应该是正确的。

If we **were** to go back to the Moon, a careful and painstaking study of its surface **could** fill in all the details of its history.

如果我们将来再次登上月球,那我们就要努力和详细地去研究它的表面并填补上它发展中的细节。

If the film **were** moving backward, the pieces **would** re-join to form a glass and jump back up onto the table.

假若电影是倒过来放的,玻璃杯碎片将重新拼合为一个玻璃杯而后跳上桌子。

If time **moved** backward, the broken pieces **could** come together in a great many ways. Only one of these ways, however, would re-form the glass.

假若时间倒流,碎掉的玻璃片可以以许多种方式聚集,而其中只有一种聚集方式,才能重新产生出玻璃杯。

2. 对过去的虚拟(主句为过去将来完成时,从句用过去完成时)

She **would have probably made** more of a mess of rearranging them if she **had left** them on the floor for me to fix.

如果她不管这些而让我来处理,那她可能还要花一些时间来弄。

The instrument **would not have been** damaged **had the voltage not been** so high.

如果当时电压不那么高,该仪器就不会烧坏了。

After the violent earthquake that shook Los Angeles in 1994, earthquake scientists had good news to report: The damage and death tool **could have been** much worse.

1994 年洛杉矶发生强烈地震,地震专家感到庆幸的是,这次地震避免了原本会更加惨重的损失和伤亡。

3. 涉及将来的情况

If one were to design a bracket to support 100 lb when it **should have been** figured for 1,000 lb, failure would surely be forthcoming.

如果一个人要设计一个能支撑 100 磅的托架,而它本应该能支撑 1000 磅,结果肯定会失败。

If new measures **were** not taken, oysters **would become** extinct or at best a luxury food.
如果不采取新的措施,牡蛎将会灭绝或至少会变为一种奢侈的食品。

The theorem is not true in general if these restrictions **be removed**.
若把这些限制条件都取消掉,一般来说这个定理就不成立了。

4. 虚拟语气在从句中的使用

虚拟语气还可以出现在主语从句、宾语从句、表语从句,同位语从句和状语从句中。

使用虚拟语气的常见动词有:require, demand, suggest, desire, propose, recommend, request, insist, order。

常见形容词有:necessary, essential, important, possible, impossible, desirable, natural, reasonable, better, preferable, sufficient。

常见名词有:requirement, suggestion, necessity, importance, request, condition, restriction, restraint, recommendation, demand, philosophy, policy。

The board **insisted** that the company hire security guards, use video monitoring, and take other steps to ensure that "no eggs can be diverted for any other purpose."
该委员会还要求公司雇佣安全护卫、采用视频监控并采取其他措施以确保"没有卵子能被挪作他用"。

The output of light and heat of the Sun **requires** that some 600 million tons of hydrogen be converted into helium in the sun every second.
太阳所产生的光和热需要每秒将六亿吨氢转化为氦。

In the last 15 years, pilots **have reported** well over 100 incidents that could have been caused by electromagnetic interference.
在过去的 15 年中,据飞行员报告,有 100 多起航空事件,可能由电磁干扰造成的。

Your eyes will begin to dart around under your eyelids **as if you were** looking at something occurring in front of you.
你的眼睛会在闭着的眼睑下迅速转动,就好像你在看着眼前发生的什么事情。

She suffered from headaches and could hardly sleep. It was **as though she had** suddenly developed a strange illness.
她眼睛灼痛,总觉得喉咙发干,头痛失眠,像是突然得了一场怪病。

Any matter, **be** it air, water or wood, has weight.
任何物质,不论是空气、水、还是木头,均具有重量。

Exercise

练习一

翻译下列句子。

1. 如果没有引力,我们人本身及其他东西就会离开地球,飞向太空。
2. 如果当时采用了这种方法,就会节省很多时间。
3. 如果当时采取了这种方法,就会节省很多时间。
4. 如果此程序被移植到另一台电脑上,即使键盘型号只是有些许的不同,其输入部分也必须改变。
5. 如果一个人携带重物在水平的地面上行走,则他没有做功。
6. 一旦这些轰炸机遇到这样的空防系统,其结果会是致命的。
7. 我们建议立即修改这项设计。
8. 极为重要的是所有的解都要代入原方程中检验。
9. 这要求该晶体管要适当地加以偏置。
10. 我们建议读者不必等掌握了本章内容后才去学习后面的章节。
11. 出现这一情况的必要条件是尤拉方程要得到满足。
12. 我们的要求是再做一个实验。
13. 当时看上去那台计算机好像被损坏了。
14. 所有这些题目,不论是容易还是困难,都可以用这种方法来解。

练习答案

第一章 词法

第一节 冠词

练习一

General Zuo Quan	Ancient Greece	Southeast Asia
the far east	the West Indians	the Kunlun Mountains
the United Kingdom	the United States of America	the Geneva Agreement

练习二

1. A, a
2. /, /
3. an
4. /

5. A,a,a 6. a,the,a,an,the
7. The,a,an,the,the,the 8. /,/,the
9. the,the 10. The,the,the,/,the,The,/,/,/,/,the,/
11. the,/,/,the 12. the,the,/,the
13. the,the,the,the
14. /,/,/,/,/,/,/,/,The,/,/,The,/,a,the,/,a,/
15. /,a,the,/ a,a,the,/,/
16. The,the,the,the,/
17. The,the,the,the,the,the,the,A,a,a,a,the,/,/

练习三

1. A computer system consists of a computer and some peripherals.
2. Chemists measure mass on a balance.
3. This is an n-value function.
4. The collector of the transistor must be connected to the positive terminal of the power supply.
5. The control of systems is an interdisciplinary subject.
6. Information is knowledge.
7. Air is matter.
8. Kirchhoff's rules are very useful to the analysis of networks.
9. Figure 6.3 shows the block diagram of a digital computer.
10. This point will be discussed in Chapter 5.
11. Mathematics is a very useful tool in science.

第二节　名词

练习一

bases	antennae	axes
formulas,formulae	indexes	maximums,maxima
minimums,minima	schemata	strata
symposia,symposiums		

练习二

1. The mechanical engineer continually invents machines to produce goods and develops machines tools of increasing accuracy and complexity to build the machines.
2. An insurance company might use a mainframe computer to manage companywide customer data.
3. A considerable amount of thought and effort is necessary in order to state it clearly as a problem requiring a solution.
4. Fasteners is a general term including such widely separated and varied materials.

5. Workstations introduced in the early 1980s are expensive, powerful desktop computers.
6. Four functions of the mechanical engineering common to all the fields mentioned are cited.
7. The version easiest to use and most closely related to the electronic structures of the atoms is the so—called long—form periodic law.
8. This microprocessor and other components necessary to make it work, are mounted on a main circuit board called the motherboard, or system board.
9. Mechanical engineering is the branch of engineering that deals with machines and the production of power. It is particularly concerned with forces and motion.
10. The third function is production of products and power, which embraces planning, operation, and maintenance.
11. As an effort to reduce confusion, the new numbers seem logical and many receive worldwide approval.
12. We will display the newer group numbers to enable you to understand both sets of group designations.
13. The cost of supercomputer ranges from several hundreds of thousands to millions of dollars.
14. Memory, also known as primary storage or RAM (random access memory), is temporary working storage.
15. Old—fashioned copper—wire telephone network, an analog system built to transmit the human voice, still exists.
16. Despite its name, this kind of memory cannot remember.

第三节 形容词、副词

练习一

1. Its external characteristic is a straight line parallel to the x-axis.
2. Electrons closer to the nucleus are held more tightly than those in the outer orbits.
3. This remote scanning service company could detect crop problems before they became visible to the eye.
4. This body interacts with other bodies present.
5. In this case, no rotation whatsoever will result.
6. These are the smallest particles obtainable.
7. Even in this case, there are two directions possible.
8. Now satellite communication is nothing mysterious.
9. Everything electronic will be done digitally.
10. The human body is made of countless structures both large and small.
11. The power rule can be used for all rational exponents, positive and negative.

练习二

1. Currently, rules on using these devices are left up to individual airlines.
2. We have to totally change our attitude toward napping.
3. Clearly, we were born to nap.
4. Usually some of these parameters are known.
5. Conventionally current flowing toward a device is designed as positive.
6. The device consists mainly of five parts.
7. These parameters are easily measured.
8. The longer vertical line always corresponds to the positive terminal.
9. This technique is used extensively in Chapter 7.
10. In the following discussion we usually assume the emf of a source to be constant.

练习三

1. The better the connections between too halves of the brain, the more harmoniously the two halves work.
2. The lower your stage of sleep, the slower your brain waves will be.
3. Such deposits are several-folder greater than total reserves of the lower viscosity conventional crude oils.
4. This kind of device has become more and more complicated.
5. This sheet of steel is as thin as a few tenths of a centimeter.
6. The distance of the terminal from the computing center is as great as three kilometers.
7. When water evaporates, the lighter molecules evaporate just a tiny bit faster.
8. The sun looks much brighter than other stars.
9. Of all the stars on the sky, the sun looks the biggest.
10. Of all these machines here, this one works most satisfactorily.

第四节　动词

练习一

1. Energy, minerals, and metals are three basic building blocks of our technological society.
2. One micron is a thousandth of a millimeter.
3. A pinhead is about a millimeter across.
4. These factors do not account for the interesting question.
5. As early as the early 1820s, it was realized that this phenomenon is of great use.
6. The productive forces were of a very low level.
7. Fasteners are of many different types.
8. The pressure at the center of a tornado is usually 13 pounds per square inch.

9. The point seems particularly clear for the young of predatory animals.

10. These submarine earthquakes sometimes give rise to seismic sea waves.

11. Most of the quartz is a variety of amethyst that heat has turned brown.

12. There are three basic processes that cause a change in oceanic salinity.

13. Cells cannot remain alive outside certain limits of temperature.

14. Ways of characterizing the difference have become more accurate and meaningful over time.

15. This classification proves inadequate.

16. It appears to be breaking the laws of thermodynamics.

17. Worms are made of in the shape of an hourglass which results in a further increase in load-carrying capacity.

练习二

A mouse is a device that is rolled about on a desktop to direct a pointer on the computer's display screen. The pointer is a symbol, usually an arrow, which is used to select items from lists on the screen or to position the cursor. The cursor, also called an insertion point, is the symbol that shows where data may be entered next, such as text in a document.

第五节　连词

1. The basic circuit components are an energy source, an energy converter and conductors connecting them.

2. Civil engineers design and construct buildings, railways, roads, bridges, tunnels, harbors, water and sewage systems, and other public facilities.

3. This device is large and complicated.

4. This machine has the advantages of simple structure and good performance.

5. To explain the circuit operation qualitatively, it is assumed that R is infinite and that the diode is ideal.

6. This method has the advantages that the phase scale is linear and that there is no ambiguity concerning the size of the phase shift.

7. Another point of view which may be adopted, and which is sometimes more convenient, is illustrated in Fig. 3 – 5.

第六节　介词

练习一

1. This measurement is of great precision.

2. Of all these instruments, this one is the most expensive.

3. The science of chemistry is very useful in the modern world.

4. The separation of gold from its ore is not easy.

5. This series can converge with rapidity.

6. The conductivity of a semiconductor varies with temperature.

7. With radar, we can see distance objects.

8. We can make an electric bell with this kind of magnet.

9. This line is parallel with the x-axis.

10. The radio waves with different wavelengths travel at the same speed.

11. Typical noise margins are usually better than the guaranteed value by about 75 mV.

12. By Eq(3), we can obtain the following expression.

13. This is the only method by which the disadvantage may be overcome.

14. This device measures 12 by 18 by 6 inches.

15. The temperature may stay constant for a long time.

16. This book is too difficult for a beginner.

17. It is necessary for us to solve this equation for x.

18. This is a manual for electrical engineers.

19. This cargo is too heavy for that crane to lift.

20. On simplifying, the result becomes as follows.

21. These are the information on the mechanical properties of the material.

22. The international conference will take place on Sunday.

23. We measure force in newtons.

24. Direct current flows only in one direction.

25. The exercises vary considerably in difficulty.

26. We can measure a slight change in pressure.

27. Its transmission over a long distance causes some loss of energy.

28. This temperature is a marked decrease over the 150 ℃ previously cited.

29. This voltage is fairly stable over a wide frequency range.

30. A bridge crane passed over our heads.

第七节　与数字有关的表达练习答案

练习一

1. Excessive speed plays a major role in as much as one fifth of all fatal traffic accident.

2. The output of diesel oil for farm use has more than doubled.

3. During this period its territory increased ten-fold.

4. The output of chemical fibre has been increased three times as against 1975.

5. Output of chemical fertilizer was more than 2.5 times greater.

6. The output is 100 times the input.

7. Its speed is three tenths that of light.

8. This box is six times heavier than that one.

9. The wavelength of this musical note is over three times longer than that of the same note in the air.

10. Its grain output was 16.5 percent higher than in 1976.

第二章 时态和语态

第一节 时态练习答案

练习一

Para A 一般现在时,是在说明解释。

Para B 一般现在时,是对存在的事实真理的描述。

Para C 一般现在时,对事实的描述。

Para D 一般过去时,对过去发生的事实的描述。

Para E 一般过去时,对过去的实验的描述。

Para F 现在完成时出现的频率最高,从全段来看,这段应该出现的文章最开始部分,说明这一成果已经带来的影响,这既是一种背景资料的介绍,也为下文引出作者所要研究的范围做了必要的铺垫。

Para G 一般将来时,表示计划。

练习二

1. A new coding system is proposed in this paper.

2. A beam of light moves through this constant density in a straight line until it reaches the interface of the core and cladding.

3. This has been discussed in Chapter 2.

4. A number of different giant molecules have been found both in the nerve cells of the brain and gut and also in gastrointestinal cells, which behave like a hormone-producing cells.

5. The temperature has kept on rising since the reaction started 3 hours ago.

6. From that moment onward, the space station will be permanent off-planet extension of human civilization.

7. In the future we will not need to work with tools in the old day. Machines will do everything for us. They will even talk and play games with us. People will have plenty of spare time. But what will they do with it?

8. In the previous section, we introduced the concept of force.

9. In the 1940s, they designed the first generation of electronic computers.

10. Until now, we have been discussing only translational motion.

第二节 主动、被动语态练习答案

练习一

1. Other problems can be foreseen.
2. Technologies for oil production can be divided into three classes.
3. Final drawings are usually made on tracing paper, cloth or Mylar film.
4. This experiment is still cited as evidence.
5. This effect accounts for chemical reactions that are forbidden by the principles of classical chemistry.
6. Although the hormone adrenaline is known to regulate memory storage, it does not pass from the blood into brain cells.
7. In experiments, vacancies have been contrived by removing an established fish from a community.

练习二

1. Many wind-pollinated species fail to release pollen when wind speeds are low or when humid conditions prevail.
2. A wire can act as an antenna.
3. When will the international conference on mobile communication take place?
4. Data indicate that the amount of carbon dioxide has fluctuates with temperature over the same period.
5. Ethanol and methanol have important advantages over other carbon-based alternative fuels.
6. The load resistance R gives an idea about the consumption of energy.
7. This paper presents an examination of the overall question of fossil fuel desulphurization.

第三章 非谓语动词练习答案

练习一

1. It is possible to determine the weight of the body.
2. The purpose of electric circus is to distribute and cover energy into some other forms.
3. The e. m. f. of the source causes a continuous and unidirectional current to circulate round this closed path.
4. In the external portion of the circuit, that is, in the load R, the current is assumed to flow from the junction a to the junction b.
5. Shelters have been constructed by civil engineers to provide a peaceful and comfortable life.
6. Since then, the term civil engineer has often been to refer to engineers who build public facilities.
7. They help to build water plants, wastewater treatment plants and dump sites.
8. Joints are designed to transmit axial load, shear, moment and torsion.

9. R is the resistance to be measured.
10. We find the theory of relativity very difficult to explain.
11. The International Telecommunication Union encourages a full array of telecommunication services to be economically provided and integrated into the world telecommunication system.
12. The first condition is necessary because systems appear to exist for a finite amount of time.
13. A liquid's particles are relatively free to move because they are held together firmly but not tightly.
14. It is hard to track the blue whale, the ocean's largest creature.

练习二

1. Electric circuits containing only elements with linear characteristic are called linear.
2. In an equivalent circuit diagram the source resistance R' may be shown connected in series with the load resistance R.
3. Depending on the relative magnitude of the voltage across R and r, we can develop two modifications of the series equivalent circuit.
4. The engineering marvels of the world, starting from the pyramids to today's shell structure, are the results of the development in civil engineering.
5. Those engaged in environmental engineering design systems to sanitize water and air.
6. Steel applied to structure is a small part. It needs some advantages.
7. Although the fundamental concepts and principles pf electronic communications have changed little since their inception, the methods and circuits used to implement them have undergo considerable change.
8. Typically, music has two structures: a melodic structure consisting of a time sequence of sound, and a harmonic structure consisting of a set of simultaneous sounds.
9. With its base grounded, Q4 is a very high impedance.
10. In gases, the particles are far apart, with empty space between.
11. Starting next year, the foundation will paint chevrons and other patterns of strips on selected roads around country.

练习三

1. As the current keeps rising, the proportionality between its value and the voltage drop across the source is upset.
2. Construction is a complicated process which involves scheduling the work and utilizing the equipment and materials so that cost is kept as low as possible.
3. In this case, the Na and Cl nuclei cease being shielded by their electrons.
4. Compressing a gas raises its temperature.
5. Let us consider doing a simple experiment.

6. By analyzing the performance of the device, we can appreciate it better.
7. We often group certain terms together in writing algebraic expressions.

第四章 从句练习答案

练习一

1. There are those who believe that most people are persuaded to sleep too much.
2. That branch of scientific analysis which deals with motions, time, and forces is called mechanics.
3. The instruction cycle is the procedure that a microprocessor goes through to process an instruction.
4. Chemistry is a branch of science that deals with matter and energy in the natural world.
5. Mechanical engineers acquired the resource of nuclear energy whose application has demanded an exceptional standard of reliability and safety.
6. No one knows the time when the first calendar was developed.
7. Memory is the computers "work area", where data and programs needed for immediate processing are held.
8. The predominant information system is now a hybrid model, whereby a variety of systems are connected, operated, and used by many people.
9. At least 63 thousand of the millions of known compounds are in everyday use in the food you eat, the air you breathe, the water you drink, and the numerous products you use.
10. There is something worries digital designers.
11. The rate at which work is done is referred to as power.
12. In a later chapter we will see the reasons for which different sources emit different types of spectrum.
13. Electromagnetic induction is the means by which nearly all the world's electric power is produced.
14. Softcopy output is typically displayed on a monitor, a television-like screen on which you can read text and graphics.
15. Work is the product of the force and the distance a body moves.
16. The damped oscillation depends on the time the switch is closed.
17. This diagram show the way the current changes with time.
18. Users may not be aware that it happens every time they switch on a machine.
19. All that one need do is push the button.
20. This is the most expensive device that there is in the laboratory.
21. The first thing that will be done is to measure the voltage across the resistor.
22. This is the only measure that we can make.
23. Anything that is hot radiates heat.
24. This is why data/information must also be stored in relatively permanent form on disks and tapes,

which are called secondary devices to distinguish them from main memory's primary storage.
25. Memory management involves keeping track of which parts of memory are in use, and which are free. It also keeps track of which programs the memory in use has been allowed to, and provides mechanisms by which programs can ask for more memory, or give back memory they no longer need.

练习二

1. As this title indicates, this chapter will deal primarily with series of complex numbers.
2. As will be seen later, acid and bases play an important role in the functioning of the human organism.
3. This material is elastic, as is shown in Fig. 2.
4. This force produces the same effect as is produced by the simultaneous action of the given forces.
5. Excess-three digits can be added by using a combinational full adder as was described earlier in this section.
6. This revision resulted in the creation of "high-speed mechanics" or, as it is called, "relativistic mechanics".
7. As with circular functions, we have the reciprocals of the above three hyperbolic functions.
8. These data are plotted on log-log paper, as shown in Fig. 2 – 6.
9. All the satellite needs in order to move in its orbits is the initial speed given it by the carrier rocket.
10. All the user has to do in order to access the records is start a web browser and visit the web site.
11. These basic rules are all we need to solve a wide variety of network problems.
12. This kind of reactor creates more fuel than it consumes.
13. A system which provides more energy at the output than is given at the input is said to be active.
14. We must first determine the limit as $c \rightarrow \infty$.

练习三

1. When electric energy is generated, transmitted and converted under conditions such that the currents and voltage remain constant with time, one usually speaks of direct-current circuits.
2. Quantum effects make their appearance as soon as the splitting of the energy levels is greater than the thermal broadening.
3. The chemical sensors have been applied to the process in pharmaceutical industry in order to control the amount of the harmful wastes discharged from the plants.
4. Every time you turn on your phone, you are asked to enter your PIN.
5. Because the chemical sensors used presently only detect the gases and electrochemical reactions, the application of chemical sensors to robots is limited to the areas of control of the gases and the concentration of ions in some media.

6. In such a situation it is necessary to resort to a multiple modulation process so that it can ease the filtering requirement.
7. The foregoing provides a basis for this theorem, although it can not be considered as a proof.
8. Since you know what a computer is, it's time to become fluent in the language and vocabulary of computing.
9. Although one or more physical properties have been altered in each of these changes, now new elements or compounds have been found.
10. In order to talk about electricity, it is necessary first to talk about the atom.
11. Although some airlines prohibit passengers from using such equipment during take-off and landing, most are reluctant to enforce a total ban.
12. The new designs should offer even greater security to cities where earthquakes often take place.
13. While the salt crust was falling, an occasional rain would drop fresh water on the salt.
14. On occasion, a crystal would form so quickly that it would grow around a droplet of water.

练习四

1. This explains the fact that the deep dream sleep is rare among prey.
2. The fifth condition follows from the fact that only real waveform can be observed in the real world.
3. The fact that aircraft may be vulnerable to interference raises a risk.
4. There is a growing awareness that these techniques are also of value in some other areas.
5. One of the main achievements is the recognition that properties of a material sould be included in the analytic model.
6. The question whether there is water on that planet will be discussed.
7. The users have no guarantee how long this kind of device will be operating.

练习五

1. It is assumed in each case that the forward-path amplifier of a negative feedback system is unilateral.
2. It is not obvious that tap water is a complex solution of many compounds dissolved in water.
3. It is clear that the equation has two roots.
4. It is still a mystery how that phenomenon was discovered.
5. It is known that molecules are made up of atoms.
6. It should be noted that Ohm's law applies only to metallic conductors.
7. It follows that there are 2π radians in one complete rotation.
8. What we have got is a source whose internal resistance is zero.
9. It is necessary for us to determine what diameter an aluminum wire must have in this case.
10. We must understand what is meant by the slope of a function.

11. A computer can do what it has been told to do.

12. What we need is an oscilloscope.

13. What we call a machine is really a kind of tool that can do work for man.

14. In 1895, a German physicist discovered what are now known as X rays.

15. These factories are quite different from what they were.

16. In this case, the magnetic induction is 5,500 times what it was.

第五章 虚拟语气练习答案

练习一

1. If there were no gravitation, we and everything else would fly off the earth into space.

2. If this method had been adopted at that time, much time would have been saved.

3. If this method has been adopted at that time, much time would have been saved.

4. If that program were to be moved to another machine, with even a slightly different model of keyboard, the input part of it would have to be changed.

5. If one were to walk along a horizontal floor carrying weight, no work would be done.

6. Should these bombers encounter such an air-defence system, the result could be fatal.

7. It is suggested that this design be modified at once.

8. It is very important that all solutions be checked in the original equation.

9. This requires that the transistor (should) be properly biased.

10. We recommend that the reader not try to absorb this chapter completely before proceeding to the subsequent chapters.

11. A necessary condition that this be the case is that Euler's Equation be satisfied.

12. Our demand is that another experiment (should) be made.

13. It appeared as if that computer had been damaged.

14. All these problems, be they very easy or difficult, can be solved by this method.

第二篇 学术论文写作

第六章 撰写论文前的准备工作

科技学术论文的写作对很多人来说不是一件轻而易举的工作。优秀的科技论文要求作者阐述自己独创的具有实验性或理论性的新看法和新观察,或是根据已有的理论发展出新角度或新认识。而用英文撰写和发表论文,尤其是在一些国际上有影响力的刊物上发表论文,则更增加了学术论文的难度,增加了作者的工作量。因此撰写英文科技论文既是一项创新性工作,也是一项系统化的工作。做好充分的资料阅读和搜集、调查研究,可以帮助我们规避有意或无意的雷同和剽窃;而周详细致的写作计划,可以明确写作目标,并在写作中始终围绕着文章的中心进行。

一、选择研究方向和课题

1. 要深入认识自己所在学科和方向以及个人的兴趣所在。
2. 经常与相关领域内的导师、同行或同学分享、交流新的理念与认识,出席和参与本学科国内国际会议。
3. 经常阅读相关领域有响力的核心刊物和著作,从中了解世界前沿的研究方向和动态、他人已经做出的研究成果以及获得很多领域内知识和资讯。
4. 确定研究课题,并试着问自己以下问题:

你的工作是原创吗?
你确定它是相关领域内最新的成果或是已有成果的新角度新观察吗?
你通过恰当的分析方法来验证你的结论了吗?它们的重要性得到论证了吗?
你采用的方法都有效并且可靠吗?
你对所用方法进行了必要的阐述了吗?
你的发现和结论完整吗?
你的方法能解决现实存在的困难和问题吗?

如果回答都是肯定的,那么说明即将要着手撰写的论文是新的、原创性的结果或方法,或者是对已发表的结果给予科学的解释,或者是对某个领域发表综述或对某个特定课题进行总结;所使用的论证方法是行之有效的,围绕论题所做的科学而可靠的论证;所得出的结论是依据论题和论证过程的,解决问题的完整的新结论、新观察和新发现。

如果在回答了上诉问题的基础上,了解国际研究动态,还能使课题与国际接轨,则论文获得发表和好评的机会更大。

二、准备资料和工具

1. 查阅和利用有关领域的检索工具

国际上六大检索系统：

（1）美国《科学引文索引》SCI（见下文）。

（2）美国《工程索引》EI（见下文）。

（3）美国《化学文摘》（Chemical Abstracts, CA。CA 报道的化学化工文献量占全世界化学化工文献总量的 98% 左右，是当今世界上最负盛名、收录最全、应用最为广泛的查找化学化工文献大型检索工具。

（4）英国《科学文摘》（Science Abstracts, SA；或 INSPEC）。包括《物理文摘》（Section A-Physics Abstracts, PA）、《电子与电气文摘》（Section B – Electrical Engineering & Electronics Abstracts, EEA）、《计算机与控制文摘》（Section C – Computers and Control Abstracts, CCA）及《信息技术》（Information Technology, IT）。

（5）俄罗斯《文摘杂志》（Abstract Journals, AJ），是世界三大综合检索统之一。

（6）日本《科学技术文献速报》（Corrent Bulletin on Science Technology, CBST；为印刷本，共12 分册）。现扩充为大型数据库"日本科学技术情报中心"（Japan Information Center Science and Technology, JICST）。是世界三大综合检索系统之一。

2. 四大索引系统

SCI, EI, ISTP, ISR 是世界四大重要检索系统，其收录论文的状况是评价国家、单位和科研人员的成绩、水平以及进行奖励的重要依据之一。我国学者在教学科研，基金资助，成果申报，晋级考评等方面工作的评议也主要以这四大检索系统为主要依据；国家科学基金和国家青年基金申报等活动也以这几个权威索引系统的查询结果为必备条件。目前我国被四大系统收录的论文数量逐年增长，论文被这些检索收录已成为我国教师和科研人员的努力方向。

（1）SCI（Science Citation Index, 科学引文索引）是美国科学情报研究所出版的一部世界著名的期刊文献检索工具。SCI 收录全世界出版的数、理、化、农、林、医、生命科学、天文、地理、环境、材料、工程技术等自然科学各学科的核心期刊约 3 500 种；扩展版（SCIE）收录期刊 5 800 余种。

SSCI（Social Sciences Citation Index 社会科学引文索引），为 SCI 的姊妹篇，亦由美国科学信息研究所创建，是目前世界上可以用来对不同国家和地区的社会科学论文的数量进行统计分析的大型检索工具。1999 年 SSCI 全文收录 1809 种世界最重要的社会科学期刊，内容覆盖包括人类学、法律、经济、历史、地理、心理学等在内的 55 个领域。收录文献类型包括研究论文、书评、专题讨论、社论、人物自传、书信等。选择收录（Selectively Covered）期刊为 1 300 多种。Social Science Citation Index（2001 年）收录社会科学领域内 1 700 余种最具影响力的学术刊物。

（2）EI（Engineering Index, 工程索引）是美国工程信息公司（Ei）出版的著名工程技术类综合性检索工具。EI 选用世界上工程技术类期刊 2 000 余种。收录文献几乎涉及工程技术各个领域。例如:动力、电工、电子、自动控制、矿冶、金属工艺、机械制造、土建、水利等。它具有综合性强、资料来源广、地理覆盖面广、报道量大、报道质量高、权威性强等特点。

（3）ISTP（Index to Scientific & Technical Proceedings，科技会议录索引）由美国科学情报研究所（ISI）编辑出版，会议录收录生命科学、物理与化学科学、农业、生物和环境科学、工程技术和应用科学等，其中工程技术与应用科学类文献约占35%。

（4）ISR（Index to Scientific Reviews，科学评论索引）由美国科学情报研究所（ISI）编辑出版，收录世界各国2 700余种科技期刊及300余种专著丛刊中有价值的评述论文。高质量的评述文章能够提供本学科或某个领域的研究发展概况、研究热点、主攻方向等重要信息，是极为珍贵的参考资料。

3. 查阅图书资料和学术期刊

通过相关书籍和核心期刊，可以了解有关领域内杰出人物研究状况、有关领域研究热点和发展趋势；以及利用网上数据库了解国际学术研究动态等有关资料。

4. 适当做阅后笔记和摘录

看文献的同时应注意随时摘录。首先纪录下他人理论和研究的成果，也许可以从中得到灵感，从而开辟出新的看法和角度；其次英语科技论文的写作包含很多固定的模式和表达方法，将这些固定用法随时做笔记，并加以复习，加上不断阅读新文献，自己动手写时也就不会举步维艰。

三、选择发表刊物

研究者们撰写论文不能"闭门造车"，论文想要被几大重要检索收录，其所发表的平台很重要。因此准备撰写论文的同时，科研工作者们也应该选定与研究方向和学科对口的期刊。

期刊的选择可以参考以下几方面的因素：

（1）依据个人的研究内容和方向，选择该领域内的相关刊物。

（2）借助期刊评价工具，参考JCI（Journal citation index）期刊被引用次数和影响因子。

影响因子（Impact factor，IF）是美国ISI（科学信息研究所）的JCR（期刊引证报告）中的一项数据，是指某一期刊的文章在特定年份或时期（一般为前两年）被引用的频率，是衡量学术期刊影响力的一个重要指标，由ISI创始人尤金·加菲得（Eugene Garfield）在1960年代创立，其创立为文献计量学的发展带来了一系列重大革新。自1975年以来，影响因子每年定期发布于"期刊引用报告"（Journal Citation Reports）。目前，影响因子已经成为国际上通行的期刊评价指标。一般来说，影响因子越大，其学术影响力也越大。

四、研究"作者须知"

期刊编排标准化进程在日益加快，我国绝大多数学术期刊在编排格式和学术用语等方面都严格执行国家制定的有关科技期刊编辑出版的标准。而国际上的知名学术刊物，他们的刊稿要求则更为标准化和规范化。因此根据不同的科研方向和成果特点，选择好期刊后，在应该对所选期刊进行深入了解和研究，注意国家、国际标准和相应的编写规范，并且按照所选该期刊征稿要求进行论文的撰写。

绝大多数期刊都在每期或某期刊物上刊登"作者须知"或称"投稿指南"或称"投稿须知"（Information for authors, Instructions to authors, notes to contributors）。

期刊征稿启事罗列的事项，除了收稿范围以外，主要是对稿件贯彻国标的具体化要求，内容如下：

（1）刊物宗旨和范围。

（2）不同栏目论文的长度、主要章节的顺序安排。

（3）投稿要求，如：投稿的分数、形式、图标、如何投寄等。

（4）是否履行同行评议。如果是双盲形式的同行评议，应如何避免在稿件中出现可识别作者身份的信息等。

（5）多长时间后能决定可否录用。

（6）采取何种体例格式？如：页边距、纸张大小、文献和图标的体例等。

（7）采用国际计量单位制（SI）。

随着时代发展，刊物的"作者须知"可能在不同时间做了调整和改变，因此，作者必须与时俱进，了解最新版本的"作者须知"。

下面本书以国际上的两本知名刊物为例，研究一下"作者须知"。

本书列举的第一个例子是《科学》杂志在2010年1月15日发行的第327期刊物上刊登的该杂志"作者须知"的精简版。

文章包含以下几个方面：

①This abbreviated version of Science's Information for Authors is printed in one issue of each year. The current, complete *Information for Authors* is available at http://www.sciencemag.org/about/authors.

此精简版"作者须知"印在每年《科学》杂志的某一期刊物上。最新的完整版可在《科学》杂志网站查询。

②Science is a weekly, peer-reviewed journal that publishes significant original scientific research, plus reviews and analyses of current research and science policy. We welcome submissions from all fields of science and from any source. Competition for space in Science is keen, and many papers are returned without in-depth review. Priority is given to papers that reveal novel concepts of broad interest.

这部分是对《科学》杂志的简短介绍：《科学》是经过同行评议的周刊，发表科学原创性研究以及对现有科技研究和理论的探索和分析。我们欢迎科技领域内各种方向成果的投稿，但由于版面竞争激烈，很多文章会被退稿，因此我们优先考虑引起广泛关注的具有新概念新想法的科研成果。

③Peer-reviewed Manuscript Types.

Research Articles (up to ~4,500 words, including references, notes and captions, or ~5 printed pages) are expected to present a major advance. Research Articles include an abstract, an introduction, up to six figures or tables, sections with brief subheadings, and about 40 references. Materials and Methods should usually be included in supporting online material.

Reports (up to ~2,500 words including references, notes and captions or ~3 printed pages) present important new research results of broad significance. Reports should include an abstract, an introductory paragraph, up to four figures or tables, and about 30 references. Materials and Methods should usually be included in supporting online material.

Brevia are brief contributions (600 to 800 words including references, notes and captions) accompanied by one illustration or table that must be contained on one printed page. Authors should also submit an abstract of 100 words or less that will appear online only. Materials and methods should be included in supporting online material (up to 500 words and one figure/table).

Technical Comments (up to 1,000 words and 15 references), are published only on Science Online; they discuss research papers published in Science within the previous 6 months. Authors should submit a brief abstract (less than 50 words) to accompany their comment that will be included in the Letters section of the print edition. The authors of the original paper are given an opportunity to reply. Comments and responses are peer reviewed and edited as needed.

Reviews (up to 3,500 words including references, notes and captions) describe new developments of interdisciplinary significance and highlight future directions. They include an abstract, an introduction that outlines the main theme, brief subheadings, and an outline of important unresolved questions. A maximum of 40 references is suggested. Most Reviews are solicited by the editors, but unsolicited submissions may also be considered.

Science's Commentary section present analysis by scientists and other experts on issues of interest to Science readers. With the exception of Letters, most items are commissioned by the editors, but unsolicited contributions are welcome.

Policy Forum (1,000 to 2,000 words plus 1-2 figures) presents issues related to the intersections between science and society that have policy implications. Education Forum (approximately 2,000 words) presents essays on science education and its practice from pre-college to graduate work. They are not meant to be research reports of an individual program. (Research results related to education should be submitted to the Reports section.) Books *et al.* (up to 1,000 words) presents reviews of current books, multimedia, exhibitions, and films of interest to Science readers. Perspectives (up to 1,000 words plus 1 figure) highlight recent exciting research, but do not primarily discuss the author's own work. They may provide context for the findings within a field or explain potential interdisciplinary significance. Perspectives commenting on papers in Science should add a dimension to the research and not merely be a summary of the paper. Perspectives are meant to express a personal viewpoint, and thus, with rare exceptions, should have no more than two authors.

Letters (up to 300 words) discuss material published in Science in the last 3 months or issues of general interest. Letters should be submitted online(www.submit2science.org). Letters are subject to editing for clarity and space. E-letters are online-only, 400-word contributions for rapid, timely discussion.

这一部分文章根据杂志的不同栏目设置分别指出了征稿的几种类型,包括研究论文(Research Articles)、报告(Reports)、Brevia(期刊博览—简讯)、技术评论(Technical Comments)、科技综述(Reviews)、政策论坛(Policy Forum)、教育论坛(Education Forum)、书评及其他(Books et al.)、研究评述(Perspectives)、来信(Letters)。这一部分对不同栏目的征稿类型、稿件字数、稿件内容和稿件所需提供的数据、示例、参考文献等做了十分简明扼要的要求。

④Manuscript Selection.

We are committed to prompt evaluation and publication of submitted papers through our fully electronic submission and review process. Papers are assigned to a staff editor who has knowledge of the field discussed in the manuscript. Most submitted papers are rated for suitability by members of Science's Board of Reviewing Editors. The editors at *Science* consider this advice in selecting papers for in-depth review. Authors of papers that are not highly rated are notified promptly, by e-mail only, within about 1 to 2 weeks. Membership in AAAS is not a factor in selection.

Papers are reviewed in depth by at least two outside referees. Reviewers are contacted before being sent a paper and asked to return comments within 1 to 2 weeks. We are able to expedite the review process significantly for papers that require rapid assessment. Papers are edited to improve accuracy and clarity and to shorten, if necessary. Authors and reviewers are expected to notify editors if a manuscript could be considered to report dual use research of concern(DURC). Papers identified as possible DURC will be brought to the attention of the Editor-in-Chief for further evaluation. If necessary, outside reviewers with expertise in the area will be consulted. Papers cannot be resubmitted over a disagreement on interest or relative merit. If a paper was rejected on the basis of serious reviewer error, resubmission may be considered. Papers submitted to *Science* but not accepted for publication may, in some cases, be eligible for publication in *Science Signaling* or *Science Translational Medicine*. Most papers are published 4 to 8 weeks after acceptance; selected papers are published rapidly online in *Science* Express(www.sciencexpress.org).

在这一部分中,文章介绍了杂志筛选稿件的具体过程。投稿会由专门领域内的编辑进行审查,评价不高的稿件会在1~2周内通过电子邮件通知作者。投稿作者和审稿人需要通知稿件是否需要汇报DUCR情况。(笔者注:DUCR,即美国国家生物安全委员会科学顾问(NSABB)定义的"两用研究关注",是指可合理预期到的知识,产品,技术等有可能被误用并直接构成"威胁公众健康和安全"的研究)。被认定为DURC的稿件将由主编进行进一步的评审。另外被《科学》杂志退回的稿件可以有机会在《科学》杂志旗下的另外两个刊物上获得发表。大部分经过审议接受的稿件会在4~8周内发表,而被选中的文章会在 *Science* Express(www.sciencexpress.org)在线出版。

⑤Submission Requirements.

Authorship. All authors must agree to be so listed and must have seen and approved the manuscript, its content, and its submission to Science. Any changes in authorship must be approved in writing by all the original authors. Submission of a paper that has not been approved by all authors will result in immediate rejection without appeal.

Prior publication Science will not consider any paper or component of a paper that has been published or is under consideration elsewhere. Distribution on the Internet may be considered prior publication and may compromise the originality of the paper. Reporting the main findings of a paper in the mass media may compromise the novelty of the work and thus its approriateness for *Science*. Please contact the editors with questions regarding these policies.

Human studies. Informed consent must have been obtained for studies on humans after the nature and possible consequences of the studies were explained. All research on humans must have approval from the author's Institution Review Board(IRB)or equivalent body.

Animal care. Care of experimental animals must be in accordance with the authors' institutional guidelines.

Related papers. Copies of papers submitted to other journals by any of the authors that relate to the paper submitted to Science must be included with the submission.

Unpublished data and personal communications. Citations to unpublished data and personal communications cannot be used to support claims in the paper.

这一部分主要讲述了投稿的要求,包括以下几个方面:著作权(文章中涉及的引用内容必须经过原作者的同意,投稿文章中如果含有未经原作者允许的内容,稿件将被直接退回)、优先发表(《科学》不接受任何发表过或文章中有已发表内容的文章,发布在网上的内容必须是原创的)、人类的研究(所有关于人类的研究必须已经获得了作者伦理审查委员会(IRB)或同等机构批准)、动物的研究(实验所用的动物的处理必须符合 IRB 的相关规定)、未发表数据和个人通讯(不可引用未发表内容和个人通信信息)。

⑥Conditions of Acceptance.

Authorship, finding, and conflict of interest. All authors must agree to disclose all affiliations, funding sources, and financial or management relationships related to a paper, including those that could be perceived as potential sources of bias before acceptance. Science now requires all authors accepted papers to affirm their contribution to a paper and agree to our policies on data and materials availability. The senior author from each group is required to have examined the raw data their group has producted. See our conflict-of-interest policy, detailed at http://www.sciencemag.org/about/authors.

Data deposition. Before publication, large data sets, including microarray data, protein or DNA sequences, and atomic coordinates and structure factors for macromolecular or chemical structures must be deposited in an approved database, an accession number must be included in the published paper, and the deposited information must be released at the time of publication. Electron micrograph maps must' also be deposited. Approved databases are listed at http://www.sciencemag.org/about/authors. Large data sets with no appropriate approved repository must be housed as supporting online material at Science, or when this is not possible, on the author's Website, provided a copy of the data is held in escrow at Science to ensure availability to readers.

Data availability and materials sharing. After publication, all data necessary to understand, assess, and extend the conclusions of the manuscript must be available to any reader of Science, and all reasonable requests for materials must be fulfilled. Before acceptance, Science must informed of any restrictions on the sharing of materials (Materials Transfer Agreements MTAs, for example). Unreasonable restriction may preclude publication.

License and Access policies. Authors retain copyright but agree to grant to Science an exclusive license to publish the paper in print and online. Any author whose university or institution has policies or other restrictions limiting their ability to assign exclusive publication rights (e.g., Harvard, MIT, Open University) must apply for a waiver or other exclusion from that policy or those restrictions. After publication, authors may post the accepted version of the paper on the their personal Web site. Science also provides an electronic reprint service in which one referrer link that can be posted on a personal or institutional Web page, through which users can freely access the published paper on Science's Web site. Science allows deposition of the accepted papers into the NIH PubMed Central or other PMC International repository 6 months after publication, in accord with the requirements of the funders NIH and Wellcome Trust, provided that a link to the final version published in Science is included. Original research papers are freely accessible with registration on Science's Web site 12 months after publication.

Press coverage. The paper should remain a privileged document and will not be released to the press or the public before publication. Questions should be referred to the AAAS Office of Public Programs (202 - 326 - 6440).

这一部分主要讲述了杂志对稿件的接收条件，包括以下几个方面：著作权、科学发现和利益冲突（文章作者须同意公开文章相关附件、研究来源、资助关系等）、数据处理（在发表前，所有文章中的数据集合必须存入在批准列入的数据库中，并在文章中公开该数据集合的登陆方式）、材料共享和数据可用性（出版后要求必须将所有和结论相关的数据向读者公开，不合理的限制可能会妨碍出版）、批准和开发政策（作者保留著作权但是须向《科学》杂志提供发表文章和在线刊登文章的授权）、新闻报道（文章发表之前不得向任何媒体发表与论文相关的信息）。

⑦Manuscript Preparing.

Title should be no more than 96 characters (including spaces) for Reports, Research Articles, and Reviews, and 64 characters plus spaces for Brevia.

One-sentence summaries capturing the most important point should be submitted for all papers.

Abstracts explain to the general reader why the research was done and why the results are important. The abstracts should present background information to convey the context of the research, descrie the results, and draw general conclusions.

Text starts with a brief introduction describing the paper's significance, which should be intelligible to readers in other disciplines. Technical terms should be defined. Symbols, abbreviation, and acronyms should be defined the first time they are used. All tables and figures should be cited in numeical order.

References and notes are numbered in the order in which they are cited, first through the text, then through the text of the references, and then through the figures and table legends. Each references should have a unique number; do not combine references or embed references in notes. Do not use op. cit. or ibid. We now accept titles in references and will include these in our online version.

Acknowledgements, including complete funding information, accesion numbers, and any information related to authorship conflict of interest, should be gathered into the last numbered reference.

Tables should be included at the end of the references and should supplement, not duplicate, the text. The first sentence of the table legend should be a brief desciptive title. Every vertical column should have a heading, consisting of a title with the unit of measure in parenthese. Units should not change within a column.

Figure legends should be double-spaced in numerical orders. The figure title should be given as the first line of the legend. No single legend should be longer than ~200 words. Nomenclature, abbreviations, symbols, and units used in a figure should match those used in the text. Units should be metric and follow SI conventions.

Supporting online material (SOM) is posted permanently on Science Online, is linked to the manuscript, and is freely available. SOM includes materials and methods plus extra text, figures, tables, references, and video or audio clips that are important for the integrity of the paper. Detailed instructions on preparing SOM can be found at http://www.sciencemag.org/about/authors/prep/prep_online.dtl.

Figures should be submitted as part of the online submission or, if necessary for large files only, on CD. No part of a figure may be selectively manipulated. When figures are assembled from multiple gels to micrographs, a line of a space should be indicated the border between the two orginal images. See our online information for Authors for information on preparing art. We can include high-resolution images as SOM.

这一部分主要讲述了杂志对稿件准备工作的建议和要求，包括以下几个方面：题目（报告、研究论文和科学综述的题目少于96个字符，简报题目少于64个字符）、一句话摘要、摘要（须陈述文章背景、研究过程、结果和结论）、正文（须有介绍部分，正文中科技语须解释）。图表缩略语等在第一次使用时应作出定义，并按照字母顺序引出图表和数据）、参考文献和注释（按顺序列出参考文献和注释，每一个参考文献须有一个题号，不允许用op, cit, ibid）、图表（放在参考文献后以补充的形式而非复制正文，每一个图表要求有图表说明）、配图说明、支持在线材料以及数字。

接着我们看看英国的权威学术杂志《自然》刊登在其中文网站上的"作者须知":

《自然》系列期刊的编辑努力为作者提供高效、公正和充满关切的投稿、同行评议及发表经历。作者期望被接受发表的投稿都是经过同行以最严格的专业标准进行过审评,他们也希望编辑是根据其提供深刻和有益分析的能力来挑选同行评审的专家。编辑在选择《自然》期刊的内容需要权衡诸多因素,但他们会在尽可能保持最高决策质量的前提下努力减少做出决定的时间。经过评审后,编辑会努力提高一篇论文的可读性,因此对读者来说,通过建议和对文章的编辑,所有的研究工作都将这样的形式呈现,即对领域内专家来说它是易读的,对直接领域外的科学家来说它是可以理解的。通过我们的高级在线出版系统,研究工作会以在线开工发布而不被延误。在每周举行的新闻发布会上,《自然》系列期刊为3000多位注册记者提供新闻,内容涉及即将出版的所有研究论文。大约80多万注册用户会通过电子邮件收到目录内容,在期刊的主页、目录页及"新闻和观点"栏目中,许多论文都以"亮点方式"突出介绍以方便非专业读者阅读。在所有的这些工作过程中,《自然》系列期刊的编辑坚守根据相关政策制定的编辑方针、伦理和科学标准,这些政策都刊登在我们期刊的网站上,我们也会周期性地评估这些政策以确保它们能持续地反映科学界的需求。	《自然》系列期刊对作者的承诺(保证)
《自然》系列期刊是由每周出版的多学科《自然》杂志和8种每月出版的期刊组成。《自然》杂志发表在某一学科内具有高影响、其他领域的科学家也会感兴趣的研究工作;8种学术期刊的名称是根据其报道领域命名的,它们都发表在其领域中质量最高、影响力显著的论文,这8种期刊的名称分别是:《自然生物技术》、《自然细胞生物学》、《自然遗传学》、《自然免疫学》、《自然材料学》、《自然医学》、《自然方法学》、《自然结构和分子生物学》(《自然》杂志的主页有它们的直接链接)。所有的这些期刊都是国际性的,它们在美国、英国和日本出版和印刷。点击这里可获得更多这些期刊间相互关系的信息。《自然》杂志和《自然》系列月刊的影响因子位居世界影响因子最高的期刊之列。每种期刊的影响因子可以都在其期刊的主页上找到。期刊的崇高声望让作者受益良多,但也意味着论文发表的竞争异常激烈,因此有许多投稿未经同行评审就被拒绝。《自然》系列期刊与绝大多数其他期刊的不同之处在于它们均没有编辑委员会,取而代之的是,论文是否出版是由具备深厚专业背景的编辑在与科学界作广泛的商议后决定的。这篇文章只是提供这些非凡期刊的常规编辑过程。虽然所有的期刊都基本相似且有共同的编辑方针,但所有的作者在投稿前都需要参考所投稿期刊的《读者指南》,以获得在该期刊准备和发表论文的至关重要的详细信息,因为期刊间存在差别。	如何在《自然》系列期刊上发表您的研究工作
下面的部分概述了期刊的编辑过程,描述了编辑在投稿和发表过程中是如何处理稿件的。可以通过进入在线投稿系统了解这一过程中的每一个步骤,并了解稿件的状态。	编辑过程

在将论文全文投稿前,研究人员也许可以从编辑处获得非正式的反馈信息。这种服务的目的是节省时间,如果编辑认为论文不适合发表,还可以将论文及时投到其他期刊,而不被耽误。如果希望使用投稿前询问服务,请使用所选期刊的在线系统发送一段话,解释论文的重要性,以及论文的摘要或概述段和相关的引用目录,以便编辑能够将投稿与其他相关工作进行对比判断。编辑也许会很快邀请作者递交完整的论文(这并不意味着发表的任何承诺),或许说明这篇论文不适合在该期刊发表。如果接到的是否定的回应,请不要回复。如果确信自己论文的重要性,那就不要在乎编辑的疑惑,可以通过期刊的在线投稿系统递交论文的全文。编辑会对此做更详尽的评估。	投稿前询问
当准备投稿时,请根据期刊的要求使用在线投稿系统。当期刊收到投稿时,它会提供一个编号并安排一位编辑,这位编辑负责阅读论文,征询科学顾问和编辑部同事的非正式建议,并将投的稿与本领域最近所发表的其他论文进行比较。如果论文看起来新颖、引人注目、所描述的工作既直接又有深远的意义,那么编辑会将论文送出去作同行评审,通常会送给两个或三个独立的专家。然而,因为期刊只能在某一领域或次领域发表极少数的论文,因此许多论文未经同行评审就被拒绝,即使这些论文描述的可能是可靠的科学结果。	初次投稿
在特殊情况下,编辑不能发表您的论文,但他(或她)也许会建议这篇论文更适合在其他的《自然》系列期刊上发表。如果作者愿意将论文重新投到所建议的期刊,那么只需要简单地链接到编辑提供的网址,将论文和审稿意见转给新期刊。这一过程全在您的掌握(控制)之中:如果选择不使用这种服务,取而代之的是可以使用期刊常用的在线投稿服务将论文投到其他的《自然》期刊或《自然》出版集团的期刊,而且还可以选择在投稿中是否包含审稿人的意见。	投稿在《自然》系列期刊间的转移
当编辑决定将论文送出去评审时,他会给通讯作者发一封电子邮件告知这一信息。编辑挑选的审稿人的依据是:独立性;对论文做出全面、公正的技术方面评价的能力;目前或最近是否评审过相关投稿;以及在规定的时间内是否能对投稿进行评审等。同时可为论文推荐审稿人(包括详细的地址信息),尽管编辑不一定会采纳这些信息,但这些信息常常是有用的。编辑会考虑作者的要求排除一定数量的指定科学家作为审稿人。	同行评议

当编辑根据审稿人的意见决定出版论文时,不仅要考虑这篇论文目前是的情况,还要考虑修订后的情况。在收到所有审稿人的意见后,编辑们讨论这份投稿,然后再给作者写信。在这封信中,编辑或是拒绝发表您的论文,或是建议修改后重投,或者说论文不需要进一步的修改就可发表。如果编辑建议修改论文,他或她会提供特别的建议,并在信中陈述这种修改的情况,以及是否会与审稿人进一步讨论再投的修改稿件。如果编辑邀请修改该论文,则应该在重投的稿件中附上一封新的封面信,信中应包括对审稿人和编辑意见的逐一回应,包括怎样修改论文以回应这些评价。	决定和修订
论文被接受以后,文件编辑(或副编辑)会对这篇论文做出版前的准备,他们会对文章进行推敲、润色,以便文字和图具有可读性,对直接领域外的读者来说也是清晰明白的,并且让论文符合期刊的风格。文件编辑将为英语为非母语的作者提供建议,并且在编辑这些论文时特别小心。	接受以后
所有的论文都会以印刷版本的形式出版,在期刊的网站上以 PDF 和 HTML 格式全文刊登。如果编辑和审稿人认为补充信息对于论文的结论至关重要(比如大的数据表格或有关一种方法的详细信息),而且许多专家对此的兴趣甚于论文的其他部分,那么补充信息将随同论文一同在电子网络版发表。许多链接和导航服务会提供给《自然》系列期刊以在线形或(HTML)出版所有论文。新闻发布服务将包括所有论文和通讯作者的详细联系方式,这意味着作者的工作会引起世界上所有主流媒体机构的关注,他们也许会选择在报纸或其他媒体中对作者的工作进行特别报道。部分论文会在《自然》杂志、《自然》出版集团的出版物和专门的网站上被突出地介绍或概述。《自然》出版集团出版的期刊不要求作者的版权,但是会要求签署一份独家的出版许可文件。	出版后
如果一位期刊的编辑不能发表一篇论文,也不建议再投稿,那么建议将论文发表在别的期刊上。然而,如果确信编辑或审稿人严重曲解该论文,那么作者可以给编辑写信,解释认为该决定不正确的科学理由。请记住编辑会优先处理最新的投稿和被邀请重投的稿件,因此会需要数周时间才能得到有关不同意见的回信。在这一期间,不允许将论文投到别处。为了研究论文能够不延期发表,建议如果论文被拒绝了,就将论文投交到别处,而不要将时间花在与编辑进一步的交流上。	对决定的不同意见

最后本书对在阅读英文科技期刊"作者须知"和与杂志联系投稿的过程中常用词或表达以及注意事项,作以简要汇总:

1. corresponding author 通讯作者:负责联系出版、校稿事宜的作者。
2. author for copy requests 副本索取作者:文章发表后,编辑部会给作者提供一些文章的副本供其他读者索取使用,作者中应有一位作者专门负责此事。

3. academic degree 学位,如 M. D. ,Ph. D. ,RN。

4. academic title 职称,如教授、副教授(associate professor),职称不能作论文署名用

5. a covering letter 附信。

6. a running head / title 页眉标题,约5个英文单词。

7. legends 插图说明,应与插图分开,另页打印。

8. unmounted prints 不加装帧的照片,即投稿用的图片、照片要保持原样,不能装帧。

9. double spacing 双行(打印),即送审的英文稿件要以空两行的格式打印。

10. prime reviewer 初审者,即负责稿件初审的专家,一般为三人,所以投稿时应向编辑部至少提供三份副本。

11. copyright transfer 版权转让:一般来说,稿件被接受的同时,其版权同时转让给了该杂志。

12. authorship 著作权:参加研究的所有作者,包括没有署名的作者,都具有著作权。

13. authorship responsibility 作者责任:

(1)作者必须是参加研究或部分研究的人,对所作研究是知情的;

(2)作者必须对所做的研究负责。

14. patients rights to privacy 病人隐私权:研究应对病人的隐私进行保护,如提供病人的照片时,必须将能识别该病人的所有特征加以掩盖或作相应处理,仅将病人的眼睛挡住是不够的。

15. informed consent 知情同意(书)、在进行新药、新技术、新方法的研究时,必须将研究的有关事宜告诉病人并征得病人的同意,在论文中必须对此有专门说明。

五、写好提纲

各种资料已经就绪之后,作者便应该开始构思写作。正式撰写论文之前,论文作者还要做以下几方面工作:

(1)组织好手边的资料,去粗留精,去伪存真。

(2)选择写作方法和过程。

(3)如何合理的组织材料,构建论文结构。

其中,后面两个步骤的差异性稍大。不同的人会选择不同写作方法,有的人对自己所研究的内容很有信心,所谓"心中有乾坤",他们直接撰写;有的人边搜集资料,边研究边写作;有的人在写作之前先做好写作计划,然后再按步就班地添加数据和论据。在这些写作方法中显然是后者最被广泛的使用。因为撰写论文是一个系统化的庞大工程,在写作前拟好写作计划可以使

得整个写作过程事半功倍、有条不紊。所谓提纲写作就是作者在撰写论文之前,按照论文主次结构和行文顺序,构筑论文中心主题、以章为单位的各分论点、以节为单位的各分论点、各章节的论据数据和分析及各章节小结和论文结论;每一部分都与论文主题相关并以线状结构组织排列。提纲可以呈现论文各个部分的主次要内容,表明各个内容的顺序和所在位置,因此可以一目了然地展现论文的主题、论点、论据及各个具体内容之间的逻辑关系,提纲写作具有连贯性、一致性、系统性和逻辑性的特点。

常见的提纲形式有句子提纲(sentence outline)和标题提纲(topic outline)。本书通过以下几个例子分别分析一下这几种提纲写作的格式。

下面的提纲为基本格式,供大家参考。

Essay Outline	
I. Introduction	
Thesis:_____	—controlling idea
II. Main idea 1:	
Topic Sentence:_____	
A. Sub-idea	
B. Sub-idea	
1. supporting detail	
2. supporting detail	
a. Fact 1	
b. Fact 2	—Body Paragraphs
III. Main idea 2:	
Topic Sentence:_____	
A. Sub-idea	
B. Sub-idea	
C. Sub-idea	
* * * * * *	
IV. Conclusion	

其次，通过具体示例展现句子提纲的撰写方法。

A Sample of Sentence Outline

I. Introduction

Thesis: Three new studies reveal that brown fat remains functional in adult keeping lean.

II. Main idea 1:

Topic Sentence: Brown adipose tissue consumes energey to generate body heat, however, physiologists thought that the tissue largely disappeared by the time we reach adulthood.

III. Main idea 2:

Topic Sentence: Now, researchers have shown that the brown fats present and working in adults

A. Sub-idea 1: Physiologists Wouter dosed 24 young men with radioactive glucose and turn down the thermostat and found that brown fat is active in the process.

B. Sub-idea 2: Endocrinologist C. Kahn scanned 2,000 patients and found 5% sported brown fat without being chilled.

C. Sub-idea 3: Enerback confirmed the tissue's identity by looking at gene activity.

IV. Conclusion: Researchers can focus on whether we can harness brown fat to help overweight patients burn off unhealthy white fat.

最后，通过具体示例展现标题提纲的撰写方法。

A Sample of Topic Outline

I. Introduction

Thesis: Three new studies reveal that brown fat remains functional in adult keeping lean.

II. Main idea 1:

Topic Sentence: Brown adipose tissue's function to generate body heat by consuming energey instead of people's long-time misunderstanding

III. Main idea 2:

Topic Sentence: researches showing that the brown fats present and working in adults

A. Sub-idea 1: Physiologists Wouter's experiment on 24 young men

B. Sub-idea 2: Endocrinologist C. Kahn's scans of 2,000 patients

C. Sub-idea 3: Enerback's study of gene activity.

IV. Conclusion: application of brown fat to help overweight patients burn off unhealthy white fat.

第七章 科技英语论文的题目和署名

一、科技英语论文的题目

(一)拟定论文题目的原则

科技论文的题目(Title,Topic)以最恰当、最简明的词语反映论文中最重要的特定内容的逻辑组合,是论文的眼睛和灵魂,是论文研究方向、主要内容及创新的高度浓缩,是反映表达论文方向与水平的第一个重要信息。论文题目的选择要求高度且具体、准确且简洁。信息时代和网络索引的趋势需要论文题目准确、简洁、重点突出且专业性强、索引性高。

基于易于读者选读、审选编排、编制索引的目的,将一篇几千字甚至上万字的论文提要为几个词汇,使其能够清楚准确地表达论文核心提要,需要作者仔细琢磨推敲,遵循以下拟题原则:

1. 内容上

好的论文题目,要重点突出,准确简洁,避免笼统空泛、冗长繁琐、华而不实、模棱两可。
例如:
Dissecting self-renewal in stem cells with RNA interference
Integrated approach to identify genetic mechaisms
上述论文题目能准确表达论文内容,恰当反映所研究的范围和深度。
试比较以下示例中二题目
例一:
(1) Study on inflorescence architectures《植物花序类型多样性研究》
(2) Evolution and development of inflorescence architectures《植物花序类型多样性的形成机制》。
这一示例中的两则题目,题目一过于广泛,毫无针对性;而题目二将植物花序类型多样性的研究细致到成长的因素,重点突出。
例二:
(1) Impacts of CO_2 on Photosynthesis《CO_2对光合作用的影响》
(2) The Progress Research of Responses and Acclimatization Mechanism of Plant Photosynthesis to Elevated Atmospheric CO_2 Concentration and Temperature《植物光合作用对大气CO_2和温度升高的响应及其适应机制的进展研究》
(3) The Impact of Elevated CO_2 Concentration on Photosynthesis and Plant Productivity《CO_2浓度升高对植物光合作用和植物多产的影响》
这一示例中,题目一过于笼统抽象;题目二解释细致,但是过于繁复,没有做到让人一目了然的效果;而题目三则简单清晰醒目。

2. 语言表达上

要求中英题目具有一致性,同时减少对没有实质性意义词汇的使用。

如:"A Study on","An Investigation of ","Concerning","On"等,当然有一些作者依照个人习惯,在题目中选择类似上述词汇,并非不可以,只是如果题目字数过长是可以省略的。

3. 题目中的常用到的词汇

例如:"作用"、"效果"、"功能"、"反应"simulation 指示,effect,impact 影响,study 研究,investigation 调查,research 研究,progress 进展,use,application 用途等。

(二)英文论文题目的构成和拟定技巧

1. 构成形式

英文论文题目主要以名词短语(noun phrase)为主,基本上由一个或几个名词加上其前置和(或)后置定语构成,即首先根据论文中心论点、研究对象、研究目的和结论等因素,确定短语型题名的中心词,再进行前后修饰。各个词的顺序很重要,词序不当,会导致表达不准。题目通常不用陈述句,因为题目主要起标示作用,而陈述句具有判断式的语义,也不够精练和醒目。探讨性质的文章有时为了增加生动性可以用疑问句,但是非常正式的学术论文不适宜用疑问句作为题目。

例如:

《补充 CO_2 对光生物反应器培养小球藻生长和光合作用的影响》

(1) Effects of CO_2 Enrichment on Growth and Photosynthesis of Green Alga Chlorella Vulgaris

(2) Enrichment of CO_2 is effective on Growth and Photosynthesis of Green Alga Chlorella Vulgaris.

(3) Is Enrichment of CO_2 is effective on Growth and Photosynthesis of Green Alga Chlorella Vulgaris?

从上述同一中文题目的英文撰写形式来看,第一句为名词短语,语序正确,层次清晰。第二句为陈述句,则显得略为繁复。第三句为疑问句,语气生动,但是不免带有言下之意,表达不十分明确。

2. 定语及语序

名词中心词由简单的定语修饰,题目中常见的定语包括形容词、名词、动名词、现在分词、过去分词、动词不定式和介词短语等。根据该定语的长度和词语性质可前置或后置,语序要合理准确安排,避免出现错误和异议。而当表示材料、用途、时间、地点、内容、类别等的名词作定语的时候,为了增强题目醒目、重点突出和逻辑清晰的效果,题目中常常不用 of 短语表示所属,而是直接用名词充当定语,这在其他专业英语中也是一个较为普遍的现象。

例如:

植物脂肪 plant fat,而不说 fat of plant

道路工程 road works,而不说 works of road

黄金储备 gold reserve,而不说 reserve of gold

3. 冠词的缺省

为了达到简洁明了的效果,冠词一般可用可不用,很多作者选择省略冠词。

例如:

(1) Functional end groups for polymers prepared using ring-opening metathesis polymerization.

(2) Latent thiol mercaptan chain transfer agents and their use in synthesis of polymers.

观察上述两个题目中,作者均没有使用冠词。尤其对于长度比较长的题目,省略冠词可以精简题目。当然省略定冠词的情况,只适用于标题中,正文撰写过程中一般不应该出现这样的情况。

4. 题目中的大小写

题名字母的大小写有以下3种格式:

(1) 全部字母大写。

例如:IMPLANT BOOSTS ACTIVITY IN INJURED BRAIN

(2) 每个词的首字母大写,但3个或4个字母以下的冠词、连词、介词全部小写。

例如:An Optoelectronic Nose for the Detection of Toxic Gases

(3) 题名第1个词的首字母大写,其余字母均小写。

例如:Ultrashort metal-metal distances and extreme bond orders

目前第一种格式较少使用,第二中格式用得最多,而第三种格式的使用亦有增多的趋势。

5. 字数

题目长度应该适当,过短便会题目空泛,没有针对性;过长则繁琐不醒目。而且无论是国外学术期刊还是国内的期刊对题目的字数一般都有一定的限制。一般中文要求在20字之内,英文要在10个词之内,不宜超过15个词。

6. 多个题目

多个题目通常指副标题(title)和系列题目(series title),使用较少,但有的期刊连续登载时会使用,来揭示文章中的关联。

常见的形式有:

(1) 破折号衔接:正标题——副标题

例如:Social Happiness——The Development of an Eighteenth-Century American Poetic Ideal

(2) 冒号衔接:正标题:副标题

例如:Euphemism: Characteristics, Structures and Application

(3) 罗马数字衔接:系列题目 I

　　　　　　　　　系列题目 II

例如:Investigation on CO_2 and Temperature(I): Response of Photosynthesis to Elevated Atmospheric CO_2

Investigation on CO_2 and Temperature(II): Responses and Acclimatization Mechanism of Plant Photosynthesis to Elevated Atmospheric CO_2 Concentration and Temperature

7. 题目中的缩略语

题目中应该慎用缩略语,已得到整个科技界或本行业科技人员公认的缩略词语,才可用于题名中。

ATP(adenosine triphosphatae,三磷酸腺苷酶)

AcOH(acetic acid,乙酸)

LASER(light amplification by stimulated emission of radiatoin,激光)

EI 美国工程索引数据库对题目的要求:

1. 题目首词尽量不出现冠词。

2. 题目首词首字母大写,其余小写。

3. 题目不可使用非公认通用符号、代号及数学公式、化学结构公式。

4. 题目中尽量避免使用缩略语、特殊字母,如数字和希腊字母。

二、科技英语论文的署名

(一)署名的目的和条件

无论是期刊论文还是学位论文,作者署名都是一项重要内容。作者署名涉及作者的权利(知识产权)、责任(包括学术责任和社会责任)及作者单位的知识产权。规范论文的作者署名,可维护作者及单位的知识产权,维护和体现科学的真实性和严肃性。署名的目的一是为了表明对论文著作权的拥有,二是承担相应的义务,三是署名和地址的编写便于读者与作者的联系及文献检索。

当然并非所有对论文有所贡献者都要在作者处署名,必须是做出实质性贡献的主要创作者、研究者或设计者才可以署名;而学生的导师、项目的领导人、对数据收集整理者起到的为指导作用、资助作用和协助工作,正确的做法是将上述人员名字列入论文致谢部分表达感谢,而非署名。

(二)署名的格式

1. 学术性期刊中署名的一般格式

将署名置于题名下方,并采用如下格式:作者姓名,作者工作单位名称及地名,邮政编码(一个作者下写下一个地址),

例如:

> Quantum dots in photonic crystals: From quantum information processing to single photon non-lineat optics
>
> Dirk Englund, Ilya Fushman, Andrei Fataon, Jelena Vuckovic
>
> (Ginzton Laboratory, Stanford University, 316 Via Pueblo Mall, Stanford, CA 94305, United States)

2. 姓名的英文书写

英语国家的人名形式为名字,中间名字,姓氏,即 first name, middle name(if have), family name,每一部分的首字母必须大写。例如:William Shakespeare, Emily Dickens, Bill Joe Jackson。

而常常出于简洁以及避免歧义的目的,中间名字简略为首字母缩写形式,即 Bill Joe Jackson 常写作 Bill J. Jackson。

我国作者的姓名书写形式很多,近些年逐渐形成较为统一的格式。1982 年我国通过了拼写中国专有名词和词语的国际标准《汉语拼音方案》,其中中国人名属于专有名词,译成外文应遵照其汉语拼音形式拼写。

因此我国作者姓名英文书写应遵循我国现行的国家标准 GB/T 16159—1996《汉语拼音正词法基本规则》:作者姓氏和名字分写,姓和名开头字母大写,姓氏在前,名字在后并连成一词,不加连字符,不缩写,省略调号。

例如:王丽英正确的拼写法应是:Wang Liying,而不正确的拼写法主要有:WANGLIYING,WANG LI YING,WANG LIYING,Wangliying,Wang-liying 等。

3. 工作单位名称、地址和邮编

工作单位名称和地址的标明是对作者身份的表示,同时也便于工作单位、作者个人的信息统计检索,以及感兴趣的读者与作者联络之用。

工作单位名称要规范、统一、稳定,一般的单位有统一的英文名称,作者切忌自行翻译。对大多数工作单位和研究机构来说,地址无需详细的列出,如某某区、某某街道、某某大厦,只要不影响邮政投递,只写出单位名称和邮政编码即可。

例一:

> Geometric Characteristic Analysis of Parameters of Slag Particle Group
> Lin Jianxiang
> (School of Civil Engineering & Architecture, Harbin Engineering University, Harbin 150001, China)

例二:对于多个作者,多作者姓名之间用逗号隔开,同一单位,直接编写单位地址即可。

> Geometric Characteristic Analysis of Parameters of Slag Particle Group
> Lin Jianxiang, Zhang Wei
> (School of Civil Engineering & Architecture, Harbin Engineering University, Harbin 150001, China)

例三:而对于多作者、多工作单位,则应按编写作者名单的序列,分别注明各自工作单位,并提供邮政编码。

> Geometric Characteristic Analysis of Parameters of Slag Particle Group
> Lin Jianxiang[1], Zhang Wei[2]
> (1. School of Civil Engineering & Architecture, Harbin Engineering University, Harbin 150001, China; 2. Inst. of Eng. Mech. of State Earthq. Bureau, Harbin 150080, China)

例四：如果作者在论文投稿后和论文发表前这期间更换了单位，那么要标明新单位的地址，一般写在脚注的位置。

Geometric Characteristic Analysis of Parameters of Slag Particle Group

  Lin Jianxiang, Zhang Wei*,

  (School of Civil Engineering & Architecture, Harbin Engineering University, Harbin 150001, China)

―――――――――――

  * Present Address: School of Civil Engineering & Architecture, Harbin Institute of Technology, Harbin 150001, China

---

例五：在很多知名杂志上，作者工作单位没有直接标注在作者姓名之下，而是以脚注的方式标注在第一页，这样做一方面可以使页面看上去更清晰明了、突出正文，另一方面很多论文是由很多作者共同完成，如果将所有作者的工作单位一一标注在题目下方，会造成一种累赘繁琐的视觉效果。

Genome-wide maps of chromatin state in pluripotent and lineage-committed cells

  Tarjei S. Mikkelsen[1,2], Manching Ku[1,4], David B. Jaffe[1], Biju Issac[1,4], Erez Lieberman[1,2], Georgia Giannoukos[1], Pablo Alvarez[1], William Brockman[1], Tae-Kyung Kim[5], Richard P. Koche[1,2,4], William Lee[1], Eric Mendenhall[1,4], Aisling O'Donovan[4], Aviva Presser[1], Carsten Russ[1], Xiaohui Xie[1], Alexander Meissner[3], Marius Wernig[3], Rudolf Jaenisch[3], Chad Nusbaum1, Eric S. Lander[1,3,7] & Bradley E. Bernstein[1,4,6,7]

―――――――――――

  Broad Institute of Harvard and MIT,
  Division of Health Sciences and Technology, MIT,
  Whitehead Institute for Biomedical Research, Cambridge, Massachusetts 02142, USA
  Molecular Pathology Unit and Center for Cancer Research, Massachusetts General Hospital, Charlestown, Massachusetts 02129, USA
  Department of Neurology, Children's Hospital,
  Department of Pathology, Harvard Medical School, Boston, Massachusetts 02115, USA
  These authors contributed equally to this work.

有时为和杂志编审联系，在论文上需要编写较为详细的地址。英文的地址撰写和中文不同，一般说来，英文地址的格式就是从小的具体的地点到大的范围书写，而区、路、街道等都可以用相应的缩写形式来简化地址书写形式。本书在这里作以简单小结：

室/房 Room,缩写为 Rm.
号 No.
宿舍 Dormitory
楼/层 Floor,缩写为 FL.
小区 Residential Quarter
甲／乙／丙／丁 A／B／C／D
巷／弄 Lane
单元 Unit
号楼/幢 Building 缩写为 BLDG
街,Street,缩写为 St.,或 Avenue 缩写为 Ave.
路,Road,缩写为 Rd.
县 County
镇 Town
区 District,缩写为 Dist.
市 City
省 Province,缩写为 Prov.

例如:

中国黑龙江省哈尔滨市南岗区南通大街 145 号哈尔滨工程大学 1 号楼 316 室,150001

Room316,Building1,Harbin Engineering University,No. 145,Nantong Rd.,Nangang Dist.,Harbin,Heilongjiang Prov.,China,150001

4. 排序问题和通信作者

如果论文由两个或两个以上作者共同完成,那么要按照贡献大小依次排列,按署名顺序列为第一作者、第二作者……。署名的排序反映了论文创造者的贡献、权利及责任大小,即第一作者是主要的贡献者、权利和责任人,其他序列的作者依次递减。当然不排除论文有多人共同完成,并列为第一作者的情况,这种特殊情况可以用脚注的方式标明。

通信作者或责任作者(Corresponding Author,CA)是指论文完成后,在投稿的实际操作过程中,统筹投稿工作以及负责与审稿专家、编辑等联系工作的作者。这是国际学术界通行的一种署名方式。

很多情况下,通讯作者是提出论文观点、确定论文构思并最终定稿及完成稿件投寄的作者,并能对实验结果的真实性、科学性负责和对论文的学术观点加以解释的主要责任人,也是学术成果的主要权利人。通常情况下在论文首页脚注处以 * 标出。

例如:

Regulatory network involved in the cell fate determination of embryonic stem cells

Jiu Zhigang, Liu Li, Xie Zhihui, Jing Naihe*

(Institute of Biochemistry and Cell Biology, Shanghai Institutes for Biological Sciences, Chinese Academy of Sciences, Shanghai 200031, China)

* 通信作者, E-mail: njing@sibs.ac.cn

通信作者的作用不亚于第一作者,不标注通讯作者的弊端有:

(1)责任不明确,无法在编校过程中与作者联系,尤其在研究生(作为第一作者)离校后将造成工作的障碍。

(2)无法为读者提供学术交流的途径;无法在发生问题后澄清责任。

(3)贡献大小不明确,无法对主要责任者的工作给与相应的肯定。

(4)不利于期刊编辑部对同行专家的遴选。

附1:

《Science》杂志"作者须知"中对"署名"一项的说明和描述:

向《Science》杂志投稿,意味着该稿件的通讯作者(corresponding author)接受了这样一个责任:保证所有的作者都同意在稿件上的署名,都看过并同意稿件的内容,也同意将其投给《Science》杂志。任何署名的改变都要有全部原作者签名同意的书面意见。

附2:

《Nature》杂志"作者须知"中对"署名"一项的说明和描述:

Being an author

The *Nature* journals do not require all authors of a research paper to sign the letter of submission, nor do they impose an order on the list of authors. Submission to a *Nature* journal is taken by the journal to mean that all the listed authors have agreed all of the contents. The corresponding (submitting) author is responsible for having ensured that this agreement has been reached, and for managing all communication between the journal and all co-authors, before and after publication. Any changes to the author list after submission, such as a change in the order of the authors, or the deletion or addition of authors, needs to be approved by a signed letter from every author.

作为论文作者:

不要求所有作者签署投稿信件,但是投稿信件提交后,即表明所有署名作者都要履行遵守《自然杂志》关于署名著作权利和义务的内容。如果投稿后有任何作者顺序上的变动,要求提交变更说明,并且要求每位作者签名。

Author contributions statements

Authors are required to include a statement of responsibility in the manuscript that specifies the contribution of every author. …*Nature* journals also allow two coauthors to be specified as having contributed equally to the work being described(most often used for co-first authors), but prefer authors to use the 'author contributions' style for reader clarity.

作者贡献的声明：

每位作者必须详细阐明各自在论文中所担任和承担的工作。《自然》杂志亦允许两个作者共同为第一作者，但是更倾向于作者们向读者阐明各自的贡献。

Corresponding author-prepublication responsibilities

The corresponding(submitting) author is solely responsible for communicating with the journal and with managing communication between coauthors. Before submission, the corresponding author ensures that all authors are included in the author list, its order has been agreed by all authors, and that all authors are aware that the paper was submitted. After acceptance, the proof is sent to the corresponding author, who circulates it to all coauthors and deals with the journal on their behalf; the journal will not necessarily correct errors after publication if they result from errors that were present on a proof that was not shown to coauthors before publication. The corresponding author is responsible for the accuracy of all content in the proof, in particular that names of coauthors are present and correctly spelled, and that addresses and affiliations are current.

论文发表前，通信作者的责任：

论文发表前，通信作者的责任是联系杂志社及统筹所有作者的工作，确保所提交的一切内容属实。

Corresponding author-responsibilities after publication

The journal regards the corresponding author as the point of contact for queries about the published paper. It is this author's responsibility to inform all coauthors of matters arising and to ensure such matters are dealt with promptly. This author does not have to be the senior author of the paper or the author who actually supplies materials; this author's role is to ensure enquiries are answered promptly on behalf of all the co-authors. The name and e-mail address of this author(on large collaborations there may be two) is published in the paper.

论文发表后，通信作者的责任：

论文发表后，杂志社将视通信作者为质疑问询的答复人，通信作者要及时地联系其他作者关于论文发表过程中的相关事宜。通信作者不要求必须为论文材料的最主要提供者或创作者，他/她的作用是代表所有作者，及时答复投稿和编审过程中出现的一切问题。在出版的论文中，要求标明通信作者的姓名和电子邮件地址。

第八章 科技英语论文摘要的撰写

一、摘要的概念和作用

摘要又称概要、内容提要。摘要是以提供文献内容梗概为目的,不加评论和补充解释,简明、确切地记述文献重要内容的短文。其基本要素包括研究目的、方法、结果和结论。具体地讲就是研究工作的主要对象和范围,采用的手段和方法,得出的结果和重要的结论,有时也包括具有情报价值的其他重要的信息。摘要应具有独立性和自明性,并且拥有与文献等量的主要信息,即不阅读全文,就能获得必要的信息。任何一篇完整的论文都要求写随文摘要,摘要的主要功能有:

(1)让读者尽快了解论文的主要内容,以补充题名的不足。现代科技文献信息浩如烟海,读者检索到论文题名后是否会阅读全文,主要就是通过阅读摘要来判断;所以,摘要担负着吸引读者和将文章的主要内容介绍给读者的任务。

(2)为科技情报文献检索数据库的建设和维护提供方便。论文发表后,文摘杂志或各种数据库对摘要可以不做修改或稍作修改而直接利用,从而避免他人编写摘要可能产生的误解、欠缺甚至错误。随着计算机技术和网络的迅猛发展,网上查询、检索和下载专业数据已成为当前科技信息情报检索的重要手段,网上各类全文数据库、文摘数据库,越来越显示出现代社会信息交流的水平和发展趋势。同时论文摘要的索引是读者检索文献的重要工具。所以论文摘要的质量高低,直接影响着论文的被检索率和被引频次。

二、英文中的几种"摘要"

在英文中 abstract 和 summary 都可以表示内容提要、摘要的意思,即表示用简短精确的文字概括论文内容。但 abstract 和 summary 还是有区别的。

Abstract 用在正文之前,是论文整体的一部分,是为方便读者阅读、提供检索而做的对论文正文的内容提要。具有一定的专业性,一般用于专业领域内的学位论文(dissertation)、期刊文章(journal paper)、学术会议论文(conference paper)、展示论文(poster)等。

Summary 用法相对广泛,广义地讲,可以指任何文章的大意概要、主要论点和观点综述;狭义地讲,也可以成为学术论文的一部分。如果正文前无 abstract,正文开始的第一段通常就是 summary;如果前面有 abstract,在短的论文中 summary 经常位于文章最后,功能相当于 conclusion。Summary 也可以用于向国际会议投稿,即作者先投寄 summary,而不是全文。

当前 abstract 的使用越来越多,由于网络检索的需要,期刊论文的撰写和投稿都要求必须有 abstract。

三、论文摘要的类型和主要内容

(一)摘要的内容

摘要是一种对论文正文基本内容的浓缩,以读者迅速掌握原文内容梗概为目的,无须做主观评论和解释,但必须简明、确切地表述原文的重要内容,从内容上要求具有逻辑性和完整性。具体地说,应该概括说明全文的以下主要内容:研究工作的目的、方法、结果和结论四个方面,而重点是结果和结论。这四个方面的具体要求如下:

1. 研究目的(aim):主要说明研究工作的前提、背景和目的以及相关联的主题范围,注意不可过于泛泛。

2. 采取方法(method and technique):主要说明理论支撑(theory)、实验条件(experimental condition)、实验手段(experimental technique)、分析方法(analytical method)、程序设计(program design)、系统设计(system design)、材料(material)、手段(approach)、设备和仪器(equipment and instrument)等。

3. 研究结果(result):主要说明观察数据(observations)、实验发现(findings)、得到的效果(effects)、性能(functions)等。可以是所获得的实验结果(experimental outcomes),也可以是理论性成果(theoretical result)等;可以包含应用的情况(applied situations)或潜在的用途(potential usages)。

4. 结论(conclusion):主要是对结果的分析、比较、评价、应用,提出的问题,今后的课题,假设、启发、建议、预测等。

例如:

Photocatalysis is the acceleration of a photoreaction in the presence of a catalyst. Recently photocatalysis is a rapidly expanding technology for treatment of polluted water. This paper discusses the photocatalytic degradation for environmental applications. The paper examines the chemical effects of degradations of pollutants of various variables, including adsorption, temperature, intensity of light, pH, and presence of anions, cations and so on. A critical analysis of the available literature data has been made and some general conclusions have been drawn concerning the above mentioned effects. The need for more work on specific points has been brought out.	研究目的以及当前研究背景 论证内容 研究方法和结果 今后的课题和建议

(二)摘要的类型

根据内容侧重的不同,摘要可分为以下三大类:说明性摘要、资料性摘要和报道-指示性摘要。

1. 说明性摘要(indicative abstract):也称为指示性摘要、描述性摘要(descriptive abstract)或论点摘要(topic abstract)。它主要介绍论文的论题和研究目的,一般只用二、三句话概括论文的主题,而不涉及论据、方法、结果和结论,不需要提供数据。因此说明性摘要多用于综述、会议报告或文选检索类期刊中。此类摘要可用于帮助读者决定是否需要阅读全文。

2. 资料性摘要(informative abstract):也称信息性摘要或报道性摘要。它是论文的高度浓缩,是原文内容要点的总结。其特点是全面、简要地概括论文的目的、方法、主要数据和结论。可以说,资料性摘要是说明性摘要的扩展,因此除了对相关问题的定性描述,还要提供一定的定量信息。读者不仅可以方便查找,还能从中获得很多信息。

3.报道-指示性摘要(informative-indicative abstract):以报道性摘要的形式表述文献中信息价值较高的部分,以指示性摘要的形式表述其余部分。

试比较下列示例:

例一:说明性摘要

This paper reviews quantum critical point. It analysizes the presence or absence of a quantum critical point and its location in the phase diagram of high temperature superconductors. Conclusions concerning the relationship between quantum critical point and temperature are made.	论文主题 论证大致过程 结论

例二:资料性摘要

Quantum dots in photonic crystals are interesting both as a testbed for fundamental cavity quantum electrodynamics (QED) experiments and as a platform for quantum and classical information processing. We describe a technique to coherently access the QD-cavity system by resonant light scattering. Among other things, the coherent access enables a giant optical nonlinearity associated with the saturation of a single quantum dot strongly coupled to a photonic crystal cavity. We explore this nonlinearity to implement controlled phase and amplitude modulation between two modes of light at the single photon level—a nonlinearity observed so far only in atomic physics systems. We also measured the photon statistics of the reflected beam at various detunings with the QD/cavity system. These measurements reveal effects such as photon blockade and photon-induced tunneling, for the first time in solid state. These demonstrations lie at the core of a number of proposals for quantum information	论文主题 论据阐述 (方法、数据) 研究步骤 结果和结论

一般说来,资料性摘要中研究方法、研究结果和结果分析或评价等应相对详细,研究目的则相对简略,即简写目的,写明采用的具体方法,详细写所得到的结果和结论。说明性摘要则相反,要明确给出该研究的目的,方法简单明了,结果部分只需给出该研究的重要结论及其研究意义即可。但无论哪种类型的摘要都应写得内容充实,不要过分抽象或空洞无物,不做自我评价。

四、摘要的文体要求及写作技巧

摘要既要有高度的信息浓缩性,又具有可读性,还要结构完整、篇幅简短及独立成篇。摘要写作是一种控制性的作文形式,通过阅读原文,吸收原文的文章结构与语言方面的长处,写出内容一致、结构近似、语言简洁的短文。抓住文章重点,避免事无巨细、一一罗列。摘要受字数篇幅限制,语言上应遵循简单扼要准确清晰的写作原则。因此英文摘要要使用正规英语、标准术语,行文符合语义和语法的要求。

1. 具体写作步骤

(1)重新审视原文。首先要仔细阅读全篇作品,然后对作品进行整体分析,掌握原文总的意思和结构,明确全文的主题(the main theme)和各段的段落大意(the main idea)。

(2)弄清要求。搞清楚是写全文概要,还是写某一部分的概要,或就某些问题写出要点。

(3)列出原文要点。分析原文的内容和结构,将内容分项扼要表述并注意在结构上的顺序。在此基础上选出与文章主题密切相关的部分。

(4)草拟写作提纲并写出初稿。将挑选出的要点作为框架草拟详细的提纲,以所列的提纲为依据写出摘要的初稿。

2. 写作时要特别注意的几点

(1)摘要应包括原文中的主要事实(main facts);略去不必要的细节(unnecessary details)。

(2)安排好篇幅的比例。摘要应同原文保持协调,即用较多的文字写重要内容,用较少的文字写次要内容。

(3)注意段落的连贯和句子的衔接。要用适当的转折词语贯通全文,切忌只简单地写出一些互不相干的句子。

(4)尽可能用自己的话来写,但不排斥用原文的某些词句。

(5)计算词数,由于篇幅所限,删减与主题无关的内容和过度修饰。学术论文摘要的字数一般为正文字数的2%～3%,国际标准化组织建议不少于250个词。

3. 时态

首先,一般现在时的使用。在摘要中使用的时态一般为一般现在时,有时用现在完成时态。因为摘要中阐述的内容包括研究目的、背景信息、主要内容、实验方法、研究结论等均为当前的状况。而对于研究过程的阐述,虽然是过去所做的事情,但是距写作时间很近,同时作者为了减轻写作难度和意思上的混淆,也可以采取现在时态写作。

例一:本文讨论了量子点与光子晶体间的耦合。

This paper discusses quantum dots in photonic crystals: from quantum information processing to single photon nonlinear optics.

其次,现在完成时的使用。尽管摘要大体可以使用一般现在时,但是也要依据具体情况适时地调整时态的使用。有的研究已经取得了一些成果,已经做了一些准备,获得的结论已经做了一些论证,这些内容可以用现在完成时态,强调其影响或作用,或者该研究工作仍然在进行。

例二:我们通过受激拉曼绝热通道技术研究了在一个四层的原子腔结构行为。

We have investigated the behaviour of an atom-cavity system via a stimulated Raman adiabatic passage technique in a four-level system.

再次,一般过去时的使用。对于描述撰写作者已经做过的工作、引用文献或已取得的结果的内容,可以用一般过去时。

例三:我们测量了反射光束光子与 QD/腔结构失谐的各种数据。
We measured the photon statistics of the reflected beam at various detunings with the QD/cavity system.

4. 人称和语态

科技论文的撰写可以以第三人称为主,如 the paper,the study,the author;可以以具体研究对象手段,如 the measurement 等作主语,辅以被动语态的句子结构;也可以以第一人称"I""We"作主语,使用主动语态,这样的用法更为简单灵活,因此为当前很多刊物所提倡。例如:

This paper describes the fundamental principles of the quantum algorithm.
本文阐述了量子算法的基本原理。
A few basic dielectric test objects are given in the paper.
本文给出了几种基本的介质实验目标。
We explore this nonlinearity to implement controlled phase and amplitude modulation between two modes of light at the single photon level.
我们探讨在单光子水平下两种模式的光之间的非线性问题以实现控制相伴和幅度调制。

五、英文科技学术摘要常用词汇和表达方式

由于摘要的英文表达要求用词简明、层次清楚,因此掌握一些特定的规范表达,甚至建立一个适合自己需要的"句型库"(stock phrases),对于摘要的撰写是很有帮助的。本文所选取的例句均源于 SCI 收录的 1992-2002 年间发表、并具较高被引频次的论文(前 100 位)摘要(选取例句时偏重于第一人称和主动语态)。

1. 介绍研究背景

(1)常用词汇有:

review 回顾	summarize 总结	present 呈现	outline 概述
describe 描述	illustrate 阐释	report 介绍	explain 解释
deal with 处理	account for 解释	introduce 介绍	
concern 关注	relate to 涉及		

例如:
This article outlines related theoretical studies of psychology and neurobiology of addiction.
本文概述心理学和神经生物学的成瘾性相关理论研究。
This paper accounts for some system features of an inhabited 3D virtual environment.
本文阐述了三维虚拟居民环境的一些系统特征。
In this thesis, we have made some meaningful works relating to the improving efficiency of organic light-emitting devices and its degradation mechanism.
本论文对提高有机电致发光器件的效率以及器件的老化机理进行了一些有意义的研究。

(2)常用句式有:

		article paper thesis dissertation	
To begin with, To start with, Firstly, At first, Above all, In the first place,	we/the author(s)	study program project research investigation	focus(es) on… proceed(s)… introduce(s)… provide(s) a brief background on…
	we/the author(s)		

例如:

In this paper, we focus on…

这篇文章我们针对…(问题)

The structure of this paper proceeds as follow.

这篇文章结构如下。

In this paper, we shall first briefly introduce the related concepts.

首先介绍一下这篇论文的相关概念。

To begin with, we will provide a brief background on the…

首先介绍一下这篇论文的相关背景……

2. 表示研究目的

(1)表示目的常用词汇有:

名词:
aim 目的　　goal 目的　　purpose 目的　　objective 目的　　object 目的
target 目标　　intention 意图　　consideration 考虑
动词:
aim at 目的在于　　　　　be aimed at 目的在于
direct at 针对　　　　　　be directed at 针对
attempt to do 尝试　　　　intend to do 企图

例如:

The purpose of this paper is to examine the rheological properties of MWNT filled polycarbonate nanocomposites formed by melt extrusion.

本文旨在研究碳纳米管填充聚碳酸酯熔融溢出形成的纳米复合材料的流变性能。

The ultimate goal of a Network Intrusion Detection System(NIDS) is to alert a system administrator each time an intruder who tries to penetrate the network.

网络入侵检测系统(NIDS)的最终目的是当有入侵者试图渗透到网络时提醒系统管理员。

This paper aims at providing methods to construct such probability distribution.

本文旨在提供方法来构造这样的概率分布。

A major objective of this report is to extend the utilization of this procedure.

本报告的一个主要目标是扩大这一过程的利用开发。

(2)常用句式有：

		is to deals with...
		is to focus on the topics of
		is to present the knowledge that...
		is to discuss...
		is to analyze...
		is to provides an overview of...
		is to gives an overview of...
The purpose	the	is to compare... and summarizes
aim	paper	is to include discussions concerning...
objective	article	is to present up to date information on...
of	thesis	is to address important topics including...
		is to strongly emphasize...
		is devoted to examining...
		is to express views on...
		is to explain the procedures for...
		is to develop the theory of...
		is to try to explore...
		is to determine...

例如：

This study is to investigate the effect of two kinds of obstacles in the chunk decomposition-a specific type of insight that contains the process of breaking up the perceptual patterns or chunks into elements so that they could be reorganized in a new manner.

本研究旨在探索两种块分解障碍的影响——这一具体研究见解涵盖了将知觉模式或块分解成元素，使其以新的方式重组的过程。

This article is to discuss the tight relationship between absolute pitch and Chinese language and to compare the differences of process character between absolute pitch and non-absolute pitch subjects when they process the Chinese language.

本研究旨在探讨绝对音高能力与汉语母语之间的密切关系并比较绝对音高能力与非绝对高音在加工汉语任务上的差异。

3. 概括论点及研究内容

(1) 常用词汇有：

present 呈现	describe 描写	report 报告	introduce 介绍
explain 解释	illustrate 阐述	deal with 处理	study 研究
consider 考虑	discuss 讨论	investigate 调查	analyze 分析
state 陈述	develop 发展	emphasize 强调	examine 审查
contain 包括	cover 包括	include 包括	measure 测量

例如：

This paper investigates an automatic frequency tuning system which is one of the most important parts of the buncher.

本文主要研究作为聚束器最重要的组成部分之一的频率自动调谐系统。

This study measures the interval-censored data of generalized proportional hazards models.

本研究测量了一种广义比例风险模型的区间截断数据。

In this paper we focus on the classification of color texture images.

本文中我们着眼于彩色纹理图像的分类。

4. This paper deals with the history of the use of hydrogen as a combustible or shielding gas in welding.

本文研究焊接中使用的氢气作为易燃保护气体的历史。

(2) 常用句式有：

The paper article thesis	presents the function of… discusses the application of an alyze the phenomenon of strongly emphasizes the significant role of… explains the procedures for… states the structure of develops the theory of…
In this study/ paper,	attention is concentrated on 重点是
there is a focus on,	重视,集中
attention is paid to,	重视
the emphasis is on,	重点

例如：

In this paper, mathematical models for calculation and prediction of melting rate in arc welding with a triple-wire electrode are described.

本文描述了计算和预测三丝电极弧焊接融化率的数学模型。

This report is a study of the potential net economic impacts that could accrue to the state.

本报道是有关网络经济对国家潜在影响的研究。

This paper introduces a three-dimensional model, for fluid flow and heat transfer in the interfacial region between the TIG arc plasma and weld pool.

本文介绍了一种研究 TIG 电子弧离子区和熔池的界面区流体流动和热传递的三维模型。

In this study, we describe a psychobiological model of the structure and development of personality that accounts for dimensions of both temperament and character. We also describe the conceptual background and development of a self-report measure of these dimensions.

在这项研究中,我们描述了解释脾气性格的人格结构和发展的精神生物学模型。我们还描述了这些范畴内的自我报告措施的概念性的背景和发展。

4. 表示研究方法

(1) 常用词汇有：

theory 理论	concept 概念	data 数据	statistics 数据
question 问题	problem 问题	argument 论据	
opinion 观点	topic 话题		
test 测试	examine 审查	experiment 实验	
analyze 分析	analysis 分析		
measure 测量	estimate 估计	calculate 计算	
use 应用	apply 应用	application 应用	

例如：

We analyzed a qualitative data set of interviews with 200 women in the IT workforces in Australia, Ireland, New Zealand and the United States.

我们采访了来自澳大利亚,爱尔兰,新西兰和美国的 200 名在资讯科技领域工作的妇女,以此进行定性数据分析。

We attempt to recover a function of unknown smoothness from noisy sampled data.

我们试图从嘈杂的采样数据中恢复未知的平滑函数。

The paper draws on a number of examples to illustrate this point and discusses the implications in terms of the requirements for genuine community participation and empowerment.

本文借鉴了一些例子来说明这一点,并讨论了在真正的社会参与和授权的要求方面的影响。

(2) 常用句式有:

> The theory is developed from the angle of …
> The concept is discussed in the light of the context that …
> The question/problem/argument is raised from the perspective of …
> The test/examine/experiment is carried out …
> Experiments are performed …
> The analysis is based on …
> The study implements some techniques …

例如:

The simulation system is utilized to perform experiments with various control strategies for the robot team organizations, evaluating the comparative performance of the strategies and organizations.

模拟系统在各种控制策略下对机器人小组和小组的组织方式进行测试、测评并比较各种策略以及组织方式的性能。

Three relevant approaches to grey scale texture analysis, namely local linear transforms, Gabor filtering and the co-occurrence approach are extended to color images.

三种相关的灰阶纹理分析方法,即线性变换、Gabor 滤波器和共现法都被运用到色彩图像分析中。

This study concerns the neural mechanisms of the cueing effects on categorization of pictures by using ERP technique.

本实验采用了 ERP 技术,对图片分类任务中的线索效应进行了研究。

5. 表示结果、结论或建议

(1) 常用词汇有:

> 阐述结论:
> show, result, present, summarise, introduce, conclude
> 说明论证:
> support, provide, indicate, identify, find, demonstrate, confirm, clarify
> 表示建议:
> suggest, suggestion, recommend(recommendation), propose, expect

例如:

The results showed that FRNs were only elicited eminently by negative outcomes, and proportional to the degree of unexpectation, which is consistent with the theory of Reinforcement Learning. As for how the FRNs reflect outcome evaluation, it will be further examined in our subsequent research.

本研究采用动态的抽奖赌博任务进一步考察了二者的关系,结果表明,和强化学习理论的观点相一致,只有不利的反馈结果诱发了 FRN,并且结果出乎意料的程度与 FRN 的波幅呈正比。

The findings of this research indicate that despite the best intentions of those involved in the project, it was implemented in a way that led to a primary focus on serving the needs of government.

这项研究的结果表明,尽管本着最好的意图参与该项目,最终它的实施导致了主要的焦点仍集中在对政府服务的需求上。

(2)常用词句式有:

The results findings outcomes experiments data analyses	show that… indicate that… present that… suggest that… demonstrate that… confirm the argument that…
The study research	concludes that… summarizes the results of this investigation. gives the conclusions and future directions of research. provides a summary and a discussion of …

例如:

In this thesis, by means of numerical stimulations and theoretical analysis, the properties of the defect modes in one-dimensional photonic crystal containing metamaterials are investigated. The most important results are given as follows.

本文通过数值模拟和理论分析,系统地研究了含特异材料的一维光子晶体中的缺陷模的性质。主要的研究成果有以下几个方面。

The aim of this study is to review the main data sources dealing with world tariffs and trade. After discussing some issues and methodology, we provide a brief description of the main datasets available in terms of the origin of the data, its accessibility, reliability and shortcomings.

本研究的目的是审查处理世界关税和贸易的主要数据来源。在对相关问题和方法论进行讨论之后,我们提供了在数据来源、可用性、可靠性和缺点方面的有效数据集的简要说明。

六、撰写 EI、SCI 期刊论文注意事项

本书前文介绍过,EI(The Engineering Index,工程索引)及 SCI(The Science Citation Index,科学引文索引)是当前世界最著名的两大科技文献检索系统,是国际公认的进行科学统计与科学评价的主要检索工具。在撰写 EI、SCI 期刊论文时,有一些事项要注意,一些错误应避免,按照相关规定或约定俗成的写作方式进行撰写。具体注意事项如下:

1. 摘要应尽量简短精练,不要过多着墨于课题研究的背景信息。一般的 EI 规定摘要一般

不超过150字(words)或1 500字母(office);SCI论文摘要一般为200~300字。另外不同期刊要求也不尽相同,如Science《科学》杂志要求摘要在125字左右;而Nature《自然》杂志则要求摘要在150字以内。

2. 摘要中不应出现图标、图表等,也尽量避免使用特殊符号,如缩写、化学结构式、数学方程式等。如果有不得不出现的缩略语或术语,应在缩略符号首次出现时给出其全称或必要解释。

3. 摘要的第一句话应避免与题名(title)重复。摘要的第一句话作用重要,应该反映文章的研究问题和研究目的等可以指示文章研究方向的内容。

4. 摘要不应包含参考文献、注脚或注解等。

5. 删去不必要的字句,如"It is reported…","Recently…","The author discusses…","In this paper"等;一些不必要的修饰词,如"in detail","briefly","here","new","mainly"等也可酌情省略。

6. 时态和语态的使用:用过去时态叙述作者的工作和研究方法,用现在时态叙述作者的结论。尽量用主动语态代替被动语态。

7. 定语的使用:能用名词做定语的不要用动名词做定语,能用形容词做定语的不要用名词做定语。

例如:用measurement accuracy,代替measuring accuracy;用experimental results,代替experiment results。可直接用名词或名词短语做定语的情况下,要少用of句型。例如:用measurement accuracy,代替accuracy of measurement;用equipment structure,代替structure of equipment。避免使用一长串形容词或名词来修饰名词,可以将这些词分成几个前置短语,用连字符连接名词组,作为单位形容词(一个形容词)。

8. 可用动词的情况尽量避免使用动词的名词形式。例如:用thickness of plastic sheets was measured,代替Measurement of thickness of plastic sheet was made。

9. 摘要中出现的词汇,如果有英美两种拼法,则两种用法皆可,但在文章中须保持一致。

10. 最后,请学习以下摘自Science《科学》杂志论文Anomalous Criticality in the Electrical Resistivity of $La_2-xSrxCuO_4$。

The presence or absence of a quantum critical point and its location in the phase diagram of high temperature superconductors have been subjects of intense scrutiny. Clear evidence for quantum criticality, particularly in the transport properties, has proved elusive because the important low temperature region is masked by the onset of superconductivity. We present measurements of the low-temperature in-plane resistivity of several highly doped $La_2-xSrxCuO4$ single crystals in which the superconductivity had been stripped away by using high magnetic fields. In contrast to other quantum critical systems, the resistivity varies linearly with temperature over a wide doping range with a gradient that scales monotonically with the superconducting transition temperature. It is maximal at a critical doping level(pc) ~ 0.19 at which superconductivity is most robust. Moreover, its value at pc corresponds to the onset of quasi-particle incoherence along specific momentum directions, implying that the interaction that first promotes high-temperature superconductivity may ultimately destroy the very quasi-particle states involved in the superconducting pairing. (164字)

量子临界点在高温超导体的图像中存在与否以及其位置目前是研究热点。明确的证据量子临界性,尤其是在已证明难以实现的重要的低温区是隐蔽的超导电性。明确证据已证明因为重要的低温区超导被掩盖,量子的临界点,特别是其交通特性难以实现。我们呈现了在离开高磁场情况下,对低温的超导平面电阻几个高度掺杂镧单晶进行的测量。与其他量子临界系统相反,电阻率随超导温度在很大范围内呈线性变化,与梯度、尺度单调与超导转变温度相关。它最大的一个关键的掺杂水平是0.19,其超导电性是最强的。此外,它在聚碳酸酯上的值与开始准粒子沿特定方向不一致的趋势相关,这意味着它们相互作用,它最初促进了高温超导但是最终可能破坏准粒子参与超导配对。

七、撰写学术论文摘要

学术论文摘要是学术论文重要的组成部分之一,是专家组评委最先审阅的部分。通过学位论文摘要,他人可以一目了然地了解到论文的研究目的、研究问题、研究内容、分析方法和结论等论文重要内容。

1. 学术论文摘要的内容要求

学术论文摘要的内容要求和期刊论文摘要一样,学术论文摘要也是对论文内容的总结概括,在摘要中应体现论文的研究目的、研究内容、研究方法、创新性成果及其理论与实际意义。无论是硕士论文(Master's thesis)摘要还是博士论文(doctoral dissertation)摘要都应体现出论文的系统性、学术性和创新之处。摘要中不宜使用公式、图表,不标注引用文献。这里要着重指出的是学位论文摘要与期刊论文摘要不同之处在于它必须指出研究结果的独到之处或创新之处。

学位论文摘要可以依序按照以下三个方面撰写:

开头部分介绍研究的背景、宗旨、意义,提出问题,说明解决某一问题的必要性或重要性等。其次介绍研究目的和研究范畴或研究领域。

中间部分介绍论文的主要内容,有必要的可以简要地提出研究方法或研究步骤。

最后概括总结研究结果或结论,特别要指出论文研究的新创造,新突破,新见解或新方法。

2. 学术论文摘要的篇幅

国内的学术论文摘要一般包括两部分:中文摘要和英文摘要。英文摘要应与中文摘要内容相对应。博士学位论文的中文摘要约3 000字左右,为了便于文献检索,应在中文摘要下方另起一行注明学位论文的关键词(不少于五个)。不同学校对学位论文编写格式的要求不同,但大体都要根据《科学技术报告、学位论文和学术论文的编写格式》(GB/T 7713—1987)和《学位论文编写规则》(GB/T 1.1—2000—审批版)等相应规范制定学位论文编写规则和格式。摘要最后另起一行,列出4~8个关键词。关键词应体现论文特色,具有语义性,在论文中有明确的出处;并应尽量采用《汉语主题词表》或各专业主题词表提供的规范词。学术论文相应的英文摘要要比中文摘要浓缩精简很多,但是通常学位论文英文摘要比期刊论文摘要长,但一般也不超过一页。国内的博士论文英文摘要较长,一般二至三段甚至以上,字数约为 500～700 字。

3. 学位论文英文摘要的格式和结构布局

英文摘要一般单起一页,上方为题目,换行居中写 Abstract,英文摘要的内容与中文摘要基本相对应,要求语法正确,语句通顺,文字流畅。摘要结束时在右下方第一行写姓名,专业名用括弧括置于姓名之后,右下方第二行写导师姓名,格式为 Supervised by。最下方一行为关键词(Key words)。

(Title)

Abstract

Background related to the present study

Problems that need to be solved

Objectives and scope of this study

Outline of the main contents

Methods carried out to prove the argument

Results

Conclusions

Key Word:××,×××,×××,×××,×××

---

4. 请参考以下博士论文英文摘要示例、来学习撰写方法和格式

Study on improving the efficiency and stability of organic light-emitting devices

Zhang Qiang

Supervised by:Prof. Li Yulong

Abstract

  As a new technology for Flat Panel Displays (FPDs), the Organic light-emitting devices (OLEDs) were paid much attention to by academia and industry for its advantages of light weight, low cost, broad visual angle, high response speed, spontaneous light-emitting, high brightness and efficiency, etc.. By the use of novel materials, the structures of the devices and the crafts have been improving and great progress has been made. However, up to date, there are still shortcomings of the devices, such as low efficiency and high turn-on performance voltage, and so on. Hence, further improvement of the performances of OLEDs is still the research focus in the world.

  In this dissertation, we have made the following work relating to the improvement of efficiency of OLEDs and the degradation mechanism of OLEDs.

  1. Time-resolved photoluminescence spectra are firstly used to study the energy transfer processes in the co-doped organic red light-emitting devices. There are five parameters affecting the properties

of fluorescent OLED and orthogonal test table $L_{16}(45)$ was used to carry out the systematic study. The parameters includes: The thickness of HTL, thickness of EML, thickness of ETL, doped concentration of DCJTB, doped concentration of Rubrene. The optimum structure for the OLED devices is ITO/ HIL(50nm)/ HTL(40nm)/EML(40nm)/ ETL(20nm)/ LiF(1nm)/ Al(100nm), the doped concentration of DCJTB & Rubrene are 1 wt%, 30 wt%, respectively. The luminance(L)-current density(J)-bias voltage(V) characteristics were recorded simultaneously with the measurement of a PR650 spectroscan spectrometer by combining the spectrometer with a Keithley 2,400 programmable voltage-current source. The brightness of OLED prepared with parameters mentioned above is 8,650cd/m^2 under the voltage of 23.5v, and relative efficiency is 2.58 cd/A@6.8v.

2. The advantage of organic electro-phosphorescent materials is discussed comparing with that of organic fluorescent materials. And the differences of energy transferring mechanism in the doping status between the organic electro-phosphorescent materials and organic fluorescent materials are also introduced. They are the theories of Forster energy transfer and Dexter energy transfer.

3. Based on the progress of spintronic, we firstly propose that the OLEDs internal efficiency maybe also, in principle, be increased if singlet excitons are created alone in the emitting layer through applying suitable ferromagnetic materials to control the spin direction of injected electrons and holes. We have studied the spin injection of organic light emitting devices preliminarily. The organic light-emitting devices with ferromagnetic metal nickel(Ni) as the spin aligner and semitransparent anode are fabricated. The structure of the devices is Ni/NPB/Alq/LiF/Al. The polarization of the light from the devices under different magnetic density is tested and analyzed.

Experiments and analyses demonstrate to performance red fluorescent OLED device and high efficiency and stability phosphorescent OLEDs

Keywords: organic light emitting diodes, micro cavity, phase shift on reflection

参考译文:

改善有机电致发光器件的效率和稳定性的研究
张强
指导教师:李玉龙
摘要

作为一种新型的平板显示技术,OLEDs由于具有重量轻、成本低、视角宽、响应速度快、主动发光、发光亮度和效率高、能实现全色显示等优点,因而备受科学界和产业界的重视。通过新材料的研究和使用,器件结构和工艺的不断完善,有机电致发光器件的发展已经取得了长足的进步。但是到目前为止,OLEDs仍存在效率偏低,开启电压较高等缺陷,因此进一步提高器件的性能仍然是各国研究人员的研究焦点。

本论文对提高有机电致发光器件的效率以及器件的老化机理做了以下工作：

1. 首次利用时间分辨光致发光光谱研究了采用辅助掺杂的方法制备有机红光电致发光器件内的能量转移过程。深入细致的考察制备基于 DCJTB 红光 OLED 器件的五个主要参数包括 HTL 厚度、EML 厚度、ETL 厚度、DCJTB 掺杂浓度、Rubrene 掺杂浓度对 OLED 的亮度、效率等特性的影响。用 Keithly2 400，PR650 及光具座搭建的测试平台测试了 OLED 的 I–V，V–B 性能，同时评价了 OLED 的 V–11 特性，优化出的红光 OLED 的最优结构参数是：HTL 厚度为 40 nm，EML 厚度为 40 nm，ETL 厚度为 20 nm，DCJTB 掺杂浓度为 1 wt%，Rubrene 掺杂浓度为 30 wt%。按优化的参数制备出的红光 OLED 器件，当外加电压 23.5 V 时，器件的亮度达到了 8650cd/m^2，最高电流效率为 2.58 cd/A，对应的电压为 6.8 V。

2. 分析了磷光发光材料相对荧光材料的优势，进而详细叙述了磷光材料掺杂与荧光材料掺杂在能量转移方面原理上的不同，即 Forster 理论和 Dexter 理论。

3. 基于自旋电子学的研究进展，我们首次提出通过选择合适的磁性材料来控制注入到有机电致发光器件中的载流子的自旋方向，使在发光区只形成单线态激子，从而提高有机电致荧光器件的效率的设想。我们初步研究了有机电致发光器件的自旋注入，制作了以铁磁金属 Ni 做电极的有机电致发光器件，并测试了 Ni 做阳极的器件所发射的光的偏振特性，对实验结果进行了分析。

实验和分析表明上述方法是改善红光荧光器件的制备工艺和新型磷光发光器件制备及器件封装方面是增加器件稳定性及处理老化机制的创新性的有效手段。

关键词：有机发光二极管，微腔，反射相移

分析：

这一篇博士论文摘要的第 1 部分介绍研究背景，即目前作为平板显示技术的有机电致发光器件的发展和研究已成为业界焦点。同时指出在目前此项技术的开发应用中仍存在很多问题。第 2 部分介绍本论文研究的主要内容，即作者在哪些方面进行了改进的尝试。第 3 部分总结并评价此项研究的价值与意义。这项研究工作是解决器件当前存在问题的有效途径和方法。这篇学术论文摘要对研究对象、研究背景，研究内容、研究结果和所得结果的科技价值都进行了简单但必要的介绍，是一篇完整的，具体的学术论文摘要。

第九章 论文正文的撰写

一篇学术论文的正文,是论文的主体部分,占据其主要篇幅。论文的研究问题,创新之处以及研究结果等都在这一部分得以充分体现。因此,要求这一部分内容充实,论据充分、可靠,论证有力,主题明确。为了满足这一系列要求,在写作篇幅较长的论文正文部分时,一般将正文分成几个部分,使用多级标题来保证文章层次分明、脉络清晰。这些段落即所谓逻辑段,一个逻辑段可包含几个自然段。每一逻辑段落可冠以适当标题(分标题或小标题)。

一般来说,正文可以包括以下部分或内容:调查与研究对象,实验和观测方法,仪器设备,材料原料,实验和观测结果,计算方法和编程原理,数据资料,经过加工整理的图表,形成的论点和导出的结论等。当然,其中的结论可以单独设一部分(或一节)展开叙述。学术论文的主体部分通常由以下几个部分构成——Introduction(引言)、Materials and methods(材料与方法),Results(结果),Discussion(讨论)及Conclusion(结论),即IMRDC结构。本书通过几方面介绍论文正文部分的写作要点。

一、引言

引言(Introduction)又称前言、序言、绪论、导论等。学术论文中的引言是对全文内容和结构的总体勾画。引言的主要任务是向读者勾勒出全文的基本内容和轮廓。一个好的引言就相当于文章成功了一半。如果引言没有内涵,过于简单,没有逻辑,没有真正体现出一篇论文的研究初衷和创新要素,那么这篇论文就不是一篇合格的论文。要写好引言,要做到内容上具体不空泛,形式上层次鲜明和逻辑清楚,将内容和形式结合起来,即要求在符合逻辑性的基础上建立内容上的层层递进。引言尽管不像摘要那样有一定的篇幅限制和相对固定的格式,但在内容和结构模式上也有需要遵循的规律。本书将介绍学术论文内容和形式上的要求,以及撰写科技英语论文所需的语言技巧。

1. 引言的内容和结构布局

学术论文引言一般要求包括以下几项内容:

(1)研究背景、范畴或领域(Research Background):介绍某研究领域的背景、意义,发展状况,目前的水平等;阐述研究领域的基本内容,语言应尽量简洁明了,因为文章的读者一般为领域内学生、学者,所以一些显而易见的知识要用概括性的而不是叙述性的语言来描述。

(2)文献回顾(Literature Review):回顾和综述该领域内前人的研究成果,对他人研究成果加以评价或比较;分析过去研究的局限性进而引出自己的研究问题和创新之处。文献回顾对于学术论文来说作用很大,要特别着重笔墨来描写。一方面要把该领域内过去和现在的状况全面概括总结出来,特别是最新进展和过去经典文献的引用。另一方面,文献的应用和数据的提供一定要准确。引用的数据也要正确,特别是间接引用的数据(即不是从原文献中查到的数据,而是从别人的文献中发现的另外一篇文献的数据)。

(3)研究目的(Objective):说明自己研究课题的目的。具体地通过文献回顾,指出前人尚未解决的问题,进而引出自己研究课题的动机与意义,即针对有待解决问题提出自己的新方法、新思路或是该领域内他人未曾研究的新课题。

(4)研究主要内容(Main Contents)用概括性的描述语言论文的主要内容,或勾勒其大体轮廓。可以分为一二三四等几个方面来描述,为引言做最后的收尾工作。

2. 引言的结构布局

虽然都是对论文的概括性描述,但是引言部分和论文摘是有区别的。

(1)摘要的格式比较固定,论文摘要一般都要包括目的、方法、结果、结论四项内容,且各自所占的篇幅大体比例一样。

(2)引言中研究背景介绍和文献回顾是非常重要的内容,因此所占比例应较大,需要详细介绍。

(3)因为很多论文正文有结论部分,所以在引言中对研究结果的介绍可以省略;而摘要则必须把主要研究结果列出。

通过以下图,引言的结构布局可以清楚地表现:

Introduction

Research Background:

Introducing the general research area including its background, importance and present level of development

....

Literature Review:

Reviewing previous research in this area

....

Objective:

A. Indicating the problem that has not been solved by previous research, raising a relevant question

B. Specifying the purpose of your research

....

Main Contents:

A. Announcing your major findings

B. Outlining the contents of your paper

下面这段引言的例子摘自一篇关于内蒙古奶业的博士论文,我们一起学习一下。

Introduction

Dairy is the competitive and characteristic industry which can make the Inner Mongolia Autonomous Region strong and their people rich. Also it has become the pillar industry in IMAR's economic growth. Enforcing the competitiveness of dairy and stimulating the growth of it are not only the vital measures in process of transforming "the number of dilated", extensive, and traditional dairy economy made to the quality, efficiency, intensive and modern one. Meanwhile these measures are of great significance in stimulating sustained, rapid and sound animal husbandry economic development in IMAR.

Based on the Michael Porter Diamond Model and current situation of IMAR's dairy industry development, this thesis has done the research in 4 major core determinants and 2 major effective elements in domestic competitiveness of IMAR's dairy industry.

The IMAR owns abundant factors of dairy production including high quality milk source, human resource, technology resource and capital resource. However the factor of production has become limiting factor in dairy industry growth, recently. The potential strong consumer demand exists due to the huge gap between the per capita possess and consumption in dairy, moreover the strong consumer demand exists in domestic and international market. The situation of dairy industry and other relatives is beneficially interactive and mutually promoting with the developing of the national economy and the improving of dairy industry's concentration. The implementation of the strategy that 2 major dairy enterprises manage the operation has formed the solid foundation for further improvement of dairy's competitiveness in IMAR. The present circumstance of dairy is the following: The opportunities and challenges exist at the same time; the opportunities are more obvious. Especially the progressive standardization of dairy industry offer a golden opportunity for the organized and healthy development of dairy. Along with the vital guarantees from the policies drew up and implemented by the authorities.

Research Background
Thesis statement—
Research objective
ain Contents

参考译文：

奶业是内蒙古的优势特色产业，是兴区富国的基础产业，近年来已成为内蒙古畜牧业经济发展的一大支柱产业。促进奶业发展，提高奶业竞争力不仅是促进内蒙古奶业经济由数量扩张型向质量效益型转变，由粗放型向集约型转变，由传统奶业向近代奶业转型的重要举措，同时对促进内蒙古畜牧业经济健康持续发展具有重要意义。

本文以波特钻石模型为理论框架，基于内蒙古奶业发展现状，研究了内蒙古奶业国内竞争力的四大核心决定因素以及两大重要影响因素。内蒙古拥有丰富的奶业生产要素，包括优质的奶源、人力资源、科技资源和资本资源，但奶业生产要素仍为目前奶类发展的主要限制因素。内蒙古居民奶类人均消费量与人均占有量差距较大，未来奶类需求还有很大空间，此外，国内外市场空间也较为广阔。随着国民经济的发展，奶业行业集中度的提高，奶业产业也与其他相关产业形成了良性互动，相互促进的良好态势。以两大巨型乳业企业为领军，乳企经营战略的实施为内蒙古奶业的竞争力奠定了良好基础。目前，奶业发展机遇与挑战并存，但机会大于威胁，特别是奶业行业的逐步规范，为奶业的有序健康发展提供了良好平台，政府的支持和相关政策的出台与实施为内蒙古奶业发展提供了重要保障。

3. 引言研究背景的撰写技巧

如何给文章破题，让作者观点一目了然，对一篇论文来说非常重要。引言开头的最主要目的是告诉读者论文所涉及的研究领域及其意义是什么，研究要解决什么问题，目前状况或水平如何。也就是说，开头要回答如下问题：

What is the subject of the research?

What is the importance of this subject?

How is the research going at present?

In what way is it important, interesting, and worth studying?

What problem does the research solve?

引言破题常用句型有：

句型1：研究主题 + 谓语动词 be…

句型2：研究主题 + has become …

句型3：研究主题 + be 过去分词（被动语态）

句型4：Recently, there has been growing interest in / concern about + 研究主题

句型5：Recently there have / has been extensive / increasing / numerous publications / literature / reporting on + 研究领域

句型6：Researchers have become increasingly interested in + 研究领域；Researchers have recently focused their attention on + 研究领域；Researchers are recently paying more attention to + 研究领域

请学习以下破题例句：

句型1：研究主题+谓语动词 be…

Adsorption of bacteria on mineral surface is the premise of deep interaction of bacteria and mineral, and is also the basic research in the application of bacteria as reagent in mineral processing.

微生物在矿物表面的吸附是微生物与矿物表面深度作用的前提，也是生物药剂在选矿中的应用的基础研究。

句型2：研究主题+has become…

Many high technologies have been applied to design and manufacture autobody covering products. CAD/CAM integrated technique is one of these applications in the automobile industry.

高科技已应用到汽车车身覆件产品的设计和制造中。CAD/CAM集成技术便是其中之一个。

句型3：研究主题+be 过去分词（被动语态）

The microbial diversity research of high concentration cassava alcohol wastewater treatment plants TLP systems was studied by clone, PCR amplification and denaturing gradient gelelectrophoresis (DGGE) based on 16S rDNA.

基于16S rDNA 克隆测序、PCR-DGGE 技术对木薯酒精厂高浓度有机废水 TLP 处理系统工艺中细菌多样性进行研究。

句型4：Recently, there has been growing interest in / concern about +研究主题

Recently, there has been growing concern about the residual organic matter produced during waste water treatment.

目前，废水处理过程中产生的居民有机物越来越备受关注。

句型5：Recently there have / has been extensive / increasing /numerous publications / literature / reporting on +研究领域

There has been an increasing awareness that many people are affected by crime.

人们越来越意识到，很多人都正受到罪恶的影响。

句型6：Researchers have become increasingly interested in +研究领域；Researchers have recently focused their attention on +研究领域；Researchers are recently paying more attention to +研究领域

Researchers are paying more attention to the technique of high pressure injection.

研究人员越来越关注高压喷射技术。

4.引言文献回顾的撰写技巧

(1)定义。文献回顾(Literature Review)是学术论文的重要组成部分，很多论文、报告、课题立项申请书都有文献回顾的部分，是作者对他人在某研究领域现有的文献、已做工作和研究成果的总结与评述，包括他人有代表性的观点或理论、发明发现、解决问题的方法等。文献回顾的目的是对某一领域某一方面的课题、问题或研究专题搜集大量情报资料，分析综合当前该课题、问题或研究专题的最新进展、学术见解和建议，从而揭示有关问题的新动态、新趋势、新水平、新原理和新技

术等,发现需要进一步研究的问题和角度,为后续研究寻找出发点、立足点和突破口。

(2)引言中文献回顾的作用。文献回顾是在对文献进行阅读、选择、比较、分类、分析和综合的基础上,研究者用自己的语言对某一问题的研究状况进行综合叙述的情报研究成果。文献的搜集、整理和分析都为文献综述的撰写奠定了基础。文献综述反映当前某一领域中某分支学科或重要专题的历史现状、最新进展、学术见解和建议,它往往能反映出有关问题的新动态、新趋势、新水平、新原理和新技术等等。文献综述是针对某一研究领域分析和描述前人已经做了哪些工作,进展到何种程度,要求对国内外相关研究的动态、前沿性问题做出较详细的综述,并提供参考文献。与背景描述(Backupground Description)不同,文献回顾(Literature Review)首先是对学术观点和理论方法的整理;其次是作者对前人已做研究和已获成果的评价;最后是研究新方向的引出。

受到篇幅限制,引言中的文献回顾一般要求用概括性语言来阐述以下内容:
①该领域的其他人已获得的研究成果和已取得的发展脉络;
②对他人的研究自己的见解和评价;
③当前的研究水平、存在问题及可能的原因;
④进一步的研究课题、发展方向的引入;
⑤本论文研究对历史空白的补充或对已有研究的创新和深入。

(3)撰写文献回顾的步骤。
第一 选题;
第二 搜集、阅读文献资料(教材、专著、学位论文、期刊论文);
第三 归纳、整理、分析出与自己研究直接相关的文献资料。
第四 成文

(4)引言中文献回顾的写作要点。

第一,引言中的文献回顾篇幅有限,因此要根据所查阅的大量文献进行综合的归类、提炼、概括,提炼出与自己研究直接相关的文献进行综述。语言要简洁准确,尽量避免大量引用原文,要用自己的语言把作者的观点说清楚,从原始文献中得出一般性结论。

第二,文献回顾不是对已有文献的重复、罗列和一般性介绍,而是以评论的观点融入作者自己对以往研究的优点、不足和贡献的批判性分析与评论。这一部分是作者自身理论水平、专业基础、分析问题、解决问题能力的最好体现。

第三,文献回顾的目的是引出自己的研究创新点。系统总结某一研究领域在某一阶段的进展情况,并结合本国本地区的具体情况和实际需要提出自己的见解。

第三,文献回顾语言要准确,叙述前人工作的欠缺以强调自己研究的创新时,应慎重且留有余地(避免"首次提出"、"重大发现"等)。

(5)引言中文献回顾常见的写作模式。引用文献时,不同的学科或领域可能采用各自约定俗成的体系或格式。在写论文时,应该了解自己学科采用的固定格式。本书将介绍几种常见的文献回顾写作模式。

模式1:作者(年代) + 谓语动词主动语态 + 研究内容/成果
模式2:研究内容/成果 + 谓语动词被动语态 + (作者年代)
模式3:It has been + 谓语动词被动语态 + by 作者(年代) + that 从句
模式4:It has been + 谓语动词被动语态 + that 从句(作者年代)研究内容/成果 + 谓语动词被动语态 + by 作者(年代)

例如:

1. Hanson et al. (1976) noted that oak mortality and decline were associated with drought and insects throughout a multi-state region of the mid-west.
2. Success at this Science Day was found to be linked to parental support(Czemiak 1996).
3. It was found by Czemiak(1996) that success at this Science Day was linked to parental support.

或:

It was found that success at this Science Day was linked to parental support(Czemiak 1996).

请学习以下例文:

(6)例文1:

In the recent years, with the development of economic globalization, an increasing attention has been paid to the economic recession. Furthermore, the economic recession, like a terrible disaster for countries and economic organizations, had also significantly impacted on individuals' lives, especially in 2008 (Barrell & Hurst, 2008). Due to the recession effecting on "commodity prices, exports, and trade barriers" which inflict a loss to the country's open economy is considerable for people(Leamer, 2008). As a result, a lot of people's incomes could be influenced by the recession(Anon, 2009). Moreover, many people's shopping behavior is decided by many causes, including their incomes(Bell & Lattin, 1998). According to their words, if the incomes of individuals decrease, the shopping behavior of them will be probably changed. To sum up, the aim of this literature review is to focus on the effects of the economic recession on individuals and gain whether or not the individuals' shopping behavior is changed by the crisis effect. In short, firstly, the literature review will demonstrate the effects of recession. Then, it will show the changes of individual shopping behaviors in the crisis. Finally, the review will argue the causes of the changes of individuals' shopping behavior.	研究背景介绍 文献回顾

例文 2：

Since the publication of *The Sound and the Fury*, it has attracted the attention of the traditional literary scholars and theory-based postmodernist critics. Nearly every critical approach has been used to interpret it such as Marxism, New Criticism, Structuralism, Deconstruction, Psychoanalysis, Linguistics, Feminism etc. Seriously scholarly and academic writings about the novel emerged after World War II and matured in the fifties. A wealth of commentary articles and books mushroomed. Critical reviews focus on the narrative technique, the use of the stream of consciousness, and the Christian symbolism of Faulkner's masterpieces.	研究背景
For example, James Burnham was the first who discussed the novel's language technique in his essay "*Trying to Say*" (1931). "*William Faulkner Celebrates Easter, 1928*" writer by Powell, is the first essay on Christian symbolism in the novel. 1950s and 1960s saw a great many readings of *The Sound and the Fury* from the angle of New Criticism. Olga W. Vickery's "*The Sound and the Fury: A Study in Perspective*" (1964) in 1954 is perhaps the first really important discussion of the novel's overall structure, and the interrelatedness of all its component parts. During the 1950s, there are another two important critics of the novel. One is Carvel Collins. The other is Cleanth Brooks. Collins wrote an essay to comment on the novel based on Freud's theory of Id, ego and superego and another essay about Faulkner's use of mythology in the novel. The most useful and influential research of the novel's overall design and significance came from Cleanth Brooks' essays in *The Yoknapatawpha Country* (1963), he pointed out universality beneath Faulkner's special brand of regionalism. Modern criticism of the novel starts in the middle of 1970s and the 1970s produced a substantial amount of psychological criticism of the novel. John T. Irwin published "*Doubling and Incest/ Repetition and Revenge: A speculative Reading of Faulkner*" (1975) in 1975 to focus on the oedipal struggle between father and son. In the 1980s and 1990s, poststructuralist theory acts as an important part in criticism of the novel. Matthews' "*The Rhetoric of Containment in Faulkner*" (1989) is regarded as one of the best poststructuralist readings of the novel. Furthermore, *New Essays on The Sound and the Fury* (2007), edited by Noel Polk, is also a good poststructuralist criticism.	文献回顾 国外研究现状 国内研究现状

In the meanwhile, the researchers of our country pay more attention to *The Sound and the Fury*. Since 1980s the research on Faulkner has been on the increase. . The study of *The Sound and the Fury* can be divided into five parts, Creation goal, theme, characters, artistic characteristics and ways of expression. First, the study of theme and creation goal. Li Wenjun summary the theme of *The Sound and the Fury* as the collapse of the plantation family of south American, Caddy's fallen means the destruction of the i south morality. Xiao Minghan in his essay point out that *The sound and the fury* is far from personal tragedy, William Faulkner imagination was largely decided by his strong historical consciousness. TaoJie explore theme of The Sound and the Fury mainly from William Faulkner's original creative motivation and creation goal. Another individual researchers think patience and sacrifice spirit is theme of *the sound and the fury* . Second, the characters. Caddy is the crucial figure of the novel. Xiao Minghan thinks that Caddy is a lovely figure, her absence represents the southern women's status: no body, no independent status, and no own voice, but determined described by other. That is to say she is just a symbol Wu Yueming made a more in-depth analysis of Caddy from the perspective of feminist criticism; he thinks Caddy is the victim of patriarchal society. Idiot Banjy is William Faulkner's original creation. Xiao Minghan thinks Banjy is the reflection of the human nature and is a mirror of the moral. Quentin is a very complicated character. Xiao Minghan thinks that Quentin is the successor and defenders of the southern tradition culture and moral; from Quentin we can see the influence of the historical burden for the young. Third, artistic characteristics and ways of expression. On the structure, Xu Wenpei analyzes the structure of the novel from the stream-of-consciousness performance and receptive aesthetics perspective. Gu Juan analyzes the novel from music angle. On the technique of expression. Liu Chenfeng studise the novel from the method of Variation space-time method and aesthetic value. Liu Jianbo discusses the significance of the archetypal of *The Sound and the Fury* in his article.

Although *The Sound and the Fury* has been explored from various points of view, not many researchers study the novel from social psychology. This study will use Karen Horney's anxiety theory as the theoretical basis, to analyze the anxiety phenomenon in *The Sound and the Fury*; the influence of the individual environment and the culture environment and the characters defensive strategies is the focus of this study.

(7)引言中文献回顾常见的表达方式。

A. 表示已有研究

XX is the first one who published a book/paper on…

The earliest study concerning the topic was done by

The earliest study could be traced back to…

B. 概述业界普遍观点

It is commonly acknowledged that…

It is commonly accepted that…

C. 表示研究空白

Although we witness great progress in this field, there is still space for the further improvement in the device.

We have witnessed in recent years the development of the techniques of…, but the study continues to work.

While many researchers have studied the issue, but not many develop the issue from the point of view.

The problem of … has not been explained.

So far there is no enough evidence that shows…

The previous studies fail to prove that…

The theory of … cannot explain …

D. 引出作者观点

Viewing this, the paper discusses…

In this regard, this paper studies…

Basing on the existing data, we intend to study…

On the basis of the existing study, we attempt to discuss…

Inspired by the idea that…we implement several experiments to examine…

In the light of shortage in this field, we carried out studies on…

To solve the existing problems, our study investigates …

Aware of the fact that…, we research…

Realizing the problem, we study…

Fully learning the previous failure, we performed experiments by using the new techniques and devices to…

二、材料与方法

1. 写作目的

材料与方法(Materials and Methods)是理工类科技论文常见的组成部分方法,它的主要作用是描述论文研究内容的实验过程。通过科技期刊发表的科学研究所得的试验结果要具有真实性,即在同样条件下研究结果能够被重复,这也是科学研究的基本要求。因此将材料与方法交代清楚,使其他研究者能够进行重复试验并得到同样结果,是论文成功与否的关键。让他人能够重复相同实验,作者首要的任务就是采用合理的方法,典型并可行的材料,准确的统计分析方法,同时要将这些材料方法步骤交代清楚。

2. 写作内容及写作要点

尽管不同学科对"材料与方法"部分应该包括的内容要求不尽相同,但是通常遵循先"材料",后"方法"的写作顺序。"材料"一般应包括试验地点、时间、材料、仪器设备、样品、实验对象、药品、试剂、准备方法等。方法主要描述"试验是如何进行的",其内容包括:试验环境条件、试验程序,测记载的项目、方法和时间、所应用的统计分析方法等。笔者自己创造的方法应详细说明"方法"的细节,以备他人重复;改进的方法应详述改进之处,若原封不动地使用现存的方法,只需注明。

在写作过程中尽量做到以下几点:

(1)对材料的描述应先概述再详述。通常首先要概述所采用材料,然后再对材料做具体的描述和规定,包括材料的结构、主要成分或重要特性、设备的功能等。材料描述中应该清楚地指出研究对象(样品、动物、植物、病人等)的数量、来源和准备方法。如果采用商标名的仪器、化学试剂或药品时,还应包括对仪器进行精确的技术说明,并列出试剂或药品的主要化学和物理性质。

(2)对方法的描述要详略。详细描述实验方法、实验步骤、实验试剂的规格、批号、型号、制造厂家名称、厂址(城市名)等;准确地记载所采用药物和化学试剂的名称、剂量、给药途径;如果是对他人方法的改进,则应给出原方法的引用出处;使用现存方法须标明出处和方法名称,无须展开描述;如果方法是被广泛熟知的,可以省去参考文献。

(3)实验过程中的图表使用。实验过程是对实验的整个操作流程的清楚描述,很多作者为了更清楚地阐述自己的实验,在文章中都附加以实验的流程图进行说明。流程图的画法很多,有的是文字式的,有的是文字和示意图结合的,根据不同的实验有不同的做法。

(4)阅读投稿期刊的作者须知了解相关的具体要求。如果是医学农业相关论文,实验对象一般是人或者动物等,实验方法步骤要符合相关道德伦理标准。尤其是国外的刊物大多对牵扯到人或者动物的实验都有一些特定的要求,有些是不允许在人或者动物身上进行实验操作的,这需要认真阅读投稿刊物"作者须知"中关于实验的详细规定。如果违反这一规定的话,可能不会被接受评审或者发表,这一点要特别注意。

3. 英语写作技巧

(1)时态和语态。

时态：

①材料与方法部分多属回顾性叙述，一般用过去时表示本实验中所采取的方法。

例如：

For neurosphere preparation, cells were plated at 105 cells/ml in neural stem cell basal medium (NeuroCult, StemCell Technologies Inc., Vancouver, BC), with differentiation supplements (NeuroCult Differentiation Supplements, StemCell Technologies Inc.) and basic fibroblast growth factor (b-FGF, 20 ng/ml). Neurospheres formed after 7-10 days in culture.

②说明研究或实验之前发生的动作或情况，用过去完成时；表示过去以前一直进行的动作，用过去完成进行时。

例如：

In vitro fetal mouse neurospheres and rat neural cells have been prepared well as described previously to assess the effects of Ang II on neural differentiation.

③业界惯用的方法、不受时间影响的事实、说明图表内容和数值表示法等，用一般现在时。

例如：

The water samples have been filtered through 0.22 μm membrane to separate the algal cells in the laboratory.

语态：

由于所涉及的行为与材料是叙述的焦点，因此描述实验步骤的句子通常用被动语态，而且读者已知道进行这些行为和采用这些材料的人就是作者本人；如果句子用的是主动语态，则一般主语也不是进行实验的人，而是仪器设备工具等。

例如：

Counting neurospheres was performed in the view at ×20 magnification with an Axioskop microscope (Carl Zeiss). They were passaged every 10-14 days by mechanical dissociation into single cells.

(2) 材料与方法部分的常用表达。

①表示材料来源。

句型1：was / were from…	来自……
句型2：was / were provided / supplied by…	由……提供……
句型3：was / were purchased from…	购自……
句型4：was / were obtained from…	从……中获得
句型5：was / were produced / manufactured by…	由……生产的
句型6：was / were donated by… was the/a gift of / from… …was a donation from…	由……赠送
句型7：using…	使用……

②表示实验方法。

句型1：was isolated by the procedure of… 用……方法分离
句型2：was prepared according to the method described by… 根据……方法制备
句型3：was carried out as previously described… 按照以前介绍的方法进行……
句型4：was determined by…；…was measured with… 用……方法测定
句型5：Samples of…were obtained/taken from… 从……取……标本
句型6：was collected/harvested under…conditions 在……条件下收集
句型7：was fixed with… 用……固定
句型8：was stained with… 用……染色
句型9：was embedded in… 被包埋在……
句型10：Samples were prepared as before/as previously described…
　　　　　　　　　　　　　　　　 和以前一样(用以前介绍过的方法)制备……
句型11：was dehydrated in… 在……中脱水
句型12：was diluted to… 被稀释到……
句型13：was incubated with…at…for…hours 用……在……(温度)保温……小时
句型14：was grown in…medium 被种植在……培养基中
句型15：was suspended to/at a concentration of… 被配制成悬浮液,浓度为……
句型16：was stored at… 被保存在……(温度)
句型17：by/by means of / with(by)the aid of / by the use of /using… 使用,采用(某方法)……

句型 18:	in a similar way	以类似方法
	in all manner of ways	以各种方法
	in much the same way	以基本相同的方法
	in a regular manner / in the usual manner	以常用方法
句型 19:	mathematically	用数学方法
	theoretically	理论上
	statistically	用统计法
	empirically	用经验方法
	experimentally	用实验方法

句型 20——各种方式的表达:

on and on / continuously / without break (intermission)	持续不断地
intermittently / with intermittence	间断地
in combination (conjunction) with	与……结合
in chronological order	按时间顺序
in descending (ascending) order	以递降(升)顺序
clockwise / in a clockwise sense	顺时针地
counterclockwise / in a counterclockwise sense	逆时针地
in groups	成群地
in a line	成直线地
in pairs	成对地
in rows	成排地
in a circle	成圆圈地
upside down	上端朝下
downside up	下端朝上
inside out	里面朝外
outside in	外面朝里
the right side up	正面朝上

③表示实验对象分类分组。

句型 1: There are … types / kinds / varieties of ……	有……种
句型 2: There are … classes / sorts of ……	有……类
句型 3: … may (might/can) be classified/divided/categorized/ grouped into	……分成
句型 4: … fall into several groups…	划分为几组

④表示实验结构成分和范畴。

句型 1:⋯consist of⋯
句型 2:⋯is made up of⋯
句型 3:⋯ranges from⋯to⋯
句型 4:⋯is a component part of⋯
句型 5:⋯is composed of⋯

⑤表示实验假设。

句型 1:Assuming that ⋯
句型 2:Assumption / Hypothesis is that⋯
句型 3:It is assumed that ⋯
句型 4:Hypothesis is tested in this study.
句型 5:⋯is composed of⋯

⑥表示定义。

句型 1:Define ⋯to be⋯
句型 2:⋯is defined as⋯
句型 3:⋯is called ⋯
句型 4:⋯is said to be⋯
句型 5:⋯is
句型 6:⋯means
句型 7:⋯signifies
句型 8:⋯is considered to be⋯
句型 9:⋯is taken to be
句型 10:⋯refers to⋯

⑦表示图表阐释。

(graph, diagram, drawing, chart, sketch)	图
curve line graph	曲线图
projection drawing	投影图
flow chart	流程图
diagrammatic sketch	示意图
key diagram	概略原理图
perspective drawing	透视图
histogram	直方图,频率曲线

plan	平面图
side view	侧视图
top view	俯视图
elevation	立面图
section	截面图
detail	大样图
scale	比例
solid(blackened // full // filled)circle	实心圆
open circle	空心圆
line of circles	圆点组成的线
(solid,open)square	(实心,空心)方块
cross	十字符号
dashed line(chain dash)	小线段(虚线)
dash-dot-dash line	─·─线
chain dot	点线(……)
dotted-dashed line	点画线
heavy(thick)solid line	粗实线
thin(light)broken line	细虚线
(solid,broken)line	(实,虚)线
(straight,wavy)line	(直,波状)线
(smooth,dotted)curve	(平滑,点)曲线
(shaded,clear)area	(阴影,空白)区
(dotted,hatched,cross-hatched) area	(布点,网状,阴影线)区
(dark,light) shaded area	(深,线)阴影区
two rows from top	前两行
the middle row	中间一行
the third column from right	右数第三列
the second row from bottom	倒数第 2 行
in unit of ……	以……为单位
as shown in Fig 2/ as given in Fig 2/ as listed(presented,summarized,evidenced)in Fig. 2	如图 2 所示

⑧常用时间表达。

2 – day lead	超前两天
2 – day lag	之后两天
once in a way/ once in a while/ occasionally/ on occasion	偶尔
at monthly intervals	每月一次
at 10-day intervals	每 10 天一次
at regular intervals	每隔一定时间一次
every other week/ every 2 weeks	每隔一周(每两周)
within a matter of hours	在大约几个小时内
in the early part of the century	在本世纪初叶
in the first decade of May	在五月上旬
in mid-May/ in the middle of May	在五月中旬
in early morning hours	在清晨
in late autumn-early winter	在深秋——初冬一段时间
in early(late)spring	在早(暮)春
in the past century and more	在过去 100 多年
during the last decades(10 years)	在最近 10 年
in the past years/ in the last years/ over the past years/ over the last years/ for the past years/ for the last years	最近几年
in recent years	近年来
in successive years	连续几年
in the current year / this year	今年
in the first half of 1998	1998 年上半年
throughout the period	在整个期间
in the subsequent months/ years / seasons	以后的
in the previous month	前一个月
in the neighboring/surrounding months	前后月份
for the next 3 weeks/ for two weeks to come(follow)	未来……
in advance	未来……
after/ subsequent to	在……之后
before/ ahead of / prior to / anterior to / by the time / not later than	在……之前
for 3 consecutive(successive)days / for 3 days together / for 3 days in succession	连续 3 天
during the night/ during the night time / during the night hours	夜晚
during the daytime/ during the daytime hours	白天

in a week/ within a week(未来的); a week later(过去的)	一周后
upon / on / as soon as / No sooner… than	一……就……
at the very moment…	一……马上就……
accordingly as + 句子/ according as + 句子	随着……

4. 范例学习

(1)下面例文摘自一篇名为:"Anisotropic Saturable Absorption of Single-Wall Carbon"(《单壁碳纳米管在聚乙烯醇中的各向异性饱和吸收研究》)。

Materials and experiments

SWNTs (single-wall carbon nanotubes) were prepared by laser ablation. Purified SWNT samples of 5 mg were dispersed in 50 ml of 0.1% water solution of sodium dodecylbenzene sulfonate(NaDDBS)(Wako Pure Chemical Industry) with strong ultrasonication(28 kHz,100 W, and 1 h). The obtained solution was passed through a glass fiber filter(Advantec GC50, retaining diameter 0.5 Lm) to remove SWNT bundles. To this solution 5 g of PVA powder(Wako, absorptiometric grade, saponification degree 78% ~ 82%) was added and dissolved. The resulting suspension was then poured into a Petri dish, and water was gradually evaporated for a period of one week. The removed freestanding film had a thickness of 120 Lm. For the alignment of SWNTs, we employed mechanical stretching of the film(stretching ratio 6) under heating to 60 ℃ in humid environment. We noted that an SWNT-undoped PVA film was broken at a stretching ratio of 4, which suggests that SWNTs contribute to reinforcement of the composite films. We observed optical microscope images using a digital microscope(VHX-100 Keyence) with a camera resolution of 4,800·3,600 pixels. We used a spectrophotometer(Hitachi U4,000) for measurement of the polarization absorption spectra. We inserted a film polarizer into an optical line of the spectrophotometer measuring a reference baseline. Next, we also inserted samples in the optical line and measured polarization-dependent absorption spectra of the samples at different polarization angles by varying the angle between the stretching direction of the samples and the light polarization direction. The anisotropic saturable absorption properties were studied by using a Z-scan system based on a polarized femtosecond erbium-doped fiber laser(Imra Femtolite 780, model B-60, tunable wavelength 1,560 ~ 1,750 nm, pulse width 100 fs, repetition 48 MHz). We focused the output light with an achromatic lens(10 mm focal length). The beam diameter profile at each position was measured with a beam profiler(Beam-Scope-P7, Data Ray), giving a minimum

1. 用一般过去时描述材料制备过程。
2. 标注材料生产厂名
3. 规定实验时间
4. 不受时间影响的事实用现在时态

beam diameter of 16.4 lm at the waist. The transmitted light was collected by another achromatic lens(30 mm focal length) and led to a semiconductor photodiode power sensor(Laser Star,Ophir). The sample was inserted into the laser beam line with its plane perpendicular to the z-axis and moved along the z-axis. Polarization dependence was measured by varying the angle between the stretching direction of the sample and the direction of light polarization. The detail of saturable absorption measurements by the z-scan method is described in [13].

([13] A. G. Rozhin, Y. Sakakibara, M. Tokumoto, H. Kataura, Y. Achiba,Thin Solid Film 464 – 465(2004)268.)

5. 用标注参考文献的方式标注其他研究已得出的结果

(2)学习下面论文中小标题的标注方法。
Carbon Nanotube – Polyaniline Hybrid Materials《碳纳米管－聚苯胺杂化材料》

2. Experiments
2.1. Materials
Aniline monomer(reagent grade, Fisher) was distilled under reduced pressure and kept below 0 ℃. The CNTs were supplied by CNT laboratory of Chengdu Institute of Organic Chemistry. The other reagents, such as ammonium peroxydisulfate($(NH_4)2S_2O_8$), dodecyl benzene sulfonic acid sodium salt(NaBS), ethanol, H_2SO_4, acetone and dimethyl benzene were analytical grade and used without further purification.

2.2. Preparation of carbon nanotubes – polyaniline hybrid materials
Polymerization was carried out in 250 mL roundbottomed four-necked flask equipped with a stirrer, an inlet of nitrogen and a condenser. Typically, 60 mL H_2O, 15 mL dimethyl benzene, 3 g NaBs were placed into the flask, stirred for 15 min, 0.1 g CNTs was added, stirred for 10 min, then 5 mL aniline added, stirred for 10 min. The polymerization was allowed by adding ($NH4)2S_2O_8$, which was dissolved in water and added dropwise into the flask. The polymerization lasted for 12 h at 0 ~ 5 ℃ under stirring. The hybrid materials were washed with acetone and ethanol three times to remove the unreacted monomer, low molecular weight polymer and NaBS. The resulting hybrid materials have been immersed into 1.5 M H_2SO_4 aqueous solutions for 2 h to dope, repeatedly separation three times, washed with distilled water three times. The products were dried under vacuum at 80 ℃ for 24 h. The exact amounts of reagents and solvent together with yield were listed in Table 1.

2.3. Measurements
The ultra-visible spectra(UV) of the samples dissolved in N, N – dimethylformamide(DFM) were obtained on UV – 3000 spectrophotometer(Japan). The infrared(IR) spectra of the samples in KBr pellets were recorded on Nicolet 200SXV Fourier transform infrared spectrometer(FTIR). The morphology was determined on a Hillachi 600 transmission electron microscope(TEM) with an accelerating voltage of 20 kV. Thermal gravimetry was performed on Perkin – Elmer TG analyzer.

X-ray diffraction(XRD) diagrams were recorded on a powder Philips PW1830 diffractometer with CuKa radiation. The conductivity of the PANI composites at room temperature was measured with a programmable DC voltage/current detector(four probe method) on pressed pellets under 20 MPa.

三. 结果

结果和讨论部分代表着文章的主要成就和贡献,论文有没有价值,值不值得读者阅读,主要取决于研究者获得的结果和所得出的结论。有些研究者在写论文的时候将结果(Results)和讨论(Discussion)两部分放在一起写,也有很多研究者将这两个部分分开写。这两种做法的选择,取决于文章的类型。如果你的结果在分析的同时进行讨论更加合适,并不适合单独阐述,则将两个部分合并撰写;反之则分别撰写。

1. 定义和内容

结果(Results)是指总结实验或理论研究中所观察到的各种现象,所得到的数据,并对这些现象和数据进行定性或定量的分析,得出规律性的东西。实验或理论研究结果是科技论文的核心,是评价论文是否有水平的关键部分。不是所有的内容都写入结果中去,而是要选择那些能说明论文主题的那些内容。

2. 结果部分的撰写方法

结果部分撰写方法通常采用表格、插图和行文撰写,即将那些有规律性的最能说明问题的数据列成表格或绘成图形,然后再用语言做必要的论述。具体地说:

(1)用图表介绍研究结果。表格能够清晰地展示第一手的研究结果,便于后人在研究时进行引用和对比。图片能够将数据的变化趋势灵活地表现出来。很多作者将表格和图片结合起来,阐述研究结果,使得结果的展现更加清楚、准确、直观。但是撰写的时候,应注意不同的期刊对于图表的要求不尽相同,因此撰写前应该仔细阅读期刊的"作者须知",根据不同期刊的不同要求分别对待。

要直截了当说明结果;不要把图表的序号作为段落的主题句,应在句中指出图表所揭示的结论(把图表的序号放入括号中):

避免:Figure 1 shows the relationship between A and B.

建议:A was significantly higher than B at all time points checked(Fig. 1).

避免:It is clearly shown in Table 1 that gold nanoparticles inhibited the growth of gallium nitride wires.

建议:Gold nanoparticles inhibited the growth of gallium nitride wires(Table 1).

常用图表:

photo	照片
drawing	绘图
diagram	示意图
flow flat	流程图
graph	线形图
pie chart	圆形图
bar chart	柱状图
structure diagram	结构图
table	表格
figure	图例

(2)用语言描述实验结果和所得观察。

3. 结果部分的英语写作技巧

(1)时态。

①说明图表时,对研究结果进行评论,推断时,不同结果相互比较时通常用一般现在时。

②描述研究结果时,一般用过去时。

(2)结果部分常用英语表达。

> The study suggests…
> The results of the experiment can be summarized as follows…
> The findings of the research demonstrate that…

4. 范例学习

"Organic light emitting diodes fabricated with single wall carbon nanotubes dispersed in a hole conducting buffer: the role of carbon nanotubes in a hole conducting polymer".

> 3. Results
>
> The $I-V$ characteristics of the devices labeled 1~3 in Fig. 4 show the different $I-V$ power dependence between the devices with and without the SWNTs. At low applied voltages (near 2.5 V), the devices with PEDOT composite show $I-V^2$ while the device without SWNTs has $I-V^5$. We note that the currents of the devices with SWNTs are abruptly increased at 3 V and then become the same $I-V$ relation with that of the device without SWNTs.
>
>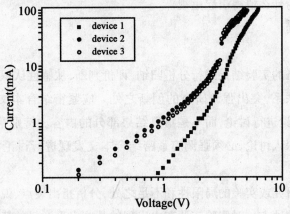
>
> Fig.4. *I-V* charactenstics for devices 1.2 and 3
>
> Fig. 5 shows the brightness dependence of the devices as a function of the applied current. In the devices with SWNTs, the emission intensity is significantly decreased compared to that of the device without SWNTs in the buffer layer. In contrast, as shown in Fig. 6, the PL spectrum of the devices with and without SWNTs shows very little difference between them. We note that the vibronic

PL feature at 2.64 eV is not shown in the EL and there is a small blue shift (0.05 eV) of the EL peak relative to the PL.

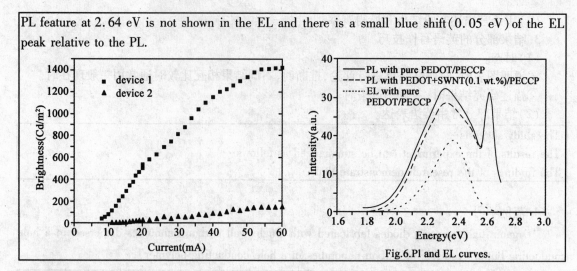

Fig.6. Pl and EL curves.

四、讨论

讨论部分是一篇论文最能够显示一个作者研究问题的深度和广度的部分。深度就是论文对于提出问题的研究到了一个什么样的程度,广度就是是否能够从多个角度来分析解释实验中的结果。讨论的重点在于对研究结果的解释和推断,并说明作者的结果是否支持或反对某种观点、是否提出了新的问题或观点等。因此撰写讨论时要避免含蓄,尽量做到直接、明确,以便审稿人和读者了解论文为什么值得引起重视。

1. 内容和结构布局

讨论内容:

①创新点。对自己的实验结果进行分析归纳,评价判断,从感性认识上升到理性认识,揭示各种观察结果之间的联系,突出强调研究的创新之处。应紧密结合本文研究所获得的重要发现,以及从中引出的结论进行讨论,而不是重复结果部分的内容。特别是要对新的发现或文献尚未报道的内容进行深入讨论,必须强调应紧密结合本文发现进行讨论,且所作的推论必须恰当。

②局限性。指出研究或实验的局限性和不足之处,分析指出疑点、说明偶然性和必然性、不确定点或应引起注意的地方。对实验或调查中出现的某些出乎意料的特殊现象,偶然结果可在讨论中作必要的说明,客观地进行解释。实事求是地分析本工作的局限性,表明作者对自己工作的自信。同时也表明作者严谨的科学态度。由于局限性是客观存在的,讨论局限性不会引起负面影响。说明本文未能解决的问题,提出今后研究的方向与问题,并不是每篇论文都必须包括以上内容,应从论文的研究目的出发,突出重点,紧扣论题。

③与他人比较。可适当概述国内外其他人员对本课题的研究近况,对其他研究成果进行对比、分析,指出异同、差距、优劣,总结本研究的结论和结果与国际、国内先进水平相比居于什么地位。应讨论本文发现和文献报道同类研究的结论有何不同,哪些文献支持本文发现,哪些文献报道与本文结论不同,从而引出自己研究的重要性,成果的新、异、优之处。切忌冗长的文献综述式的阐述。

④应用价值。根据研究的目的客观地阐明本研究结果的理论意义、实际应用的可能性和实践意义;提出进一步的研究方向、展望、建议和设想。

结构布局:

> **Discussion**
>
> The author should tell the reader what the results mean by placing them in the context of previous published studies of the problem.
>
> A. 简要说明研究背景(background)
> B. 简要介绍总的发现(general findings)
> C. 介绍具体要点(introduction of points)
> D. 与现有发现(若有)进行比较(comparison in the context of other studies)
> E. 意义(suggested meaning)
> F. 结论(conclusion)
> G. 前瞻研究(future studies)

2. 讨论部分的撰写要点

(1)对结果的科学意义和实际应用效果的表达要实事求是,适当留有余地;要谨慎使用"For the first time"等类似的优先权声明。

(2)突出本部分应阐述内容,避免重复。突出自己的创新点,要有自己见解,不要大量引用他人资料;不要过细地重复已在引言或结果中详细描述过的数据或其他资料;不要做文献综述,重复引言中的工作。

(3)在讨论中应选择适当的词汇来区分推测与事实。例如,可选用"prove","demonstrate"等表示作者坚信观点的真实性;选用"show","indicate","found"等表示作者对问题的答案有某些不确定性;选用"imply","suggest"等表示推测;或者选用情态动词"can","will","should","probably","may","could","possibly"等来表示论点的确定性程度。

(4)讨论本工作将来在可能领域里的扩展。作者可以在这一部分进一步强调本文的重要性。但是常常出现的问题是:扩展领域过于泛泛而言,没有实际内容;凭想象而不是有根据地讨论将来本研究的发展。

3. 讨论部分的英语写作技巧

(1)时态的运用。

①回顾研究目的时,通常使用过去时。

例如:

This study investigated the effects of two different learning methods.

In this study, the effects of two different learning methods were investigated.

②阐述结果时,如果作者认为所概述结果的有效性只是针对本次特定的研究,需用过去时;相反,如果具有普遍的意义,则用现在时。使用现在时的原因是作者得出的是具普遍有效的结论或推论(而不只是在讨论自己的研究结果),并且结果与结论或推论之间的逻辑关系为不受时间影响的事实。

例如:

In the first series of trials, the experimental values were all lower than the theoretical predictions. The experimental and theoretical values for the yields agree well.

The data reported here suggest that the reaction rate may be determined by the amount of oxygen available.

Our findings are in substantial agreement with those of Smith(1985).

③说明结果和阐述相关推论时,使用一般现在时。

例如:

It is possible that adding water causes the reaction rate to increase.

The data reported here suggest that the reaction rate may be determined by the amount of oxygen available.

Our findings may be only valid for females.

Our findings may be useful to others involved in curriculum development.

(2)结果部分常用英语表达。

(1)如果观点不是这篇文章最新提出的,可用:We confirm that…

(2)对于自己很自信的观点,可用:We believe that…

(3)据推断出一定的结论,可用 Results indicate, infer, suggest, imply that…

(4)对所提出的观点不完全肯定,可用:We tentatively put forward(interpret this to…) Or The results may be due to(caused by)/ attributed to /resulted from…Or This is probably a consequence of…It seems that .. can account for this…

Or It is possible that it stems from…

(5)评价他人工作不足时,可用:Their studies may be more reasonable if they had considered this situation.

Their results could be better convinced if they …

Or Their conclusion may remain some uncertainties.

(6)谈论自己研究不足时,可用:

It should be noted that this study has examined only…

We concentrate(focus)on only…

We have to point out that we do not…

Some limitations of this study are…

(7)谈论结果不足时,可用:

The results do not imply.

The results can not be used to determine / be taken as evidence of…

Unfortunately, we can not determine this from this data.

Our results are lack of …

(8)介绍对不足的弥补时,可用:

Notwithstanding its limitation, this study does suggest…. However, these problems could be solved if we consider …

Despite its preliminary character, this study can clearly indicate…

4. 范例学习

示例1:

"Organic light emitting diodes fabricated with single wall carbon nanotubes dispersed in a hole conducting buffer: the role of carbon nanotubes in a hole conducting polymer".

Discussion

We have investigated the role of SWNTs in a hole conducting polymer by comparing the OLEDs performance when PEDOT composite and pure PEDOT is used as a hole conducting buffer. As we have shown in Fig. 4, the I – V 5 power dependence of the device with pure PEDOT originates from the continuous trap charge limit (C – TCL) [12] due to the structural or chemical defects in the conjugated polymer chain. It has been reported that the charge traps in a polymeric material are generated by organic dopants [13]. The organic dopants usually have a higher trap concentration than the host, thus redistributing the trap charge near the highest occupied molecular orbit (HOMO) of the host. The redistribution of the trapped charge is followed by the introduction of discrete traps near the HOMO of the host polymer [14]. In the case of the devices with SWNTs, the lower power dependence of the current at low applied voltages implies that the injected holes are initially trapped by SWNTs. The abrupt increase of current in OLEDs with SWNTs at 3 V is probably due to the filling of the traps generated by the SWNTs and then followed by a sudden jump to the C – TCL regime.

In Fig. 5, the significant decreasing of the EL intensity in OLEDs with SWNTs in the buffer is also an evidence of the hole traps, thus there is less chance of forming excitons in the PECCP layer. A very small difference in PL data between the devices with and without the SWNTs is probably due to the scattering effect of the SWNTs. This also implies that the electronic interactions (hole traps as we proposed) between the SWNTs and the host polymer in a polymer composite should be taken into account to explain the large decrease in the EL intensity.

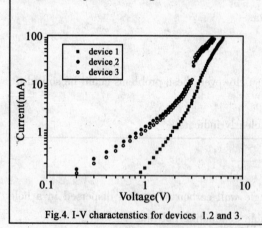

Fig.4. I-V charactenstics for devices 1.2 and 3.

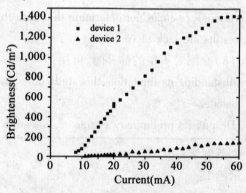

Fig.5. The brightness dependence of the devices as a function of the applied current.

示例2:

"Crystallization and Orientation Studies in Polypropylene/Single Wall Carbon Nanotube Composite"

Results and discussion

The individual SWNT diameter determined from Raman spectroscopy was in the 0.77~1.16 nm range. The individual nanotubes rope into bundles or fibrils, which have an average rope/fibril diameter of about 40 nm as seen by SEM(Fig. 1). TGA(not shown) of this purified SWNT powder in air showed 7 wt% residue above 800°C and is a result of the catalytic impurity remaining after purification. Catalytic impurity in the as produced HiPcoTM SWNTs is typically above 20 wt%. Using the continuous purification process, HiPcoTM SWNTs with purity greater than 99% have been obtained [26].

The optical micrograph of the PP/SWNT composite in the melt state (Fig. 2) shows significant nanotube aggregates. Crystallization behavior as observed from optical microscopy is shown in Fig. 3. The spherulite size in polypropylene is much larger than in PP/SWNT, suggesting that nanotube ropes or nanotube aggregates act as nucleating sites for polypropylene crystallization. However, the issue of the development of transcrystallinity has not been addressed in this study. The residual weight (0.8%) in the TGA study of PP/SWNT composite in Fig. 4 above 500 °C represents the weight of the SWNT. DSC scans in Fig. 5 show that when cooled at 10 °C/min, polypropylene crystallized at 114.5 °C, while crystallization in PP/SWNT occurred at 125.8°C. In addition, both the melting and crystallization peaks in PP/SWNT composite are narrower than in pure polypropylene. For example, the full width at half maximum for PP and PP/SWNT crystallization peaks are 5.7 and 4.4 °C, respectively. Narrower crystallization and melting peak would suggest a narrower crystallite size distribution in the PP/SWNT composite as compared to pure polypropylene. A narrower melting peak was also observed in the PET/nanocarbon fiber composite as compared to pure PET [30]. Higher thermal conductivity of the carbon nanotubes as compared to that of the polymer, at least in part may be responsible for the sharper crystallization and melting peaks, as heat will be more evenly distributed in the samples containing the carbon nanotubes.

Polypropylene in the β-crystal form melts at lower temperature than the α-crystals [31]. A peak at about 165°C in Fig. 5(b) is attributed to the melting of a-crystals in PP/SWNT and the appearance of broad peak in the 145~160°C temperature range can be due to the melting of β-crystals, or smaller or imperfect α-crystals. However, as discussed later, X-ray diffraction of the PP/SWNT fiber does not show the presence of β-crystals. Enthalpy of melting for PP and PP/SWNT composites from the second heating curves was 93 and 100 J/g, respectively.

The half crystallization time as a function of isothermal crystallization temperature is given in Fig. 6 and the isothermal crystallization parameters (n and k) determined by the Avrami equation are given in Table 1. A value close to 3 for the Avrami exponent implies a three-dimensional heterogeneous crystal growth and is practically unchanged with the addition of SWNTs. The addition of 0.8 wt% SWNT increases the crystallization rate by as much as an order of magnitude or higher and is attributed to enhanced nucleation, resulting from the presence of SWNTs.

SWNTs show resonance-enhanced Raman scattering effect when a visible or near infrared laser is used as the excitation source [32-34] and polypropylene as well as most other polymers do not show such a resonance effect. Therefore, the Raman spectroscopy is an ideal characterization technique for the orientation study of SWNT [25,35].

In Refs. [25,35], the orientation of SWNT was treated as if they were distributed around the fiber axis in a 2D plane. While 3D distribution depicts fiber cylindrical symmetry more accurately [36,37], for simplicity, we have also used 2D distribution approximation to study the orientation of SWNTs in PP/SWNT composite fibers. Fig. 7 shows the tangential mode Raman spectra (1,500 – 1,700 cm^{-1}) of the SWNT/PP composite fiber with a draw ratio of 4.5 at VV configuration, where the Raman scattering intensity monotonically decreases with increasing the angle between the fiber axis and the polarization direction of the polarizer. Using the height of 1,592 cm^{-1} peak and based on the Gaussian distribution, Herman's orientation factors1 of SWNT in PP/SWNT composite fibers were 0.81 and 0.95 for the as spun and the drawn fiber (draw ratio 4.5), respectively. Herman's orientation factor was also calculated using Lorentzian distribution, and the corresponding orientation factor values for the as spun and drawn fibers were 0.72 and 0.92, respectively. The orientation factor calculated from Lorentzian intensity distribution is lower than that calculated from Gaussian function and the difference between them diminishes with increasing SWNT orientation. This is due to the fact that the Lorentzian function is more weighted on the tail than the Gaussian function. A mixed Lorentzian and Gaussian function may be a better distribution function for the orientation of SWNT in SWNT/PP composite fiber. A detailed SWNT orientation study in fibers will be published elsewhere [38].

Fig. 8 shows 1D integrated X-ray diffraction intensity profile of the drawn SWNT/PP fiber of 4.5 draw ratio, which is extracted from its 2D wide angle X-ray image shown in the inset of Fig. 8. The integrated X-ray diffraction intensity of SWNT/PP shows the typical α-form PP crystals and exhibited complete absence of the β-crystal form, which shows [39] two strong peaks at 2θ of 16.2 ℃ and 21.2 ℃. While certain nucleating agents can promote β-crystal formation in polypropylene [39], this study shows only the α-crystal formation in PP/SWNT composite. In addition, the diffraction of SWNT bundles, which posses a 2D hexagonal lattice structure [40,41], was also not observed.

From the X-ray diffraction of drawn SWNT/PP fiber, the Herman's orientation factors for (040) and (110) PP planes were calculated to be 20.40 and 20.45, respectively. The Herman's orientation factor for the (001) plane determined using the Wilchinsky equation [42] is 0.86. Compared to the Herman's orientation factor of SWNT (0.92 for the Lorentzian distribution and 0.95 for Gaussian distribution) in SWNT/PP fiber of same draw ratio, PP shows somewhat lower orientation. This is expected to be a result of higher PP chain flexibility as compared to SWNT.

For effective reinforcement, good nanotube dispersion is necessary. Data in Table 2 show that the fiber mechanical properties are mostly unaffected with the presence of SWNTs. Micrometer size single wall nanotube (SWNT) aggregates (Fig. 2) in PP/SWNT composite did not negatively affect the mechanical properties. This would suggest that such large nanotube aggregates either did not act as stress concentrators, or if they did act as stress concentrator, their effect was nullified by those nanotubes or nanotube ropes that may be well dispersed, providing effective reinforcement. When carbon nanotubes are well dispersed in polymer matrix, improvements in mechanical properties are observed. Examples include 50% increase in PP fiber modulus with the addition of 5 wt% carbon nanofibers [18], and 60% increase in PBO fiber tensile strength with the addition of 10 wt% SWNT [26]. It is noted that improved tensile strength PBO/SWNT fibers were obtained when SWNT with .99% purity were used. Fibers processed with high catalytic impurity resulted in lower tensile strength [43]. With good SWNT dispersion and purity, similar tensile strength improvements in PP and other polymers can be expected. Current efforts are aimed at improving nanotube dispersion in polypropylene and other polymer matrix systems.

五、结论

1. 内容和结构布局

内容：

多数科技论文的正文都以结论为结尾，也有的论文将结论的内容融入讨论中。结论又称结束语、结语或归结，是在对研究结果进行理论分析和讨论的基础上，通过严密推理形成的富有创新性和指导性的，且与论文前文相互呼应的概括总结。除了最终总体的概括，也可写建议、对策、设想，或提出研究中发现的尚待解决的问题。它是在理论分析和实验验证的基础上，通过严密的逻辑推理而得出的富有创造性、指导性、经验性的结果描述。它又以自身的条理性、明确性、客观性反映了论文或研究成果的价值。结论与引言相呼应，同摘要一样，其作用是便于读者阅读和为二次文献作者提供依据。

结论并不是正文内容，尤其不是结果与讨论部分的简单重复，而应该是对研究结果更深一步的认识，是从正文部分的全部内容出发，并涉及引言的部分内容，经过判断、归纳、推理等过程而得到新的总观点。

主要包括：

(1) 归纳性说明论文揭示出来的原理、规律或发现——本研究结果说明了什么问题，得出了什么规律性的结论，解决了什么理论或实际问题；对论文创新内容的概括，措辞要准确、严谨，不能模棱两可，含糊其辞。不用"大概"、"也许"、"可能是"这类词，以免使人有似是而非的感觉，从而怀疑论文的真正价值。

(2) 对前人有关问题的看法做了哪些检验，哪些与本研究结果一致，哪些不一致，作者做了哪些修正、补充、发展或否定。

(3) 前瞻性说明未解决的问题。本研究的不足之处或遗留问题；对研究中所发现的例外结果所进行的分析和解释；也可提些进一步研究本课题的建议。

结构布局：

一般来说，结论部分的具体内容及其组织框架如下：
(1) 概括说明本课题的研究内容、结果及意义与价值。
(2) 比较具体地说明本研究证明了什么假设或理论，得出了什么结论，研究结果有何实用价值，有何创造性成果或见解，解决了什么实际问题，有何应用前景等。
(3) 与他人的相关研究进行比较。
(4) 本课题的局限性、不足之处，还有哪些尚待解决的问题。
(5) 展望前景，或指出进一步研究的方向。
在上面五项内容中，第一、二项是必不可少的。第三、四、五项内容可以根据需要而定。

2. 结论部分的撰写要点

(1) 论证的成果。主要包括取得了哪些重大发现、对主要论点的重申与归纳、对核心问题提出总体评价与解决方案三方面要点。

注意事项

① 该部分是对本论分析、论证的问题加以综合概括而得出的基本论点，要写得简要具体，使读者能明确了解作者独到见解之所在。

② 结论必须是绪论中提出的，本论中论证的，自然得出的结果。切忌论证得并不充分而妄下结论。

(2) 论证的不足。主要包括理论框架的疏漏、研究方法的缺憾、内容安排的不足三方面要点。

注意事项

① 不要触及论文的根本缺陷。

② 不足之处条数不宜列出过多。

③ 对论文不足的阐述不宜过于详细。

(3)研究的展望。主要包括对当前论题的拓展、对相关课题的发展、作者的下一步研究计划三方面要点。

注意事项

①展望应切合实际,应具有一定的可行性,切忌不着边际。

②展望应有助于解决本论文研究工作中的遗留问题,或者还需要进一步探讨的问题,并提供可能解决的途径。

(4)如果结论段的内容较多,可以分条来写,并给以编号,如1)、2)、3)等,每条成一段,包括几句话或一句话;如果结论段内容较少,可以不分条写,整个为一段。结论里应包括必要的数据,但主要是用文字表达,一般不再用插图和表格。

3. 结论部分的英语写作技巧

(1)时态的运用。

过去时:

①涉及本研究的内容。

②涉及他人研究过程的内容。

③作者认为只适用于本研究环境和条件的结论。

现在时:

①指示性说明。

②普遍接受的思想、理论或结论。

③作者认为本研究结论具有普遍意义。

④前瞻性说明。

例如:

To expand the capacity of the online test, we devised a displacement-force mixed control technique.

The online test with the proposed mixed control was successful, with accurate displacement and force control achieved for both jacks.

In the case of the polyethylene carbon precursor, thin-walled carbon nanotubes are formed.

The strong anisotropy in the observed optical and saturable absorption properties of stretched SWNT-PVA film indicates that SWNTs are aligned in PVA in a nanoscopic scale in the direction of mechanical stretching.

(2)结果部分常用英语表达。

表示对全文进行归纳总结:

1. The specific conclusions derived from the present study can be listed as follows.
2. The main conclusion drawn from the present study is that…
3. From the above results, we can conclude that…
4. The findings of both studies lead us to conclude that…
5. A future paper will extend this research to include…
6. Further research is needed to find out how generalizable the findings are.
7. Additional research is needed to continue the task of …
8. Future research should consider…
9. The research of solving these issues will be reported in future literature.
10. From/Through/According to what has been discussed above, we can come to/reach/arrive at/draw the conclusion that…
11. All the evidence supports a sound conclusion that…
12. Our findings suggest that …
13. These findings lead the auther to a conclusion that …

表示研究结果的意义:

1. The findings reported here are (quite) striking (remarkable, fascinating).
2. These preliminary findings are very reliable (encouraging, promising. Convincing, ambiguous).
3. The results reported here prove (confirm, suport, bear out) the hypothesis (assumption, observation) that …
4. The above findings can be viewed (approached) as follows (in terms of.., from other standpoint).
5. We can consider (interpret, look at) these results as fully reliable (consistent with) …
6. This fruitful work gives explanation to …

表示研究方向展望:

1. Further investigations are under way to…
2. Further refinement of the models is needed to…
3. Our data leave open the question of whether …
4. In the future, we will extend the persent studies to …
5. Further progress can be provided by this experiment…
6. Our work has contributed to the understanding of …
7. The research work has brought about a discovery of …

例如:

These data confirm the presence of at least two major HCV genotypes in Nigeria.

These results do not support the idea that treatment to lower cholesterol concentration cause mood disturbance.

There is no evidence that NIDDM produces any change in bone metabolism or mass. However, the relation of insulin resistance to hypertension remains to be further studied.

4. 结果部分范例学习

示例1：

"A Modified Operator Splitting(OS) Method for Collaborative Structural Analysis(CSA)"

CONCLUSION

This paper presented a modified OS method for the CSA system with the goal to save computation time and enhance the capability of using commercial finite element programmes. The major findings are summarized as follows:

1. The conventional OS method is formulated in an incremental form for CSA, and a scheme for incorporating the OS method into the CSA system is proposed.

2. The modified OS method, which treats unbalanced forces in the current step as pseu-doexternal forces in the immediate following step, is developed.

3. An example structure is analyzed using the CSA system. The applicability of the OS methods to CSA is demonstrated.

4. Comparison between the conventional and modified OS methods are conducted, and the modified OS method exhibits better numerical stability than the conventional OS method in the CSA considering geometrical non-linearity.

示例2：

"Catalytic Synthesis of Carbon Nanostructures from Polymer Precursors"

CONCLUSION

In summary, a catalytic synthesis route to the different species of carbon nanotubes was presented starting from different carbon precursors in the presence of an iron catalyst uniformly distributed in the bulk polymer via heating to 750 ℃ under a nitrogen flow. The catalytic synthesis of carbon nanotubes involves the catalytic decomposition of the polymer precursor to amorphous carbon and the simultaneous reduction of the iron hydroxide, used as the catalyst precursor, to iron metal at 600 ℃ and 750 ℃. In the case of the polyethylene carbon precursor, thin-walled carbon nanotubes are formed, whereas, cockle-shelled filaments and multiwalled graphite nanotubes are formed from the polyvinyl alcohol as a carbon precursor under the same conditions. The catalytic synthesis of carbon nanostructures via graphitization of amorphous carbon obtained from polymer precursors demonstrates a new route to produce different types of carbon nanostructures.

第十章 论文致谢和参考文献的撰写

一、致谢

作者在进行科技研究的时候不仅仅是依靠一己力量完成的,而是在构思、设计、实验等过程中得到他人或组织单位的帮助、支援或服务。因此,在论文正文后面,作者向曾对自己研究提出过意见、给予过帮助或提供资金设备支持的人员或单位致谢。

1. 致谢的对象和范围

对于不够署名条件,但对研究成果确有贡献者,可以以"致谢"的形式列出。作为致谢的对象通常包括以下内容:

(1)指导或协助本研究工作的实验人员。
(2)在撰写论文过程中参加讨论或提出过指导性意见和提供帮助的人员。
(3)研究提供方便(仪器、测试等)的机构或人员。
(4)被论文采用的数据、图表、照片提供者。
(5)资助研究工作的国家科学基金、资助研究工作的奖学金基金、合同单位、资助和支持的企业、组织或个人(但不宜列出得到经费的数量)。
(6)提供过某种信息,但又非论文的共同作者,且不对论文负责的人员。
(7)给予转载和引用权的资料、图片、文献、研究思想和设想的所有者。

2. 致谢的写作技巧

学术论文作者可以在论文末尾对他人给予自己的指导和帮助表示感谢,即致谢。致谢一般置于结论之后,参考文献之前。有时期刊论文,致谢部分也可放在全文第一页下面,作为脚注先算好要几行,用横线使其与所写文章分开即可,致谢两字不必写,直接写内容。致谢的文字表达要朴素、简洁,以显示其严肃和诚意。

致谢主要包括致谢者、被致谢者和致谢原因,其基本形式如下:

"本文曾得到×××帮助(赞助、指导、修改),谨此致谢(特此致谢或深表谢意)。被致谢人可直书其名,也可写敬称,如×××博士、×××教授、×××导师等。

例如:

> **Acknowledgment**
>
> I am greatly indebted to my thesis supervisor, Professor Blair. In the preparation of the thesis, she has spent much time reading through each draft and provided me with inspiring advice. Without her patient instruction, insightful criticism and expert guidance, it would not be possible for me to complete this thesis in such a short period of time without reducing its scholarly quality. Truly, without her painstaking efforts in revising and polishing my drafts, the completion of the present thesis would not have been possible.

My sincere thanks should also go to all my teachers for their scholarly advice and generous help during my study. Any progress that I have made is the result of their profound concern and selfless devotion. Among them the following requires mentioning: Professor Smith, Professor Lee, and Professor Wang.

Finally, my thanks would go to my beloved family for their loving considerations and great confidence in me all through these years. I also owe my sincere gratitude to my friends and my fellow classmates who gave me their help and time in listening to me and helping me work out my problems during the difficult course of the thesis.

参考译文:

致 谢

我非常感谢我的导师,教授布莱尔。在准备论文的过程中,她花了很多时间阅读每份草稿并给予我很多具有启发性的建议。没有她的耐心指导、有见地的评论和专业指导,我就不可能在如此短的时间内保质保量地完成这篇论文。应该说,没有她对我的草稿精心的修改和润色,完成本论文将是不可能的。

我还要感谢所有在我学习期间给予过我学业指导和慷慨帮助的老师。我的一切进步都离不开老师们的深切关怀和无私支持。不得不提的包括以下老师:史密斯教授,李教授和王教授。

最后,我还要感谢这些年来我亲爱的家人给予我的爱和信心。还要真诚地感谢我的朋友们和我的同学们在我完成论文过程中遇到困难时,抽出时间聆听我的问题,帮助我走出困境。

3. 致谢的常用英文表达
(1)表示"致谢"。
例如:

The author is grateful for …
I am indebted to … for …
The author wishes to express the sincere thanks to…
We would like to thank … for…
Great thanks are owed to … for…

(2)表示"资金资助"。
例如：

The author is very grateful to the National Science Foundation of China (NSFC) for the financial support.
The work has been written out with the support of the National Science Foundation of China (NSFC).
The research is supported by the National Science Foundation of China (NSFC).
The work was largely funded by the National Science Foundation of China (NSFC).
The research described in this paper was in part sponsored by the National Science Foundation of China (NSFC).
This work was supported by NFS Low Temperature Physics Program Grant DMR H0056, ARPA Grant MDA 901, and the Texas Center for Superconductivity at the University of Houston.

(3)表示"建设意见以及技术援助"。

The author is very grateful to Professor Wang for reading the draft / manuscript carefully.
The author is very grateful to Professor Wang for giving / offering valuable advice.
The author is very grateful to Professor Wang for helping analyze the data.
I am very indebted to Professor Wang for his expert technical assistance in operating the transmission electron microscope during the experiment.

(4)表示"他人无须负责的说明"。

The research described in this paper are those of the authors and are not related to those of Professor Wang.
The views expressed in this research do not necessarily reflect the policy of the sponsors.

(5)表示"作为研究基础的引用资料的说明"。

The paper is based on the doctoral dissertation of Professor Wang.

4. 范例学习
示例1：

Acknowledgment

The research and writing of this book has been my preeminent preoccupation these years. I would like to thank all those people who have helped to make this a better book than it would be otherwise having been. Among them, my colleagues and friends, John Hall and Roger Fort who were generous enough to send me valuable and detailed comments on the whole book in manuscript, so I am are particularly grateful to them. I am also indebted to Professor Richard Duncan especially who gave me great constructive criticisms of certain sections of the book. We thank Hilary Dave for helping throughout, especially with proof reading, and Karl Lomas who has earned out gratitude for being our excellent and long-suffering typist.

Advanced Research, through Space and Center San Diego

示例2：

Acknowledgment

I would like to thank my advisor, Prof. Ralph Roth, for his guidance, concern and advice in all matters academic. He originally suggested the some ideas on which this paper was partially based-especially some aspects of the program design, implementation and analysis. Without his dedication, kind and unselfish advice and hard work, this thesis would not have been written. Truly, without him, none of this thesis paper could have happened. I thank him for his kindness and support theoretical, technical, editorial, emotional, and existential.

Secondly, my family and friends have all endured this difficult time with the greatest support and encouragement. To them, I offer my sincerest thanks and gratitude.

Thanks to all of you.

示例3：

Acknowledgment

I thank the members of my committee, Professor XX and Professor XX of XXX University for their invaluable time and comments. I thank my family members, and many friends and colleagues for always supporting me and offering me great help.

Secondly, my advisor, Professor XX, helped me immensely both as a mentor and reader. He fought through countless drafts of countless papers, listened carefully to half-worked ideas, and never wavered in his commitment.

Finally, this research was sponsored in part by the National Science Foundation under grant N66001. The results and opinions expressed herein do not necessarily reflect the position or policy of the Government, and no special endorsement should be inferred.

5. 我国部分常用科学基金英文名称

通常,国内期刊多习惯于将基金资助项目的信息作为论文首页的脚注,国外期刊则多将其作为"致谢"的一部分标注。通常情况下只需列出项目的资助号即可,不必标注具体的项目名称。如:Supported by the National Natural Science Foundation of China (Grant No. 60171009), the Major State Basic Research Development Program of China (Grant No. G2000077405) and the Key Project of Science and Technology of Shanghai (Grant No. 02DZ/5002). 对于国家自然科学基金资助项目,通常只需要统一标注"National Natural Science Foundation of China"和项目的资助号即可,不必再分别标注"面上项目"(General Program),"重点项目"(Key Program),"重大项目"(Major Program)等进一步信息。

我国常见基金资助项目名称如下:

(1) 科技部基金项目。

国家自然科学基金(面上项目、重点项目、重大项目):The National Natural Science Foundation of China (NNSFC) (General Program; Key Program; Major Program)

国家高技术研究发展计划(863 计划):The National High-tech Research and Development (R&D) Program of China (863 Program)

国家科技攻关计划:The National Key Technologies Research and Development (R&D) Program of China

国家基础研究计划:The National Basic Research Priorities Program of China

国家重点基础研究发展计划项目(973 计划):The Major State Basic Research Development Program of China (973 Program)

国家重点基础研究专项基金:The Special Foundation for State Major Basic Research Program of China

国家重点基础研究项目特别基金:The National Key Basic Research Special Foundation of China (NKBRSFC)

国家 985 重点建设项目:The Key Construction Program of the National ("985" Project)

国家"十二五"科技攻关项目:The National Key Technology Research and Development Program of China during the "12th Five-Year Plan"

国家科技支撑计划:The National Key Technology Research and Development Program of the Ministry of Science and Technology of China

国家科技基础条件平台建设项目:The National R&D Infrastructure and Facility Development Program of China

国际科技合作重点项目:The Key Program for International Science and Technology (S&T) Cooperation Projects of China

国家科技重大专项:The National Science and Technology Major Project of the Ministry of Science and Technology of China

国家重点实验室发展项目：The State Key Laboratories Development Program of China

国家攀登计划：The National "Climbing" Program

（2）教育部基金项目。

教育部科学基金：The Science Foundation of Ministry of Education of China

教育部重大项目基金：The Research Foundation from Ministry of Education of China

教育部科学技术研究重点（重大）项目：The Key (Key Grant) Project of Ministry of Education of China

教育部博士点基金资助项目：The Ph. D. Programs Foundation of Ministry of Education of China

高等学校博士学科点专项科研基金：The Research Fund for the Doctoral Program of Higher Education of China (RFDP)

教育部博士点专项基金：The Doctoral Fund of Ministry of Education of China

中国博士后科学基金：The China Postdoctoral Science Foundation

跨世纪优秀人才计划：The Trans-Century Training Program Foundation for the Talents by the State Education Commission

教育部新世纪优秀人才支持计划：The Program for New Century Excellent Talents in University of Ministry of Education of China

教育部优秀青年教师资助计划项目：The Excellent Young Teachers Program of Ministry of Education of China (EYTP)

高等学校优秀青年教师教学、科研奖励基金：The Research Award Fund for Outstanding Young Teachers in Higher Education Institutions

教育部高等学校骨干教师基金：The Foundation for University Key Teachers from the Ministry of Education of China

教育部高等学校优秀青年教师研究基金：The Foundation of the Ministry of Education of China for Outstanding Young Teachers in University

"长江学者奖励计划"：The Chang Jiang Scholars Program of China

教育部长江学者和创新团队发展计划：The Program for Chang Jiang Scholars and Innovative Research Team in University of Ministry of Education of China

教育部和人事部留学回国人员基金：The Scientific Research Foundation of the State Human Resource Ministry and the Education Ministry for Returned Chinese Scholars

教育部留学回国人员科研启动基金：The Scientific Research Foundation for the Returned Overseas Chinese Scholars of Ministry of Education of China

全国优秀博士学位论文作者专项基金：The Foundation for the Author of National Excellent Doctoral Dissertation of China (FANEDD)

霍英东教育基金:The Fok Ying-Tong Education Foundation, China

霍英东教育基金会高等院校青年教师基金:The Fok Ying-Tong Education Foundation for Young Teachers in the Higher Education Institutions of China

(3) 中国科学院基金项目。

中国科学院基金:The Science Foundation of the Chinese Academy of Sciences

中国科学院重点资助项目:The Key Program of the Chinese Academy of Sciences

中国科学院基础研究重大项目:The Major Program for the Fundamental Research of the Chinese Academy of Sciences

中国科学院知识创新项目:The Knowledge Innovation Program of the Chinese Academy of Sciences

中国科学院"十二五"基础性研究重点项目:The Key Basic Research Foundation of the Chinese Academy of Sciences during the "12th Five-Year Plan"

中国科学院"十二五"重大项目基金:The Funds for Key Program of the Chinese Academy of Sciences in the National "12th five-year Plan"

中国科学院百人计划:The "Hundred Talents Program" of the Chinese Academy of Sciences

中国科学院千人计划:The "Thousand Talents Program" of the Chinese Academy of Sciences

中国科学院院长基金:The Special Foundation of President of the Chinese Academy of Sciences

中国科学院对外合作重点项目:The External Cooperation Program of Chinese Academy of Sciences

中国科学院留学经费择优支持基金:The Foundation for Selected Young Scientists Studying Abroad of the Chinese Academy of Sciences

中国科学院青年科学工作者研究奖励基金:The Foundation for Study Encouragement to Young Scientists of the Chinese Academy of Sciences

中国科学院知识创新工程重要方向性项目:The Main Direction Program of Knowledge Innovation of the Chinese Academy of Sciences

(4) 国家自然科学基金委。

国家自然科学基金面上项目(重点项目、重大项目):The General Program (Key Program, Major Research Plan) of National Natural Science Foundation of China

国家自然科学基金专项基金:The Special Funds of the National Natural Science Foundation of China

国家杰出青年科学基金:The National Science Foundation for Distinguished Young Scholars

国家杰出人才科学基金:The Chinese National Science Foundation for Outstanding Scholarship

国家自然科学基金国际合作与交流项目:The NSFC Projects of International Cooperation and Exchanges

海外及香港、澳门青年学者合作研究基金：The Joint Research Fund for Overseas Chinese, Hong Kong and Macao Young Scholars

外国青年学者研究基金：The Research Fund for International Young Scientists

国家自然科学基金创新研究群体科学基金：The Science Fund for Creative Research Groups of the National Natural Science Foundation of China

国家自然科学基金国家基础科学人才培养基金：The Fund for Fostering Talents in Basic Science of the National Natural Science Foundation of China

国家自然科学基金国际（地区）合作与交流项目：The Funds for International Cooperation and Exchange of the National Natural Science Foundation of China

国家自然科学基金联合基金：The Joint Funds of the National Natural Science Foundation of China

二、参考文献

作为严肃的学术杂志，不可能接受没有参考文献的投稿；对于一篇学术论文，参考文献的著录是必不可少的工作。科学的发展是一种接力跑，前人已经解决的问题，后人不必再花力气去做重复劳动。同样，已在期刊上公开发表的科技论文或出版社出版的学术著作中论述的观点数据或材料，不允许在其后的论文中重复阐述。在论文编写过程中凡是引用前人或他人的观点、数据和材料等，只需对它们进行简单的交代，并在文中出现的位置用方括号予以标明，在文末按顺序列出参考文献即可。有经验的编辑，从作者标引的文献中就可以评估论文的起点和深度。有的期刊甚至要求责任编辑亲自核对论文参考文献的著录事项。现在，参考文献表项目著录不齐全、著录项疏漏、事后补齐困难是编辑和作者修改稿件时遇到的最多的问题。因此，在科研工作开题、查阅文献阶段，就要为撰写论文的最后事项：罗列参考文献表做准备。在摘录文献观点的同时，要按照参考文献的著录项目仔细记录，切勿漏记、错记，这是论文撰写不可忽视的问题。

1. 参考文献的目的和内容

科技论文不同于一般作者直抒胸臆的写作，它是对作者科研成果和科研见解的介绍和阐述。科学有继承性，新的科研工作是建立在前人研究的基础之上的，因此科技论文一般也是建立在相关领域前人研究成果之上的。在学术论文后一般应列出参考文献，这样做既可以表明对前人的科学成果的尊重而且可以反映出作者对本课题的历史和现状的了解程度，便于读者衡量论文的水平和可信度，也能真实地反映论文的科学依据，体现论文作者严谨的科学态度，分清是自己的观点或成果还是别人的观点或成果；同时可以指明引用资料出处，便于检索。

因此，在科技论文中，引用或参考他人文献的数据、材料和论文等，都应按照一定格式和顺序予以标明。参考文献的来源是一般期刊、报纸、资料汇编、技术报告、专著、档案资料、学位论文、专刊等。

不同的发表媒介对科技论文参考文献的内容和格式的要求不尽相同，因此在发表期刊论文和撰写学位论文时,作者在把握参考文献基本原则的前提下,应该仔细阅读所投刊物的"作者须知"对参考文献的要求,或留意同一期刊中的其他论文参考文献的注录格式,使自己论文的文献列举和标注方法与所投刊物相一致。

参考文献应包含以下三项内容:作者/ 题目/ 有关出版事项。其中出版事项包括:书刊名称、出版地点、出版单位、出版年份以及卷、期、页等。

参考文献的具体编排顺序有两种:

(1)按作者姓氏字母顺序排列(alphabetical list of references)。

(2)按序号编排(numbered list of references),即对各参考文献按引用的顺序编排序号,正文中引用时只要写明序号即可,无需列出作者姓名和出版年代。

2. 参考文献的格式

在撰写学位论文或研究报告时,国际上通常遵循的格式有两种:**APA** 参考文献格式和 **MLA** 参考文献格式。由于 APA 格式和 MLA 格式都较为繁杂,因此本书只做以简单介绍,详细内容请参阅最新版本的《APA 出版手册》和《MLA 科研论文写作规范》。

(1)**APA** 参考文献格式:APA 参考文献格式由美国心理学会(American Psychological Association)制定,多适用于社会科学和自然科学类论文,其基本格式为:正文引用部分注明参考文献作者姓氏和出版时间,正文后列参考文献项,以 **References** 为标题。

APA 格式文内引用的用法:

第一,正文中引文应使用括号夹注(一般不使用脚注或者尾注)。括号放在所引用句末标点以内,但不得放在引文的引号以内。但是如果引用的是语段,而不是单句,则不将括号放在句末的标点以内。第二,括号内标明作者姓名、出版日期,姓名和出版日期之间用逗号隔开;直接引语都必须标明页码,以便读者查找,使用页码 page 的缩略形式 p. 或 pp.。第三,如果文中同一句内已经提及引用作者的姓氏,则括号内无须再次重复作者的姓;同样地,如果已经提及年份,则括号中也无须再重复年份。第四,如果引用多个位作者撰写的文献,用逗号将每一位作者隔开,最后的作者前用"and"或"&";如果是二次引用或五位以上的作者,则可只写一位作者,其他用 *et al.* 代替。

例如:

The advantage of the multiple regression analysis is that it cannot show the complex interrelations between independent variables (Bryman & Crammer, 1990, pp. 135-139).

Taylor claims that Charlotte and Emily Bronte were polar opposites, not only in their personalities but in their sources of inspiration for writing (1990).

In a 1990 article, Taylor claims that Charlotte and Emily Bronte were polar opposites, not only in their personalities but in their sources of inspiration for writing.

Empirical studies on student learning carried out since the 70's have found that students' learning outcomes to a great extent depend on their choice of learning approaches (Gardner & Lambert, 1972).

The major finding from the earlier studies (Barley *et al.*, 1978) was that learners with an integrative motivation tended to obtain better achievement than those with an instrumental motivation.

APA 格式的参考文献部分的用法：

按照 **APA** 格式的要求，所有正文引用文献须著录在 References 之下，按作者姓氏的字母顺序排列，不得以正文中出现的先后编码排序，不得使用阿拉伯数字。每一条目中的各项内容都必须按 APA 规定的次序和格式编排。

①引用专著、论文集、学位论文、研究报告的格式：

作者名字.（出版年份）.书名(斜体).出版社地址:出版社名.

例如：

Dancygier, B. (1998). *Conditionals and Prediction: Time, Knowledge, and Causation in Conditional Constructions*. Cambridge: Cambridge University Press.

②引用期刊的格式：

作者名字.（发表年月）.论文标题(斜体).期刊名称(斜体),第几期,页数.

例如：

Pringle, J. (2004). *Women Senior Managers: Successful Individuals or Markers of Collective Change. Women's Studies Journal*, Dept. 2, 79-96.

③引用电子资源的格式：

作者名字.（发表年月）.文章标题.期刊名称(斜体).卷,页码.Retrieved on 年月日. from:网站

例如：

Adler, M. (2005). Women's Employment Concentrated In Service Industries. Retrieved on 20th September, 2005 from: http://www.stats.govt.nz.

Cacicedo, Al. (2005, April). [Private parts: Preliminary notes for an essay on gender identity in Shakespeare.](*Working paper*.) [On-line]. 27 Aug. 1997. Available: http://www.arts.ubc.ca/english/iemls/shak/private_parts.txt

（2）MLA 参考文献格式：MLA 参考文献格式由美国现代语言协会（Modern Language Association）制定,适合人文科学类论文,在一般书写英语论文时应当使用 MLA 格式来保证学术著作的完整。其基本格式为:在正文标注参考文献作者的姓和页码,正文后列参考文献项,以 Works Cited 为标题。

MLA 格式文内引用的用法：

第一,引用时标明引用文献的作者和页码,不用标点隔开。第二,正文中引文应使用括号夹注。括号放在所引用句末标点以内,但不得放在引文的引号以内。但是如果引用的是语段,而不是单句,则不将括号放在句末的标点以内。第三,如果文中同一句内已经提及引用作者的姓氏,则括号内无须再次重复作者的姓,只需写页码。第四,如果引用多个位作者撰写的文献,二三位用逗号将每一位作者隔开,如果是三位以上的作者,则可只写一位作者,其他用 *et al.* 代替。

例如：

Charlotte and Emily Bronte were polar opposites, not only in their personalities but in their sources of inspiration for writing (Taylor 432).

In The Age of Voltaire, the Durants portray eighteenth. century England as a minor force in the world of music and art (214 – 48).

MLA 格式的参考文献部分的用法：

①引用专著、论文集、学位论文、研究报告的格式：

作者名字. 书名(斜体或下划线). 出版地：出版者，出版年.

例如：

Dancygier, Bob. *Conditionals and Prediction：Time, Knowledge, and Causation in Conditional Constructions*. Cambridge：CUP, 1998.

②引用期刊的格式：

作者名字."论文题名."期刊名称(斜体或下划线) + 卷. 期号 + (出版年)：起止页码

例如：

Barthelme, Frederick."Architecture." *Kansas Quarterly* 13.3 – 4 (1981)：77 – 80.

③引用电子资源的格式：

作者名字."文章名称."出版信息(例如电子期刊名、或出版名称). 发表日期. 登陆查看日期. 网址(放在＜＞中).

例如：

McCracken, Even."Desiderata." Bold Type. 28 Oct. 1996. 20 Apr. 1997 ＜http://www.bookwire.com/boldtpe/ mccracken/read. article ＄197＞.

（3）期刊论文的参考文献。

不同期刊对所投论文的参考文献格式有不同要求，编排顺序、字体变化及标点符号等方面都不尽相同，因此在投稿之前，论文作者应当仔细阅读所投期刊的"作者须知"，按照要求撰写参考文献。下面列举了来源于《自然》杂志和《科学》杂志中两篇文章的参考文献部分，以供参考。

示例1：

1. Kirchhausen, T. Clathrin. Annu. Rev. Biochem. 69, 699 – 727 (2000).
2. Marsh, M. & McMahon, H. T. The structural era of endocytosis. *Science* 285, 215 – 220 (1999).

3. Perry, M. M. & Gilbert, A. B. Yolk transport in the ovarian follicle of the hen (*Gallus domesticus*): lipoprotein-like particles at the periphery of the oocyte in the rapid growth phase. *J. Cell Sci.* 39, 257–272 (1979).

4. Marsh, M. & Helenius, A. Virus entry: open sesame. *Cell* 124, 729–740 (2006).

5. Brodin, L., Low, P. & Shupliakov, O. Sequential steps in clathrin-mediated synaptic esicle endocytosis. *Curr. Opin. Neurobiol.* 10, 312–320 (2000).

6. Schmid, E. M. *et al.* Role of the AP2 β-appendage hub in recruiting partners for CCV assembly. *PLoS Biol.* 4, e262 (2006).

7. Owen, D. J. *et al.* A structural explanation for the binding of multiple ligands by the α-adaptin appendage domain. *Cell* 97, 805–815 (1999).

8. Owen, D. J., Vallis, Y., Pearse, B. M., McMahon, H. T. & Evans, P. R. The structure and function of the β2-adaptin appendage domain. *EMBO J.* 19, 4216–4227 (2000).

9. Blondeau, F. et al. Tandem MS analysis of brain CCVs reveals their critical involvement in synaptic vesicle recycling. *Proc. Natl Acad. Sci. USA* 101, 3833–3838 (2004).

10. Praefcke, G. J. *et al.* Evolving nature of the AP2 α-appendage hub during CCV endocytosis. *EMBO J.* 23, 4371–4383 (2004).

[来源于：Eva M. Schmid & Harvey T. McMahon. Integrating molecular and network biology to decode endocytosis. Nature 448, 884–887 (2007).]

示例2：

Reference and Notes

1. G. R. McGhee, *Theoretical Morphology* (Columbia Univ. Press, New York, 1999).
2. K. J. Niklas, *The Evolutionary Biology of Plants* (Univ. of Chicago Press, Chicago, 1997).
3. D. M. Raup, A. Michelson, *Science* 147, 1294 (1965).
4. D. M. Raup, J. Vertebr, Paleontol. 41, 43 (1967).
5. R. Raff, *The Shape of Life* (Univ. of Chicago Press, Chicago, 1966).
6. J. Maynard Smith *et al.*, *Q. Rev. Biol.* 60, 265 (1985).
7. R. O. Erickson, F. J. Michelini, *Am. J. Bot.* 44, 297 (1957).
8. I. M. H. Ethemington, *Proc. R. Soc. Edinb.* 59, 153 (1939).
9. W. Troll, *Die Infloreszenzen I* (Gustav Fischer Verlag, Stuttgart, Germany, 1964)
10. W. Troll, *Die Infloreszenzen II* (Gustav Fischer Verlag, Stuttgart, Germany, 1969)

[来源于：Przemyslaw Prusinkiewicz *et al.*, *Science* 316, 1455 (2007).]

第三篇 实用科技应用文写作

第十一章 实用文体写作前的准备

写作是一个记录思想并分享给相应读者的过程。总的说来,写作可分为三大步骤,即构思、起草及修改。在构思阶段需要仔细考虑文章的具体要求,如所写文章的格式、目的、读者、及其写作方法。不管是写哪种题材的文章,要清晰地表达思想,首先要有清晰的思路,在写作前对所掌握的材料深入理解,进行梳理,归纳整合,有取有舍。在构思阶段准备充分,后两个阶段就游刃有余,变得相对容易。写作也是一个循环的过程。经过几轮的构思、起草、修改、再构思、再起草、再修改才会最终得到令作者满意符合读者要求的作品。

具体来讲,在写实用科技类文章之前,应做到以下几点:

1. 明确写作目的

实用科技类文体在日常生活中应用广泛,其种类随着社会的发展变得更加多样。概括来讲,这类文章的目的包括以下几种:

(1)记录并呈现出所做测试及实验的数据。
(2)展示写作人理解了某种原则原理,概念理论,并试图予以应用。
(3)显示作者可独立完成某种研究。
(4)对作者解决问题的能力进行确认并把令人信服的解决方法进行分享。
(5)显示出作者对某一问题的批判性或创造性的思考。
(6)证实作者在某一领域的专业性。
(7)展示作者概括能力。
(8)记录某一项目的发展及完成的各个阶段的情况等。

有的文章只涉及其中之一,而有的则需要多种综合考虑。

2. 明确研究问题

明确了写作目的也就明确了研究问题。所谓研究问题就是此文章的主题,要解决的中心问题、论点、观点等。通常研究问题可以用一句话加以概括,而这句话十分具体,是整篇文章的灵魂。如写作目的为:Reducing overhead expenses,对应的研究问题可能是:We can reduce overhead expenses by centralizing all administrative functions at headquarters. 对于掌握材料的安排取舍也都将围绕相应的研究问题进行。

很多人在写作前并没有明确研究问题,希望在写作过程中文章的主题可以自动显现出来。对于科技应用类文体,这种做法十分危险,很容易导致文章内容不集中,重点不突出,顾此失彼,逻辑混乱,从而难以达到预期的写作目的,因此应避免这种没有计划性的做法。

还需要注意的是一篇文章不能有多个研究问题,因为重点过多的文章难以让读者理解。有时写出文章需要读者采取相应的行动,而多中心削弱了文章的力量,事倍功半。以下为某电子邮件的第一段,以此展开的文章难免包含多个研究问题:

Sales last quarter were down 20% in our northern region. This may have been due to increasing competition in that area, a subject that probably should be addressed at our next sales meeting. (Incidentally, we have not set a date for that meeting and probably should do so as soon as possible.) Getting back to the decline in quarterly earnings, I think we should also consider that a possible cause might be our new sales representatives. They may not thoroughly understand the products they are trying to sell, and may be creating some misunderstandings among our customers. Perhaps they just need more time in the field or perhaps we should design an intensive sales training program for them as soon as possible.

此段文章在一段中陈述了多个观点,读者会迷惑这篇文字到底要说明什么问题。就此段而言,可就下列其中一点为中心,其他的内容为这一点服务成为一个有机的整体:

◇Sales in the northern region during the past quarter;
◇Increasing competition in the region;
◇The upcoming sales meeting;
◇The performance of the company's sales representatives;
◇A training program for the new representatives.

3. 明确读者

有的文章读者比较具体,比如某一专业的导师或专家,而有的则会比较宽泛,有层次不同的读者,从对此问题精通的专家到对文章的相关内容只有基本常识的普通读者。实用科技类文章读者的针对性较强,考虑到读者的具体需求是成功完成写作任务的关键,因此在写作前要清晰回答以下几个问题:

(1)读者可以在此文章中得到什么收益?

这种收益可能很具体,如可以帮助读者节省时间或金钱,获得物质或精神上的提升等。对于一些提议及可行性报告来说,这一点尤其重要。若此文章对于读者来说没有任何意义,读者就没有必要阅读,写此文章也就没有了价值。

具体来讲,比如要写一则备忘录,提醒收阅人用一种新的方式上交财务报告,若开头像如下例子所示,读者就看不出此则备忘录对于他们的意义:

The Controller's office has just designed a new expense report that will replace the one you are currently using. Designing this report required a great deal of time and thought, as well as many revisions until we developed the finished product. We hope you will use this report when you submit your expenses.

而稍作修改，像下面这样来写，效果则会完全不同：
We've just developed a new expense report that will be faster for you to fill out. What's more, if you do it promptly, you will get paid much faster.

或：
The Controller's office has just developed a new expense report form. It's essential that you fill it out correctly, or you won't get paid.

(2) 对于读者来说，哪些内容是新的？
像报纸上的新闻一样，只有新的东西才会抓住读者的注意力，而对于读者已经熟知的部分则可以略去不写。比如要对一工程的进展情况进行说明，下例中就包括了读者已经知晓的部分，难免降低工作效率：
As you know, the construction of the new research facility fell behind schedule in the last quarter. We had delays due to inclement weather as well as a brief strike by one of the unions involved in the project. We discussed these problems in our last report and a series of meetings was held with our contractors to resolve the union issues. I am pleased to report that we have made up all the lost ground and the R&D project is back on track. In fact, we have even begun pushing ahead of schedule and may even beat our projected completion date.

对以上备忘录的开头进行修改，如下所示则增强了时效性，更加符合此项要求：I am pleased to report that all the problems we encountered in the last quarter have been resolved and the R&D project is now ahead of schedule and may beat our projected completion date.

(3) 读者的知识水平是怎样的？
有时，文章涉及专业知识，要考虑到读者是否有相应的知识背景；如果没有，需要对提到的理论、概念及专有名词进行说明或解释，帮助读者更好地理解文章的内容。

(4) 读者的地位级别是怎样的？
读者的级别影响到文章的基调，而文章的基调涉及语言的使用。同级之间的书信与写给法官的法律文件其语言在正式程度上是不同的；同是书信，家人之间和公司与客户之间的语言相差迥异。需要注意的是在正式文体如法律文件、工程说明书、学术论文及报告等中应避免使用口语及俚语，谨慎使用缩写。

4. 进行头脑风暴
文章的影响力不仅需要有清晰的写作目的，明确的写作主题，准确地理解读者的需求，还需要具体的信息及观点来支持支撑说明所要传达的内容。头脑风暴即是调动作者的聪明才智思考出相关的想法来支持文章的主要观点。根据写作内容的复杂程度，头脑风暴需要的时间会有不同。以下几点可以帮助头脑风暴顺利进行：

（1）一旦想到与要写内容有关的想法就立刻记下来，不管什么时间什么地点，不要认为自己会永远记住这一想法。可随身携带笔记本、卡片或是使用可随身携带的可输入类电子设备，如录音笔、平板电脑及手机等。

（2）在头脑风暴阶段不要放弃任何想法，不论其看起来多细小或是多疯狂。让自己的思维活跃起来，充分展开联想，不要设置任何限制，稍后再对各种想法进行筛选组合等处理。

（3）有些时候，可以在写作前与相关人员或是同事就要写的内容进行讨论，或是对此方面的专家进行采访，发挥团队优势，虚心向周围的人学习，找到别人思想的闪光点，也会得到有益的启发。

（4）有效利用网络、图书馆等资源。

5.明确文章结构

一篇文章基本分为介绍、主体及结论三个部分。不同的文章会依此模式产生不同的变化，比如科技报告，首先要表明实验或是测试的结果。很多时候在介绍部分可以概括整篇文章的中心句即可显示出该文章主体的主要结构。大体上有以下几种情况：

（1）依照时间顺序阐述，常用的句式如：There are several steps in the development of _____。

这种结构用于解释某件事发生的过程或步骤，可以从最早发生的开始到最新发生的；也可以使用倒序，从最近的事实开始往前推，比如在简历中叙述个人经历就经常使用倒序的方式。

（2）依照空间顺序进行描述，如：_____ has several features 或 _____ has several constraints。

按照空间顺序描述一般会用到以下词汇作为连接词：below, next to, overhead, behind, adjacent to, above 等。

（3）按类别进行陈述，如：There are several types of _____ 或 There are several criteria for _____。

（4）在不同类别间进行比较，如：Although A is different from B, they share certain characteristics.

这种形式比较侧重两者或多者之间的共同点。

（5）在多者间进行对比，如：A and B are different.

对比侧重两者之间的不同点。

（6）按提出问题到解决问题的顺序进行陈述。

（7）按因果关系进行描述。很多报告采用此种方式，常用的句式如：_____ has several causes 或 _____ has several effects.

此类比较常用的连接词包括：therefore, consequently, based on, because of, due to, as a result 等。

确定了文章的结构就要开始构思文章的提纲。

编写提纲即是把文章的主要信息进行合理的编排，是写作前很关键的一步。具体来讲包括以下几个步骤：

（1）确定文章要点及结构。提纲是文章内容的雏形，通过提纲就可判断出文章的大概内容和行文方向。因此，在动笔前要明确文章的几大要点，通过大标题和小标题显示出各个要点之间的关系，再填入恰当的材料，形成全文的内容提要。

（2）分配各部分字数。确定好文章提要之后，要根据各种文体的具体要求考虑篇幅的长短从而确定文章各个部分所占的比率。有了这样的考虑，更有利于资料的安排，可集中注意力于文章的重点部分，而避免主要内容没有说透，次要内容占大量篇幅的情况。

（3）编写提纲。概括来讲，提纲可以分为简单提纲和详细提纲两种。简单提纲是高概括的，只用短句短语提及文章的要点，而不涉及具体展开方式及内容。简单提纲虽然短小，确是深思熟虑的结果，编写过程并不简单，但一旦完成可保证写作的顺利完成。详细提纲是把文章的要点及展开的部分较为详细地呈现出来，进一步扩充内容便可完成文章的编写，因此需要投入更多的时间和思考。

简单提纲和详细提纲都是文章的骨架和要点，如何选择使用两种提纲要根据具体的情况和需要。总之，拟好提纲十分重要。

6. 明确文章格式

文章的格式包括文章的外观、设计排版、长度及风格。文章的格式既要考虑到读者的需求又要注意各种文章的基本要求。各种文体在文章的格式上相差很大，在此书的以下章节将对各种实用文体进行详细说明。

写作前的这六个步骤会对接下来的写作起到事半功倍的作用，可以使整个写作过程比较顺利，重点突出，不会虎头蛇尾或是头重脚轻，明确文章需要达到具体的目的不会跑题，因此需给予充分的重视。

第十二章 简 历

简历即用个人信息推销自己的书面表达,目的是让收阅人在短时间内对自己感兴趣从而得到工作的机会。简历在美国常称为 Resume,在英国叫做 CurriculumVitae,简称为 CV,有时也称为 DataSheet。据业内人士称,多数雇主只要看几秒钟就能做出是否录用该申请人的决定,随后的面试再进一步验证最初的判断。因此要想在简历海选中脱颖而出,一份书写恰当的简历必不可少。总体来说,书写简历要注意以下几点:

(1)求职简历最好不超过一页,因此只选择最相关最重要的材料,切忌把简历写成自传。
(2)用词要具体客观,不要用空洞浮夸或主观性过强的词汇,具体的业绩及成果才是简历收阅人最关注的部分。
(3)简历整体外观整洁,重点醒目,各项内容之间要留有适中的空白空间。
(4)简历中省略主语"I"并多使用短语。
(5)避免任何形式的错误。

大体来讲,简历主要分为三种,要根据不同的情况做出明智的选择,应用最合适的简历类型。

第一节 标准简历

标准简历就是最常见的以时间顺序为主线展开的简历(Chronological Resume)。当应征者的受教育经历与工作经历朝着应征职业方向稳定地前进,中间没有空当时即可采用这种简历。简历中的信息需要真实准确,不能编造,信息的编排组织需做到最大的优化。具体来讲,通常是把最重要,与应征职位关系最密切的经历置于最前,比如教育背景或是工作经历。另外,从时间上来讲,简历应按倒序撰写,即把最近发生的事件列于最前。简历要力求简洁。任何职位的雇主都要考查应征者的专业技能、沟通技能和组织技能。因此,应征者在书写简历时要做到在最短的时间及篇幅内展示自己这三方面的素质,抓住收阅人的注意力,回答雇主对自己的疑问,给其留下深刻的良好印象。另外,简历要书写规范,任何拼写方面等细小的错误都会给雇主留下不专业不认真的印象,从而导致该申请的失败。

标准简历需要包括以下内容:

(1)姓名(Name)。姓名以大写字母置于页面上部,可应用比简历字体稍大的黑体字表示强调使姓名醒目。若简历多于一页,则每一页顶部的页眉部位(Running Head)均需注明姓名。

(2)联系方式(Contact Information)。包括有效的邮箱地址、电话号码、传真号码及电子邮箱地址。有时也要标明随着时间的推移联系方式的变化,这尤其适用于即将毕业的在校大学生,需注明毕业后的联系方式。

(3)职业目标(Career Objective/Optional)。即注明求职目标。目的明确的简历会避免浪费雇主及应征者的时间，如：A position as an accountant involving。

（4）教育经历（Education）。在此部分要注明获得的所有学历学位及资历证书，就读各大院校的入学及毕业时间，如有必要，也可列出学习过的与所应征职位有关的课程，方便雇主就专业方面对应征者进行深入了解。

（5）个人简况（Personal Information）。此部分有时可以省略，主要包括申请人的性别、出生日期、出生地、健康状况、婚姻状况等。对于一些对身高等体态有一定要求的职位，在简历中最好提供相关的信息。

（6）获奖情况（Academic Awards or Honors）。按年份列明所获奖励或荣誉，必要时可作简短说明。

（7）工作经历（Working Experience）。列明主要雇佣单位的名称、地址、具体工作职位、职务及工作的起始时间（具体到年月）、工作中取得的成绩，如有必要，也可加入志愿者工作及兼职工作的经历。

如：Designed, administered, and reported on a public awareness survey.
Supervised a three-member field crew.

（8）特长（Special Skills/Expertise）。拥有一技之长通常会给雇主留下深刻印象，起到画龙点睛的作用，比如擅长电脑科技或某种运动，精通多种语言或是乐器等。

（9）其他兴趣爱好（Other Interests/Optional）。建议所列项与应征职位有关或是不同于他人特殊的兴趣爱好。读书及音乐几乎每个人都喜欢，写出来价值不大。

（10）其他推荐材料（Reference）。通常用"References available upon request"来表示如有需要将出示更多推荐及参考资料。如有以前教授或是雇主的推荐信，可附在此处，增强说服力。

（11）时间（Date）。这一项也可以省略。随着时间的推移简历也会发生变化，留下日期便于雇主及个人参考。

标准简历范例1：

姓名用黑体书写，清晰明了 给出不同时期的联系方式，方便雇主随时找到该申请人 各部分之间留有空隙。 职业目标，通常写在简历的前部。可根据不同的需要对职业目标进行概括或大体的描述。 教育经历中说明与该职位相关的部分。在此例中就写明了毕业论文，供雇主参考。 获得的荣誉及奖励是简历不可或缺的部分。 工作经历按照倒序的顺序详细说明。在工作中的具体成绩是简历中为自己加分的关键。为节省篇幅，详细内容用短语表达，过去的工作经历通常使用一般过去时时态。	**MICHAEL BENSTON** **Present Address**（until March 2010）： **Permanent Address**： Garfield Rd Mederrian St Tacoma NS A1H 3O1 Puyallup WS W1W 8I9 Phone：254 – 341 – 098 Phone：250 – 131 – 996 Fax：254 – 341 – 099 Fax：250 – 131 – 997 E-mail：michael@ university.com E-mail：benston@ internet.com **Career Objective**：An entry-level position in software development, where my background in commercial applications would be an asset. **Education**： ◇ M. Eng. In Electrical and Computer Engineering, Dalhousie University, expected in June 2008 (Thesis："Machine Architecture and Linear Memory"). ◇ B. Eng. In Electrical and Computer Engineering, University of Victoria, 2006. Honors and Awards： ◇ Dean's List, 2002 ~ 2006, University of Victoria. ◇ NSERC Industrial Undergraduate Research Award, 2005. **Working Experience**： Summer 2006 - Software Engineer for Texas Instruments, Toronto ◇ Performed software validation and provided quality assurance. ◇ Designed a multi-headed debugging driver with Visual Studio C + +. Summer 2005 – Systems Engineer for Ford Motor Company in Windsor, Ontario ◇ Migrated paper forms to online format. ◇ Provided tech support for a variety of computer systems. ◇ Trained a college co-op student to take over plant website maintenance. Summers 2003, 2004 – Research Assistant for Path Technologies, Gibson B. C. ◇ Performed daily and weekly lab tests and prepared reports of results.

特长及经历部分也通常使用短语及一般过去时态表达	**Specialized Skills and Experience**： ◇Extensive computer skills. Operating Systems：MS-DOS，Windows XP，Solaris，Linnux. Languages：C/C++，SQL，HTM，DHTML/CSS，and JavaScript. Applications：Xemacs，Matlab，AutoCad，Cygwin. ◇Strong background in tech support. Took courses in integrated circuits and high-speed PCB design and used these skills in my position with Texas Instruments. ◇Certified in Standard First Aid & 2-Person CPR，WHMIS，and PADI Open Water Scuba Diving.
兴趣爱好及所获成绩能够表达出应征者的性格，如此例可说明该应征人热爱体育及社团活动，比较开朗活跃。 通常用这种方式结束简历。	**Interests and Achievements**： ◇Member of University of Victoria varsity basketball team，2002–2004. ◇University of Victoria Engineering Society Director，2004–2005. **References**：Available upon request.

标准简历范例2：

可以看出这也是一位应届毕业生的简历。 注意英语地址的写法，此例为美国地址，先是牌号街道名称，接着是城市名称，州名称，邮政编码。也可如此例，注明电话及电邮。	**Michael Solomon**	
	School Address（until June 20，2009） 689 Canyon Street， Kent，WA83000 253–490–0098 michaels@email.com	Address（after June 20，2009） 126 Woodlake Avenue Pond，WA 83201 253–098–256
此例教育经历部分比较简单。	**Education**	**Washington Technical University**，Kent，WA Bachelor of Chemical Engineering. Minor in Chinese. Expected graduation，June 2009

此部分为参军经历，已经在此过程中的学习经历，得到的成绩。	**Military Training** June 2004 – December 2008	◇ Special Forces Qualification Course, Ft. Bragg, 2004 ◇ Advanced International Morse Code Course, Ft. Bragg, 2005 ◇ Airborne School, Fort Benning, 2005 ◇ Class A Electronics Technician School, Ft. Gilmore, 2006 ◇ Class A Chinese Scholl, Joint Service Defense Language Institute, Wahington, 2007 ◇ Infantry Squadron Leadership Schol, Ft. Benning, 2008
工作经历，包括固定工作及兼职。	**Experience** January 2005 – present	**Kent Fire Department**, Kent, WA *Firefighter* II, January 2005 – January 2006; *Firefighter* I, February 2006 – present. Apparatus operator and unit supervisor.
	January 2005 – present	Washington National Guard, Kent, WA *Special Forces Communications Sergeant* ◇ Operate and repair communications equipment ◇ Deployed to Puyallup, April – July 2006
	June 2002 – May 2004	**ComputExperts**, Kent, WA *Computer Service Technician* ◇ Repaired hardware for all makes of personal computers ◇ Managed listserv for three clients
其他特殊技能包括计算机、语言、乐器等特长。	**Expertise**	◇ Program in C++ ◇ Speak, write, and read Chinese fluently ◇ Use AutoCad for design projects ◇ Piano
其他参考资料，给出三位可以索要该申请人推荐材料的个人信息，包括姓名、职位、单位名称、单位地址、电子邮箱地址。	**References**	Dr. Reebon, Professor, Department of Chemical Engineering, Washington Technical University, Kent, WA 83001. reeba@wtu.edu Dr. Jane, Assistant Professor, Department of Chemical Engineering, Washington Technical University, Kent, WA 83001. jana@wtu.edu
在最后注明日期，方便日后参考。	**26 March 2009**	CPT Minon IYCA Company, 33 Woodland Street, Washington National Guard, The Armory, Kent, WA 83000. minon@hotmail.com

第二节　电子简历

除了向用人单位递交纸媒简历,也可通过网络直接发送电子简历。电子简历在当今应用越来越广泛,具有不受地域限制,方便快捷的特点。由于发送电子简历比较经济快捷,要在众多电子简历中被挑选出来就更需要精心设计和编排,具体来讲要注意以下几点:

(1)电子邮件的名称要突出重点,根据招聘的要求说明应征的职位,即使不查阅电子邮件,受阅人也会知道该邮件的大致内容而不是把其当成垃圾邮件删除。如 Process Engineer,或以应征者的姓名作为电子简历的名称,如:benstoncharry.doc。

(2)根据用人单位的招聘广告,电子邮件的称谓要尽量做到具体化,落实到主管相关方面的个人,如找不到具体的收信人,可用"Dear Hiring Committee"代替。

(3)把简历用附件的形式附加于邮件,以保证简历的格式能够正常显示。

(4)在发送电子邮件之前要反复检查,确保准确无误。

(5)由于收到电子邮件数量的巨大,很多公司应用检索工具通过关键词对大量的电子简历进行检索筛选,因此要确保电子简历中包含对于应征职业有关键性联系的信息,确保能够被检索出来。在列明姓名及联系方式后,可加入关键词(Key Words)这一项,用名词列出最重要的与应聘工作有关的个人素质等信息。

以下所示,仅供参考:

电子简历例文:

粗体姓名更加醒目虽然是电子简历,同样要给出详细的联系方式。	**CHARRY BENSTON** Medernian St Puyallup WS W1W 8I9 Phone:250-131-996 Fax:250-131-997 E-mail:benston@internet.com
关键词部分十分重要,能确保在众多电子简历中被索引出来,关键词通常为名词或动名词。 不论在哪种简历中都要注明职业目标。	KEY WORDS: Electrical and computer engineering,software engineering,debugging,website maintenance,tech support,systems,research POSITION DESIRED: Software developer
此例中教育经历比较简单。若雇主找到了需要的信息,将会进一步与应征者联系。	EDUCATION:Dalhousie University,2006-8,M. Eng. in Electrical and Computer Engineering (Thesis:"Machine Architecture and Linear Memory")

第三节 功能简历

功能简历即是用来强调应征者某一方面素质或信息的简历,使收阅人迅速了解应征者的优势。比如用来强调个人在学术研究、实习工作、管理、销售或设计等方面的建树,或是个人在某方面优秀的能力等。此种简历不强调时间顺序,而是着重于多样性,因此格式也呈现多样化。

功能简历例1:

首先注明姓名及联系方式。	REID DENNIS 2110 S 90th St Tacoma,Washington 253-426-6798 reiddan@internet.com
职业目标在此例中十分具体,即为废水管理环境顾问。 在功能简历中可以没有具体的教育经历,但要突出和应征职位关系紧密的经历。在此例中主要说明该应征人为环境工程师,接着说明环境工程师的主要工作职责及范围。 其他所经历的实习工作及实验经历。	**Objective**: Work as an environmental consultant in wastewater management. **Profile**: A highly organized environmental engineer (B. A. Sc, University of Tacoma, 2007) with a positive attitude and consistent ability to meet deadlines in challenging, high-pressure surroundings. **Environmental Engineering**: ◇Developed MATLAB code for modeling atrazine transport in an aquifer. ◇Assisted in site characterization and site selection for active and passive water treatment systems. ◇Conducted an audit of a paper mill freshwater system. **Field Work**: ◇Conducted water and sediment sampling at a mine site. ◇Planted a constructed wetland for treatment of wood-waste landfill leachate. **Laboratory and Analysis**: ◇Identified, prepared, and analyzed specialized bacterial cultures for wastewater treatment. ◇Constructed thermo-graximetric analysis (TGA) and direct-current plasma (DCP) analysis of samples. ◇Carried out experiments using a variety of biotechnology lab techniques (aseptic technique, culture growth, enumeration, gram staining, etc.).

因为此应征职位为顾问,对沟通能力的要求很高,因此在简历中详细说明该应征者的沟通素质。	**Communication Skills**: ◇ Fluent in Italian, both written and spoken. ◇ Part-time teaching and research assistant at the University of Tacoma, January 2005 to present. ◇ Instructor/Counselor for Engineering Science Quest (a summer camp for pre-teen amateur scientists), Summers 2004, 2005	
所掌握的软件工具	**Software Tools**: ◇ Skilled in HYSYS. Plant, including extensibility, and Aspen. ◇ Proficient in Msffice and Visual C++; working knowledge of MATLAB and Visual Basic.	
其他成绩及参加的活动。在此例中列明的各点均与应征职位有关。	**Other Achievements & Activities**: ◇ Six-time recipient of the UW engineering Upper Year Scholarship for academic excellence. ◇ Member of the Dean's Honours List from 2002 – 2007. ◇ Enjoy playing guitar and Celtic whistle. ◇ Acid cyclist and runner. ◇ Interested in environmental remediation and international development. References available upon request.	

功能简历例2:

	Michelle Brown 789 Lakeland Street 806 – 900 – 0987 Lubbock, TX 79000 michella@hotmail.com www.tx.edu/~nameam	
此例中的职业目标比较广泛。此处给出学习成绩具体分值,便于雇主判断此应征人是否适合研究型工作。因为此工作对于写作能力要求很高,因此在此部分,应征者详细说明自己在各个领域的写作经历、成绩及才能。	**Objective**	To research, design, and write descriptions for displays at museums, zoos, and entertainment parks.
	Education	West Texas College, Lubbock, TX Bachelor of Arts in English, June 2005 GPA: Major 3.50, Overall 3.21
	Writing Experience Technical Writing	◇ Developed documentation for file management features in Windows XP. ◇ Performed a substantive edit on grant proposal for Plains Museum of West Texas, Lubbock, TX. ◇ Wrote a style guide for major grant proposals. ◇ Interviewed prospective users, compiled a user analysis, and oversaw user testing. ◇ Designed page layouts in WordPerfect.

具体包括实用文体写作、编辑、网络设计、研究、讲演、创造性写作等。		Technical Editing	◇ Developed style guidelines including font, justification, and spacing for grant proposals. ◇ Completed numerous copyediting and proofreading tasks using standard symbols.
		Web Design	◇ Created a personal Web site containing online resume and portfolio. ◇ Self-taught basic- and intermediate-level HMTL codes. ◇ Researched Web page layout and design.
		Research	◇ Researched guidelines for entertainment park information for customers. ◇ Investigated the use of symbols, such as #, @ and ∗ in technical documents. ◇ Interviewed the chief editor for Technology Today, a global scholarly magazine.
		Presentation	◇ Developed a 30-minute/20-slide presentation on Plains Museum of West Texas information signs for visitors. ◇ Created a 20-minute/15-slide presentation on online editing
		Creative Writing	◇ "Life on the Way", poem published in Enthusiasm, the college student literary magazine (Spring issue, 2008).
此应征职位涉及的电脑技能主要是办公软件的使用,因此在这一部分详细说明。		**Computer Knowledge**	Basic Microsoft Access; Windows XP; WordPerfect 11; Microsoft Word 2003; Corel Presentations; Microsoft PowerPoint. Intermediate HMTL; Basic Microsoft Excel.
在相关领域受到的奖励及荣誉具有很高的说服力。		**Honors**	◇ Sigma Tau Delta, English national honor society ◇ Sigma Tau Chi, national honor society of the Society for Technical Communication. ◇ Dean's List, Fall 2005, Spring 2006, Fall 2006, Spring 2007.
列明志愿者活动说明该个人积极热心。		**Volunteer Activities**	◇ Plains Museum of West Texas College, Children's Group Leader. ◇ Buddy Holley Museum, Lubbock, EX, Student Docent.

相关技能已经详细说明，工作经历只是简单概括。可以看出整个简历没有严格按照时间顺序进行，而是突出与应征职位相关的经历与技能。	**Work Experience** Summer 2007 Summer 2006 **References** 16 **August**, 2007	◇Camp Greylock, Becket, MA, Junior Counselor, Soccer Instructor ◇Auntie Ethel's Pizza, Lubbock, TX, Driver See attached sheet.

除了以上所述的三类简历，根据需要有时也可以把传统的标准简历和功能简历结合在一起，发挥两种简历的优势，而避免每种简历在某方面表现不足的缺点。如下例所示：

标准简历与功能简历相结合范例：

在此例中每项包含的内容是否丰富。 此部分着重该应征者的沟通技能，更符合功能简历的特点。	**Lily Ron** 789 **Lakeland Street**　　　　　　　　　　　　　806-900-0987 **Lubbock**, **TX** 79000　　　　　　　　　　　　　　　lila@hotmail.com **EDUCATION** Bachelor of Arts in English, West Texas College, Lubbock, TX. Date of graduation, 10 May 2005. GPA in major, end of Fall 2004 Semester, 3.50. Overall GPA, end of Fall 2004 Semester, 3.21 **COMMUNICATION EXPERIENCE** **Technical Writing** Developed documentation for file management features in Windows XP; Performed a substantive edit on grant proposal for Plains Museum of West Texas, Lubbock, TX; Wrote a style guide for major grant proposals; Interviewed prospective users, compiled a user analysis, and oversaw user testing; Designed page layouts in WordPerfect. **Technical Editing** Developed style guidelines including font, justification, and spacing for grant proposals; Completed numerous copyediting and proofreading tasks using standard symbols **Web Design** Created a personal Web site containing online resume and portfolio; Self-taught basic- and intermediate-level HMTL codes; Researched Web page layout and design **Research** Researched guidelines for entertainment park information for customers; investigated the use of symbols, such as #, @ and * in technical documents; Interviewed the chief editor for Technology Today, a global scholarly magazine

	Presentation Developed a 30 – minute/20 – slide presentation on Plains Museum of West Texas information signs for visitors; Created a 20 – minute/15 – slide presentation on on-line editing
此部分按照时间的倒序列明应征者的工作及学习经历,更符合标准简历的特点。	**Creative Writing** "Life on the Way",poem published in Enthusiasm,the college student literary magazine(Spring issue,2008) **IMPORTANT COURSE WORK** Work Document Design, Proposal Writing, Project Management,Professional Editing,information Architecture,Writing User Guides,Interviewing,Web Writing. **HONORS** Sigma Tau Delta,English national honor society;Sigma Tau Chi,national honor society of the Society for Technical Communication;Dean's List,Fall 2005,Spring 2006, Fall 2006,Spring 2007 **EXPERIENCE(LAST 3 YEARS)** **Volunteer docent,Plains Museum of West Texas,Lubbock,TX**,August 2003-May 2004;November 2004-present. Worked on grant proposals,prepared informational signs for museum visitors,conducted tours and classed for public-school children. **Editorial intern,Lubbock County Prairie Dog Sanctuary,Lubbock,TX.** August 2004 – November 2004. Prepared guidelines for visitors to the sanctuary. Approximately 2,000 visitors a month. **Junior counselor,soccer instructor,Camp Greylock,Becket,MA.** Summer 2004. Counseled 8 months and led soccer instruction for approximately 32 campers. **Student docent,Buddy Halley Museum,Lubbock,TX.** August 2002 – May 2003. Conducted tours for individuals and small groups. **Delivery Driver,Auntie Ethel's Pizza,Lubbock,TX.** Summer 2003. Drove approximately 200 miles each week and handled \$500 weekly with accident-free driving and no errors in cash accountability. **REFERENCES** See attached list 18 April 2005

总体来说,不管应用哪种简历,书写简历都要力求突出优势,增强表现力,回避弱势,同时做到实事求是。

第十三章 书 信

第一节 正式书信的基本原则

对于正式的英文书信,首先要求表达清晰明了(Clarity)。另外,结构清楚、语法正确恰当、讲求礼貌也十分重要。

(1)清晰明了。要做到清晰明了需要注意以下几点:
①在文化上公正并保持中立;
②句子不要过长;
③尽量使用常用的词语;
④避免废话;
⑤在句子中有明确具体的动词;
⑥人称可多使用 I 或 We,I 代表个人,We 代表所在的单位或组织,如:Because company policy does not allow payment for transfers, we cannot refund your costs in this matter. 再如:I have reviewed your proposal carefully, and my reaction to it is favorable;
⑦尽量多地了解收阅人,要考虑到发文人视为理所当然容易理解的信息收阅人可能并不知晓,对于这种情况需要做出必要的介绍或解释;
⑧反复检查避免错误;
⑨避免使用缩写,避免使用表示情绪的符号,如:)微笑或:(皱眉等。

(2)结构清楚。清晰规范的结构会有效地提高书信的效力。在架构结构时要考虑到书信的收阅人、书信的目的及背景。具体来讲,首先,在书信的开头部分要对整个书信内容进行介绍,让收阅人迅速了解此信件的相关内容,如:In this letter, I provide the credit analysis of the C. L. Company that you requested on January 26, 2010. The analysis covers three areas: customer evaluation, financial situation, and credit structure. 有时也可首先对收到的上封信件表达感谢,再引入此封信的正题,如:Thank for the good suggestions about the problems with the computers. Below is a list of the faulty computers that need replacing. 接着,对于书信内容的展开可以有多种选择,选择的标准为收阅人的兴趣和要求。如要建议一种新的工艺,可以从其优点、缺点两方面来讲,把信件分为两大部分,也可以从其成本、功能及技术要求的角度来讲,把信件分为三大部分。最后,完成整篇信件后可使用一些格式工具让文章的结构一目了然,如高亮、黑体及斜体等。

(3)语法恰当。书信中的语法要求拼写正确,标点使用准确,句子结构清晰。语法恰当会使书信的含义准确传达,也是对发信人的专业素质及专业经验的基本要求。有的语法错误通过办公软件可以检查出来,有的则需要发信人反复仔细阅读才可发现。

(4)讲求礼貌。讲求礼貌可以帮助同级之间或上下级之间更好地合作。应注意不同的国家和地区对于礼貌有不同的要求。以英语为主要语言的大部分西方国家在表达上比较直接,习惯开门见山,直抒胸臆,并习惯在文章的结尾抒发感激之情,而很多的亚洲国家崇尚含蓄文化,反映在书信表达中先是抒发感激的情绪,再把要说的事情娓娓道来。另外,对于不同级别的收阅人采用的礼貌的等级也是不同的。如:Your plan for reorganization will never work. 就不能使用在下级对上级的情况下,而最好换一种表达方式,如:Here is an alternative plan that seems promising.

讲求礼貌也要适度,过于谦卑或表达过于婉转也可能无法让收阅人理解书信的内容,从而弄巧成拙,事与愿违。

礼貌因素还要注意尊重收阅人的其他表达习惯,尊重其在日期、时间及度量衡单位的使用及书写习惯。不同的国家和地区在表示日期、时间、长度等方面形式及单位是不同的,在发信前要对相关细节做到周到的考虑。如表示日期,欧洲人习惯的书写方式是把日期写在月份的前面,如:1/11/10 表示 2010 年 11 月 1 日,而在美洲国家,这样的写法则表示 2010 年 1 月 11 日。所以在书写日期时,通常要写出月份的名称,避免歧义及误解。时差问题在当今这个讲求全球同步的时代也十分重要。如发信给外国的机构或是个人,要考虑到本地及收阅人当地时间的差异,可标明本地时区或使用格林尼治时间。其他的度量衡也要考虑周到,最好的做法是把书信中出现的度量衡换算为对方熟悉的形式及单位,如发信给英美国家,要把米换成英尺,把摄氏度换成华氏,把公斤换成磅等。

第二节　书信的分类

随着社会的发展,世界各国之间联系日益频繁广泛,英文书信变成一种应用性极强的实用文体。较常使用的书信从形式上可分为一般书信、备忘录及电子邮件三种;从内容上分包括致谢信、求职信、申请信、推荐信、邀请信、确认信、证明信、祝贺信及慰问信等。书信要求格式规范,在表达方面不同类型信要符合不同的要求。

第三节　一般书信的格式

从信的外观上来讲,在书信用纸方面(Stationery),以单位或是公司的名义写信最好使用印有单位信息的信头纸。如没有信头纸,应选用质量好的白纸。质量低劣的纸张是对收阅人的不尊重。在字体及打印(Fonts and Printers)方面,信的主体内容应使用标准字体,如 Times New Roman。在正式信函中使用变化多样的字体会被视为不严肃不专业。打印信函时要确保字符的清晰,颜色不易太浅。在信函的版式方面要注意适当地留白(Margins),确保整个页面看上去和谐,不要太密集或是内容都集中于纸张的上半部而显得头重脚轻,不要吝惜使用空格及空行。

工作中使用的正式信件要遵循固定的格式,以便收阅人在信的固定位置找到相应的信息,提高效率。具体来说英文书信一般由以下成分构成:

（1）信头（Heading）。信头包括发信人地址（Writer's Return Address）及写信的日期。发信人地址不包括发信人的姓名。英文地址要从小到大来写，顺序如下：房间号码，门牌号码，街道，区或乡镇，市或县或郡，省或州，邮编（位于省或州之后），国家名称。

地址中常用的缩写如下：

Dept. = Department　　　　　　　　Univ. = University
Inst. = Institute　　　　　　　　　　Bldg. = Building
Ave. = Avenue　　　　　　　　　　Str. = Street
Rd. = Road　　　　　　　　　　　　E. = East
W. = West　　　　　　　　　　　　S. = South
N. = North

在美国，每个州的名称都由两个字母缩写，请参考下表。

美国各州名缩写表：

英文名称	简称	中文名称
1. Alabama	1. AL	1. 阿拉巴马州
2. Alaska	2. AK	2. 阿拉斯加州
3. Arizona	3. AZ	3. 亚利桑那州
4. Arkansas	4. AR	4. 阿肯色州
5. California	5. CA	5. 加利福尼亚州
6. Colorado	6. CO	6. 科罗拉多州
7. Connecticut	7. CT	7. 康涅狄格州
8. Delaware	8. DE	8. 特拉华州
9. District of Columbia	9. DC	9.（华盛顿）哥伦比亚特区
10. Florida	10. FL	10. 佛罗里达州
11. Georgia	11. GA	11. 佐治亚州
12. Hawaii	12. HI	12. 夏威夷州
13. Idaho	13. ID	13. 爱达荷州
14. Illinois	14. IL	14. 伊利诺伊州
15. Indiana	15. IN	15. 印地安纳州
16. Iowa	16. IA	16. 爱荷华州
17. Kansas	17. KS	17. 堪萨斯州

英文名称	简称	中文名称
18. Kentucky	18. KY	18. 肯塔基州
19. Louisiana	19. LA	19. 路易斯安那州
20. Maine	20. ME	20. 缅因州
21. Maryland	21. MD	21. 马里兰州
22. Massachusetts	22. MA	22. 马萨诸塞州
23. Michigan	23. MI	23. 密歇根州
24. Minnesota	24. MN	24. 明尼苏达州
25. Mississippi	25. MS	25. 密西西比州
26. Missouri	26. MO	26. 密苏里州
27. Montana	27. MT	27. 蒙大拿州
28. Nebraska	28. NE	28. 内布拉斯加州
29. Nevada	29. NV	29. 内华达州
30. New Hampshire	30. NH	30. 新罕布什尔州
31. New Jersey	31. NJ	31. 新泽西州
32. New Mexico	32. NM	32. 新墨西哥州
33. New York	33. NY	33. 纽约州
34. North Carolina	34. NC	34. 北卡罗来纳州
35. North Dakota	35. ND	35. 北达科他州
36. Ohio	36. OH	36. 俄亥俄州
37. Oklahoma	37. OK	37. 俄克拉荷马州
38. Oregon	38. OR	38. 俄勒冈州
39. Pennsylvania	39. PA	39. 宾夕法尼亚州
40. Rhode Island	40. RI	40. 罗得岛州
41. South Carolina	41. SC	41. 南卡罗来纳州
42. South Dakota	42. SD	42. 南达科他州
43. Tennessee	43. TN	43. 田纳西州
44. Texas	44. TX	44. 德克萨斯州
45. Utah	45. UT	45. 犹他州
46. Vermont	46. VT	46. 佛蒙特州
47. Virginia	47. VA	47. 弗吉尼亚州
48. Washington	48. WA	48. 华盛顿州
49. West Virginia	49. WV	49. 西弗吉尼亚州
50. Wisconsin	50. WI	50. 威斯康星州
51. Wyoming	51. WY	51. 怀俄明州

信头靠左齐行(Left Justified)，每项信息分行排列。若使用信头纸，信头则是印好的信息，位于信纸顶部中心位置，表示发信者所属的机构或公司等。

信开头的日期位于信头信息下方，可隔一至两行，左对齐或是中间靠右的位置，使用月－日－年或日－月－年的形式，表示具体的日期不用序数词，直接使用阿拉伯数字。月份不使用缩写，如：January 17, 2010，或 17 January, 2010。应避免全部使用阿拉伯数字来表示日期的方法，因为此写法容易引起歧义及误解。

信头举例如下：

此地址表示第7大街南18210号克特市 华盛顿州邮编为98031日期为2010年3月23日	18210 7th Avenue S. , Kent, WA 98031 March 23, 2010

（2）信内地址（Inside Address）。信内地址即收信人的姓名及地址，位于日期下方隔两至四行的位置，靠左齐行，每行后面不加标点，而且需要注意以下几点：

①注明收信人姓名及其称谓，称呼用于姓名之前。

☆根据性别，主要的称谓包括如下所示：

Mr. 男性通用

Mrs. 用于已婚女性

Ms. 女性通用。

Miss 未婚女性（较少使用）

☆根据身份职务或头衔，主要的称谓包括如下所示：

Dr.（Doctor）博士

Prof.（Professor）教授

SG（Sergeant）警官

②收信人地址的写法参看信头部分发信人地址的写法。

③收信人若是一个机构，则写清该机构的地址。

④若发信到国外，需注明国名。

（3）信函题目（Reference and Subject Lines）。信函题目表明信的主要内容或是表明此封信函为某封来信的回信，可让收阅人迅速了解此封信的背景，提高工作效率。有时用"RE："或"Re："表示可参见某封邮件或文件，re 为 reference 或是 regarding 的缩写；也可以用"Subject："加邮件的名称表明此信函的目的及内容。有时，在一份信函中可同时使用 RE 及 Subject。也可在此部分使用黑体字表示强调。如下所示：

Re：Information on new fall products

Subject: Information on new fall products

(4)称呼（Salutation）。通常以问候语开始一篇书信,具体来讲,常使用到以下的称呼方式：
①Dear Sir/Madam（当不清楚收信人的姓氏性别时）
②Gentlemen（不认识收信人时使用,注意前面不加 Dear,也不能用单数）
③Dear Mr. + 姓;Dear Mrs. + 姓;Dear Dr. + 姓;Dear Ms. + 姓
④Dear + 名（只在熟人间使用）后加冒号。
如:"Dear Ms Brown:","Dear Professor King:","Dear Mr. Hartman:"等。

若不知道具体收信人的姓名,比如发给某一个组织或机构,除以上所示,还可用 Dear 加该组织或机构的名称,加冒号的形式,如:"Dear Student Health Center:","Dear Greenwell Company:"。

在一些正式的信函如一些法律文件中,也常常使用"To Whom It May Concern",即敬启者。可视具体情况而定。

(5)正文（Text Body）。正文是信的重点,通常是左对齐顶头书写。书信的正文,尤其是英语的书信习惯开门见山地写明书信的主要内容及目的,然后征求收阅人的建议或想法,没有过多的客套或官话。如果是回复对方的信函,需要首先就对方上封书信进行回应。在每段中要将主要信息放在每段的开头,然后再具体说明。尽量使用常用正式的词汇,避免使用口语体的语言。在信的结尾通常有如 I am looking forward to your response 等的礼貌用语。

正文部分要注意行间距,尤其是一些内容较少的信函,行与行之间可以使用单倍行距,段与段间使用双倍行距,而对于内容丰富的信函,段与段之间空一行即可。

(6)信尾敬语（结语）(Complimentary Close)。信尾敬语表示发信人态度的诚恳,对收信人的礼貌及尊敬。对于上级或不太熟悉的收信人,较多使用"Sincerely"或"Sincerely yours"加逗号,也常见"Yours Sincerely,"及"Respectfully,","Gratefully,"等;而对于同级别或关系比较近的收信人,可使用"Warm regards"或"With best wishes"等后加逗号。

如果日期是左对齐,信尾敬语则也左对齐;如日期是中间靠右,信尾敬语也要在与日期对齐的位置。

(7)发信人签名（Writer's Signature）。在信尾敬语的下面,留出两至四行空白手写签名,再加上打印姓名,也可在姓名前加上发信人的职位或头衔。中国人的打印姓名即是拼音,手写签名可以是汉字也可以是拼音。信函打印好后,不要忘记加上个人手写签名,对于英文信函这个步骤非常重要。

(8)附言及附件提示（Postscript and Enclosure Notice）。附言即通常见到的 P.S.,在信尾表示对正文内容的补充。如果和收阅人关系不熟或是收阅人属于上级,应避免使用附言,而是把其合理安排于正文之中。附件提示即提醒收阅人查收该信函的附件。可直接用"Enclosure"表示此信函附有附件,或用"Enclosure（number）"的形式表示此信函附件的数量,数量由"number"部分表示;还可以用"Enclosure:Subject"的形式表示出附件的题目或主要内容。Enclosure

有时缩写为 Encl. 或 Enc.，如：

  Enclosure（2）：表示此封信有两份附件

  Encl. Quality Certificate：表示此封信的附件为质量证明

  Two Enclosures：

    ①The Application Form

    2. School Report 表示此封信有两份附件，一份为申请表格，一份为成绩单

  （9）抄送提示（Distribution Notice）。通常情况下，若一封信函发给多个收阅人，要根据情况通知最主要的收阅人此封信的副本另外发给的个人姓名。

  可用 Copy，C 或 CC（Carbon Copy），cc 表示，置于附件信息的下面，如：

  Copy：V. R. Natajan

  C：V. R. Natajan

  CC：Carol King

  cc：Carol King

  （10）打字员身份确认（Identification of Typist）。有时，正式信函的打印者并不是发信人本人，发信人可能只是在信打印好之后审阅同意而签上姓名，此时就需要注明打印人信息。通常用发信人姓名大写开头字母后加冒号或斜线，再加打印人姓名小写开头字母，如：CB：lg 或 CB/lg 可表示发信人为 Charry Benston，此信由 Linn Gleen 打印。

  另外，若信件超过一页，只有第一页需要用信头纸。从第二页开始在左上角标明页码，页码下注明日期。确保最后一页至少有三行内容，否则，利用排版技巧压缩或延展前面的内容。

  一般英文信函模板：

```
Company/Organization's Name
Address
Telephone & Fax
（空一至两行）


Date（Month Day, year）
（空两到四行）
```

Receiver's Name
Receiver's Title
Receiver's Address
(空一行)
Dear Sir or Madam：
(空两行)

Text Body (正文对齐顶格号) _____
_____

(段落之间空一行)
_____
_____

(空两行)

Yours truly,
(空两至四行,用于手写签名)

Sender's Printed Name, Title
(空两行)

Enclosure
(空两行)

CC：

一般英文信函举例：

信头公司名称大写 公司地址	STRENGTHEN & FRESON CO. ,LTD. 89 Willian Street New York, NY 10007
对于机构,通常注明 电话及传真信息	Tel: 585 - 303 - 0999 Fax: 585 - 303 - 0998

· 209 ·

隔两行写明日期。	February 12, 2010
隔四行注明收信人信息。	Mr. T. Mara Chris Clerk Solidstone Technical Co., LTD. 366 Blank Street Dallas, TX 75200
首先感谢上封来信,并说明此封信的主要内容,即欢迎奥利维亚先生来此公司实习。	Dear Mr. Chris: Thank you for your letter. We are glad to see your intern worker, Mr. Olivia Barclay who will come here next week.
对本公司的实习项目进行说明,明确奥利维亚先生达到了公司的相关要求。正文简洁明了,没有废话。	The Internship Program Criteria Bulletin specifies a minimum GAP of 3.2 for the year previous to joining the internship Program and a grade of at least 80 percent in the relevant introductory course. Mr. Olivia Barclay has attained the standard and he will be welcome all the time.
	Sincerely yours,
不要忘记手写签名。	Sophie Huang
打印签名部分注明职务。	Ms. Sophie Huang, Human Resources Manager
	Enclosure

第四节 信封的写法

　　信封上的信息一律用大写字母书写并要保证与信中信息一致。发信人地址写于信封的左上角。先写姓名不加职务或头衔,再按从小到大的顺序写出发信人详细地址,最后注明邮编。
　　收件人地址写于信封中央偏右。姓名行要加称谓或头衔。
　　信封上可加入附注信息,写于信封左下角。如该信函需要收信人亲启,可注明"PERSONAL"或"CONFIDENTIAL"的字样,PRIVATE 表示此为私人信件,IMMEDIATE 表示机要信件,URGENT 表示紧急信件等。c/o 表示由某人转收。

如下例：

```
LISA H. BENSTON
71550 GAFIELD STEET
TACOMA, WA 98343

                                                    PLACE
                                                    STAMP
                                                    HERE

            MR. PAUL BOLE
            SALES SERVICE
            FRED MAYER
            6789 MEDERIAN AVENUE
            PUYALLUP, WA 90876

PERSONAL
```

第五节　书信的特殊形式

1. 备忘录

备忘录即录以备忘，是一种简单的书信，在工作和生活中比较常用，即为了以后工作的查阅或是提醒、督促某人要做某项工作而留下的记录，或就某个问题提出看法或意见。备忘录一般不需要邮寄，而是转交或是直接放在或贴在办公室比较醒目的位置。收发备忘录的双方多属同一机构中的同级，表示礼貌的客套话通常省略。如需向上级传达信息或是在比较正式的情况下，建议使用一般书信而非备忘录。

有很多公司或组织备有印好的专用备忘录用纸，上面印有该机构的基本信息，如名称，地址、联系方式等，并标明书写日期、备忘录收发人、备忘录标题等信息的位置。

具体来讲，备忘录主要由三部分组成，即题头（Heading）、正文（Body）及其他信息（Miscellaneous Elements）。

题头：

以左对齐的形式，每条信息独立成行，依次书写公司的名称及标志、收阅人姓名及职务、备忘录发文人姓名及职务、备忘录标题、发文日期、发文机关的电话等。在备忘录发出者信息部分，需要亲笔签名或是签上姓名开头字母，表明对此备忘录内容负责。在发文标题前面可加Re，或Docket，Subject等。多用几个词而非句子来表示，目的在于让收阅人在最短时间了解其内容，即时处理。

正文：

正文与书写信件的要求一样，保持版面的美观，注意行间距及留白，如有需要，也为进一步添加或标注信息提供方便。

备忘录开篇要介绍主要内容,即要回顾备忘录要讨论的问题的背景,又要提出主要观点。如:Because of our inability to serve our present and future clients as efficiently as in the past, I recommend we hire an additional claims representative and a part-time receptionist.(主要观点)Last year we did not hire new staff because of the freeze on hiring…(背景)

使用逐条列明的方式可以起到强调的作用,在备忘录中经常被用到。若是要向一个充满疑惑的收阅人说明一个问题,使用逐条列明的方式,从最重要的到一般重要的理由进行说明,要比把其混为一个很长的段落效果更好。另外,在比较长的备忘录中也可使用分级标题,以便让收阅人很快找到最想阅读的部分。

建议一份备忘录只说明一件事,如果是多件事,最好再写多份备忘录。

其他信息:

备忘录和信件一样,也会有附件,抄送等信息,相关要求与书信中的相关内容相同。如备忘录超过一页,相关格式也同书信超过一页的情况。

英文备忘录第1页模板:

Company's Name & Logo(名称大写)
(空一行)
Date:month day,year
(空一行)
To:name
  title
  simple address(邮寄地址)
(空一行)
From:name(亲笔签名或姓名首字母缩写)
  title
  simple address
(空一行)
Subject:
Text Body(<u>左起不空格</u>)
_____
_____
_____

(段落之间空一行)
_____
_____
_____

Enclosure and Others:
Copy:

英文备忘录第2页模板

Page 2（标明页码）
Date：month day，year
（空一行）
Text Body _____
_____
_____
_____

（空一行）
_____
_____
_____
_____

              sincerely,（从此至职务部分
                可以省略）
              (signature)
              Printed Name
              Title

Enclosure：

Copy

英文备忘录实例1：

备忘录的题头，通常事先印好。		**OUTSTANDING LIFE INSURANCE**
	Date：	January 18, 2010
日期和收阅人地址间空一行。	**To**：	Ted Roemer Development Manager Mail Stop 316
备忘录的发文人和收阅人通常来自同一个公司。	**From**：	Ross Ingram R. I. Policy Specialist Mail Stip 567
注明备忘录标题。	**Suject**：	Loan Form Requested

第一句话交代整篇备忘录的主要内容，在此例中告知收阅人可在退休金账户中借款。接着介绍有两种借款，并给出相应的说明，最后提示随备忘录附有借款申请表。	You are entitled to take out a loan from your retirement account. There are general loans and residential loans offered for you. The general loan doesn't require explanations of application and shall be repaid within two years; the residential loan does require explanations of application and shall be repaid with three years. An application form was enclosed in case you with to request one kind of them.
注明附件内容。	Enclosure: Loan application form

英语备忘录实例2：

题目栏中的 critical 表示此会议重要，提醒收阅人注意。	Date: January 20, 2010 To: Production Cell Members Fm: Robert Warner Re: Critical Reorganization Meeting
备忘录开头就告知收阅人参加此会议的重要意义，即参与改组生产部，同时说明会议的时间和地点。第一段开门见山，点明主题。	If you want to participate in the reorganization of our production cells, please make sure you attend the meeting on Wednesday, February 17. It will be held in conference room 9, at 5:00 p.m..
使用黑体标题一目了然，并保证信息简明扼要。需注意的是在备忘录中避免使用过长的句子。	**Agenda items under discussion** The following items will be on our agenda:
使用分条呈现的方式使表达的信息条理清晰，并起到强调的作用。	◇Changing the physical layouts of the cells. ◇Purchasing new equipment. ◇Retraining for cell employees. ◇Reducing rework in the cells. ◇Improving on-time delivery of finished product. If there are other issues that you want to discuss during the meeting, please don't hesitate to raise them.

最后详细说明此会议的重要意义。整篇备忘录的信息以倒序的方式呈现,先是最新的关于开会的信息,再介绍相关的背景,意在第一时间让收阅人对此备忘录重视起来。	**Importance of the meeting** As you know, we have been receiving a great deal of pressure from top management to improve manufacturing operations. Over the past nine months, quality problems have increased rework has also been on the rise, and the customers have been complaining about reveiving products late. Now we have an opportunity to deal with all of these issues, but only if you attend this meeting and give us your opinions. I look forward to seeing you there.

2. 电子邮件

因为高速便捷经济的特点,电子邮件正有取代纸质邮件之势,收发电子邮件也已经变成现代人每天生活的一部分。虽然发一封电子邮件非常容易,但书写电子邮件仍然需要构思完整,字斟句酌,并认真修改和检查。轻易发出的电子邮件可能会造成难以挽回的损失或失误,因此,要谨慎使用电子邮件,并要像对待其他邮件一样认真。具体来讲,需注意以下几点:

(1) 句子开头第一个字母不能小写,不要用 i 代替 I,u 代替 you,以及避免其他不规范的缩写及表情符号。

(2) 在发邮件之前,首先要考虑用电子邮件这种沟通方式是否恰当得体。电子邮件的篇幅不能过长,有时面对面的交谈或是打电话可能效果更好,比较机密敏感的内容也不适合使用电子邮件。

(3) 确保自动签名包括发信人的各种必要信息。

工作中正式的电子邮件不同于私人邮件,遵循着固定的格式。电子邮件主要包括题头、正文、签名档及附件四个部分。

题头:

题头包括发信日期、发信人电子信箱地址、收信人电子信箱地址、抄送地址(CC 或 cc)、匿名抄送(BC,BCC)(Blind Copy)地址及邮件题目栏。其中发信日期及发信人电子信箱地址由电脑软件自动生成,其他部分则需要仔细填写,因为任何小的错误都可能导致电子邮件的发送失败。注意题目栏书写要规范,不要加入过多复杂的标点符号,更不要空着不写,以免被当成垃圾邮件或是病毒邮件被邮件过滤器直接筛选出来转移到垃圾文件夹或是被收件人直接删除。清晰明了反映邮件中心思想的题目还可以为收件人节约时间,提高工作效率。另外,要在题目栏尽可能地吸引收件人的注意力,可使用大写或感叹号,如:ATTENTION! Late warehouse deliveries!

正文:

正文书写的要求同书信及备忘录。多数邮件软件可支持长达 25 页的邮件,但通常情况下电子邮件不会很长。

签名档：

签名档即信的结尾，包括发信人的姓名、职务、地址、电话、传真、邮编等，也包含一些结束语，比如："Thank you"，"Sincerely，"等。

附件：

随着网络技术的强大，一封电子邮件可以附加的附件容量越来越大。为了保持文件的排版不发生变化，可以在电子邮件中附加各种文字文件。另外，除了文字文件可以作为附件随发，一些图像文件，影音文件也可以附于电子邮件之中，十分便捷。发送附件时要注意该文件是否可以成功打开，提醒收件人查收相应附件，并且最好避免在一封邮件中附加多个过大的附件。

还需注意的是电子邮件的整体外观，如字体最好使用 12 号或 14 号的 Times New Roman 或 Courier 字体以易于阅读，避免使用花哨样式的字体；不要通篇使用大写字母，那样会给阅读带来麻烦；不要通篇使用小写字母，在各种正式的书信中都要做到书写规范；保持段落长短均衡，避免邮件很长只有一段；段与段之间要空一行，要强调一句话时也可此句话独立成段；可以适当地使用实心圆点等项目符号，条理分明；对于强调的部分可以使用黑体或斜体等。

电子邮件模板：

```
Date：weekday，day month year time（电脑自动生成）
From：Sender ＜sendername@ internet. com＞（电脑自动生成）
To   ：Receiver ＜receivername@ internet. com＞
      Other Receiver ＜otherreceivername@ internet. com＞（可多于一个）
Cc   ：＜copytosomeone@ internet. com＞
Bc   ：＜copywithoutnotifingreceiver@ internet. com＞
Subject：Topic of E-mail

Text Body _____
_____

（空一至两行）
_____
_____

（若带有附件，提醒收件人查收）
Sincerely yours，

Name
Title
Address
Telephone & Fax
```

电子邮件英文实例 1：

日期和发信人系统自动生成	Date：Mon,18 January 2010 15:15.1 From：Martin ＜mata@ internet. com＞ To ：Lee ＜leela@ internet. com＞ 　　　Thomas ＜tommie@ internet. com＞
抄送和暗送地址要书写正确，避免不必要的麻烦。	Cc　：＜lizhen@ internet. com＞ Bc　：＜maggieliu@ internet. com＞ Subject：Something Wrong in Storage Unit 8
首先交代邮件最主要的信息，告知收信人仓库屋顶漏水需尽快维修解决。	There is something wrong in the storage unit in which the goods are located. Some water keeps leaking from the roof and that may cause some damage after the hard rains.
注意邮件美观，注意留白。	Would you please come to my office at your convenience so that we can discuss how to solve the problem. I attach the ichnography of the storage unit to this email and I hope that will do some help. If you should have any questions, don't hesitate to contact me.
通过设置，发信人信息可以自动生成	Thank you, Martin Aniston Maintenance Manager 755 Office Building 253 – 466 – 909

电子邮件英文实例 2：

	Date：Mon,8 January 2010 18:05.1 From：Liv ＜Liva@ internet. com＞ To ：Joean ＜Joeana@ internet. com＞ Cc　：＜lizhen@ internet. com＞ Bc　：＜manager@ internet. com＞
题目醒目清晰，易引起注意。	Subject：ATTENTION! Updating Presentation Program
第一句话点明主题。句子不长，语言简单易读。	Several students have recently e-mailed me to say that our current program in presentation skills needs updating. Specifically, our instructors should spend far more time explaining how to create visual aids with software such as PowerPoint. I think we need to revamp our program immediately.

解释所述事件的重要性,同时也表明此邮件需要收信人重视。	Since the students are our only customers, we must take any criticism they make seriously. The presentation skills program must be as relevant to their needs as possible.
提出问题的解决方法。	I think we need to put together a team as soon as possible to revamp our current presentation skills program and add a large component about developing visual aids with software such as PowerPoint. I would be happy to lead this team. Thank you, Thomas King Technology Manager 606 Office Building 253-400-900

第六节　传　真

随着社会的发展,传真的使用变得越来越普遍。传真最突出的特点就是快速,甚至有时比电子邮件还要快。这是因为若是遇到网络拥堵,收一封电子邮件可能需要几个小时,但是传真即时就可收到。另外,可以在给某人打电话的过程中给其发传真传输一封文件,几秒钟后对方即可收到,双方可立即对该文章进行讨论。

虽然发传真十分简单,但在撰写传真的过程中仍需注意以下几点:

(1)在传真第一页的顶端注明发文人的姓名、地址、电话号码及传真号码等信息;写清此份传真的总页数以便收传真方核实。

(2)写明收传真方的姓名、职务、所在机构及传真号码。

(3)注明传真的主题及是否紧急。收传真方可能同时接收到很多传真,而标明紧急字样的会先被阅读,以免耽误要事。

(4)传真的每一页都要标明页码。

(5)若传真内容十分重要或属机密内容,最好先致电对方,确认是否做好接收的准备,并在传真发出后再次致电,确认传真被相关人士收到。

通常传真要有一个首页,相当于信头,有利于传真的收藏及管理。

以下为一传真首页,仅供参考:

Fax	
To:	From:
Company:	Pages:(including this cover sheet)
Fax:	Date:

传真的目的就是即时传递最重要的信息,因此有时在传真中可以使用短语来代替完整的句子。一篇短小的传真信息,开头可如下所示:

Reaction to your proposal. Robert said No - too costly. Bright liked it, but thought it should be tested first …

和正式的书信相比,传真不需要开篇的称呼,也不需要在结尾处签名。

传真形式多变,有时也允许手写。比较常见的是传真的大部分内容为打印,而在重要的部分及结尾手写需要注意的内容。

以下实例,仅供参考:

传真的开头,注明收发人的信息,传真页码及日期等。	To: Jason King		From: Simon Hilton
	Company: Necor Company		Pages: 2 (including this cover sheet)
此传真为纺织品的报价单,询问对方是否可以接受相关报价以继续合作。	Fax: 253 - 990 - 0987		Date: March 12, 2010
	Here is the quotation you requested for the Rose textile. My embroiderer and I have worked on it to assess the time it will take to do the work. This is a major job on which I will have to bear substantial labor and material costs - so I must ask you for acceptance in writing, and a third of the payment in advance. I hope the fair went well. Detailed quotation follows on next sheet.		
若超过一页,每页传真都需标明页码。 首先注明发传真人详细信息。	Page 2: Simon Hilton 403 Garfield Street, Tacoma WA 98400 Tel: 253 - 990 - 0987; Fax: 253 - 990 - 0987		

遵循信件的格式,此处为收传真人的详细信息。
 	
第二页为详细报价单。
	March 12, 2010
	Jason King
	Necor Company
	123 Lakewood Street
	Puyallup, WA 98300
	
	       ESTIMATE
	     To Conserve Embroidery
	
	Embroidery with Rose Pattern
	
	Patch the holes with suitable linen fabric. Conserve the existing embroidery. Line with linen and attach velcro strip.
	
	            Materials $ 7,000
	            Labor $ 2,000
	            VAT $ 525
	            Total $ 9,525
	
	VAT No: 12345667
	
	Terms
	
	Acceptance in writing. First $2,000 payable in advance. Insured at owner's risk. job.

第七节　其他各种类型的书信

1. 传递信息类书信

  大多数书信都属于传递信息类,即对相关的信息发出要求或做出答复。对于信息的要求或答复分为两类,一般请求及答复和特殊请求及答复。

  一般请求即一方向另一方提出某种要求,回复此类请求比较简单。有时回复此类请求对本身有益,如客户需要某种产品的信息,销售人员向潜在客户介绍该产品。此类请求信如下例所示:

一般请求的电子邮件：

	Date： 20 Jan 2009 09:23.12 From： Ciasinc@hotmail.com To ： Electronicscm@gmail.com Subject：Request for Information on Fuel Device
因不知明确的收信人,信的开头部分省去了称呼及问候。 第一句话就点名了整封信的目的,即索要某种型号的产品的如下信息。	
	Please send me the following information about your new electric fuel device, type TY321I.
逐点列出问题,比较清晰,也暗示收信人请逐点回答问题。	1. Can it be located anywhere and in any position? 2. Does it come with a locating bracket? 3. Does it operate independently of the engine? 4. How many pounds of pressure does it adjust to?
发出请求要具体,否则收到的回复可能毫无价值。 同时注意语法用词准确得体。	If you have information available that answers these questions, I would be pleased to receive it.
由于发信人的身份和立场,整封信省去了自我介绍和客套,因发信人确认此信会被认真对待。	Thank you, Victor Stanneen Sales Manager Ciasinc Company 1356 Garfield Street Tacoma, WA 98443

另一方面,书写特殊请求信件则不那么简单,如需要对方完成某种任务,或是回复此请求对于对方并没有直接利益,因此书写此类信件尤其要注意用词得体。发出及回复特殊请求的书信如下例：

以一般书信形式发出的特殊请求范例：

发信人地址及其他信息。	78 Neeleen Street Miracle Technical College Bailey Springs, MS 93922 12 February, 2009
收信人地址及其他信息。	Mr. Michael Brady Manager of Human Resources Ale West Transport Company

· 221 ·

2000 Evergreen Avenue E

Menphis, TN 28888

Dear Mr. Brady:

I am a technology student at Miracle Technical College. I am writing a paper for my Transportation Communication 2678 class on how firms such as yours screen for employment recent graduates of college programs.

I have done library and Internet research on the subject, but I want to augment them with information collected from some of the larger firms in the area. The results of my study will be shared with my classmates. I would also be happy to send a copy of my final report to you.

Would you please spend some time answering the following questions about the way you firm screens employees?
1. What priorities do you place on applicants' academic performance, experience and on campus interviews?
2. What do you expect of applicants' behavior and dress when they report for an interview?
3. How much importance for you place on recommendations from faculty, school officials, and previous employers?

My report is due 19 May. I appreciate your taking the time to read my letter and hope to receive a reply from you in early May.

Kelly Keon
Kelly Keon

在此封邮件中，发信人首先介绍自己的身份，希望得到对方的信任，并说服对方提供书写论文的过程中所需的相关的信息资料。

对于收阅人，发信人能做的即是把此研究成果与同学分享，无形中为该公司做了免费广告，并把写好的报告副本发给收阅人，供研究参考。发信人以此说服对方给予自己帮助。

整篇书信用语礼貌谦逊。发出特殊请求都要做到这样。

给出详细的时间，期待对方在有效时间内给出答复。在此例中并没有使用"Thanking you in advance."作为结尾，礼貌谦逊也要讲求适度，避免过犹不及。

· 222 ·

以一般书信形式发出的特殊请求回复范例:

	ALE WEST TRANSPORT COMPANY 2000 Evergreen Avenue E · Memphis, TN 28888 26 April, 2009 Ms. Kelly Keon 78 Neeleen Street Miracle Technical College Bailey Springs, MS 93922 Dear Ms. Keon: It's my pleasure to answer your questions on how we screen applicants who are recent college graduates. I will take your questions in the order you ask them.
根据对方的要求,逐条回答问题,显示出专业水准。尽管对本公司好处有限,此封信也给出相关问题的详细回答,表现出大公司的风范。	1. Our first priority is generally to consider whether the applicant's major field of study fits his or her for the job sought. For instance, we like to hire drivers who have been through an extensive training program, such as those now provided in may three-year college. In descending order, we consider academic performance, work experience, and interviews. The only exception to this priority order might be when someone's extensive work experience makes up for a lack of academic preparation. 2. We expect that applicants come prepared to ask good questions of us and to listen to us as we will listen to them. They should be clean and neat in appearance. 3. Recommendations from people who have worked with the applicant, either on the job or in school, serve primarily as a check on what we find out from an applicant's resume and records and rom the interview process.
根据对方的需要,提供参考建议,赢得对方的感激及尊重。虽然是回复信件,也讲求礼貌,以建立良好的社会形象。	A useful source you may not have fun across in your library search in the Wheel Owner, which frequently publishes information about the hiring and training of employees in our industry. I would be happy to receive a copy of your paper.

· 223 ·

Sincerely,
Michael Brady
Michael Brady Manager of Human Resources

2. 好消息书信

人们都希望收到促进事物良性发展的好消息。如果是这样的书信,要把好消息在书信的开头就传递出去,如:We are pleased to tell you that …; Congratulations on … 等。接着就必要的细节、解释、分析等进行阐述。如果是针对客户的书信,接下来还可以继续建立与客户间的友好关系,促进进一步的合作。如下例所示:

以备忘录形式发出的好消息范例:

	Sheridan Electronics Company
	Date: 27 March,2009 To: Adriana Julian From: Jimmy Maxwell Manager Subject: Council Approval of Childcare Center
此篇备忘录有四个目的。第一个在第一句话交代清楚,即提议被通过。第二个,表达对提议的赞赏,用 quite convincing, particularly impressed 来表达。	Jimmy, I'm delighted to tell you that the Sales Council has approved your committee's recommendation concerning a company childcare center. The case your committee made for it was quite convincing. The Council was particularly impressed by your figures on the number of mothers working in the company with preschool children.
第三个,希望给计划定下时间表,建议和收阅人制定时间会面已就具体实施过程进行讨论。	As you requested, Human Resources will be in charge of the project. The Council hopes you can have the center in place by June 1. I will be your coordinator with the Council for space and funding. Please schedule an hour's appointment with me at your earliest convenience.

最后,再次表达祝贺,建立与收阅人良好关系,对其进行鼓励,为该项目顺利进行创造条件。	Once again, congratulations to you and your committee. You have already put much time and enthusiasm into this project. The Council knows you will continue your good efforts in carrying your plans through to completion.

3. 坏消息书信

工作中的书信难免也会传递不好的信息,比如告诉某人提薪晋升未被通过,某项目无法按计划进行等。书写这样的书信更需要技巧。通常是开篇表达友好礼貌,接着客观公正地分析或解释存在的问题及碰到的困难,然后很自然地过渡,清楚地陈述不尽如人意的消息并提供可能的补救方式或其他的选择,最后友好地收尾。具体如下例所示:

以一般书写形式发出的坏消息范例:

此例中,该书信有两个目的。一个是让对方明白此种情况不在保修范围内,另一个是保持与对方之间良好的关系。此信需要向对方解释清楚造成该问题的原因并不伤害对方的感情。为避免出现对方不接受此消息的尴尬场面,所以用信件的方式而不选择打电话。该类信件也为纠纷可能产生的诉讼留下有用证据。	**PIERCE APPLIANCE** 3356 West Main Road · Denver, CO 80221 9 May, 2009 Ms. Diana Rein 2212 North Goldengiven Street Denver, CO 80978 Dear Ms. Rein:
整封信的基调公正中性。开篇先是表达感谢,营造友好气氛。	Thank you for your call about your dryer. As you know, following your call, our service representative Sonia Montanian examined your dryer.
第二段,客观指出并分析发现的问题。	She found that the dryer's motor had been overheated so much that it is damaged beyond repair. She also noted that the lint filter was so clogged with lint that it was not functioning properly. As a result, the lint packed into the motor, causing the overheating. At that time, she showed you the warning in your operating manual that points out that failure to clean the lint filter after every use of the dryer may result in overheating and damage to the motor.

第三段,告知坏消息,即对方无法免费更换新的发动机。	Your replacement guarantee covers only defects by the manufacturer and improper installation by us. Since neither was a factor in the motor's overheating, we cannot replace your motor free of charge as you have requested.
第四段,详细陈述其他的解决方案供对方选择采纳。	However, we are anxious to help you get dryer working again. If you want our service representative to install a new motor, please call us. We can bill the installation as a continuing service call at ＄50 rather than the normal installation fee of ＄80, saving you ＄30. The cost of the motor itself is ＄220, so your total cost would be ＄270.
最后,表达友好及礼貌。	We value you as a customer, and we hope that our solution for replacing your motor will be acceptable to you.
	Sincerely, **Jason Mineon** Jason Mineon Sales Manager

4. 求职信

除了递交简历,有时还需随简历一起递交求职申请信来表达诚意,提高被雇佣的几率。书写求职信需注意以下几点:

(1)整洁,准确,书写规范。求职信需使用打印版,所用纸张质量要好,即保证一定的厚度及白度,并且避免使用学校或单位的抬头纸。

(2)尽量把信发到具体的个人以表达诚意。为获得相关信息可以给该雇佣单位打电话询问或是上网查询。

(3)在信的开头部分,介绍要应聘的职位及相关信息,及如何获得该应聘信息等。求职信中要注意用词的礼貌谦逊又不失自信。

(4)在信中交代清楚目前所处的受教育及工作情况。如正在上学,需要说明毕业的时间或可以开始工作的时间。

(5)在求职信中应体现出对该应聘单位的了解,让雇佣者看出应聘人对该职位的诚意。

(6)加深对雇佣者的了解可以帮助选取合适且有帮助的信息。用具体的事实来说明,而不是简单发表自己的想法。教授或前任雇主的推荐信(Reference Letter)有很强的说服力。求职信中也要交代自己的受教育经历及工作经历,以及与应聘工作有关的业余爱好或特长。这一部分可能与简历有交叉的部分,要做到体现出整个简历最重要的部分。

(7)若是针对一个招聘广告来写求职信,写信时不妨把招聘广告放在旁边,确保求职信中包含招聘广告中出现的关键词,如所需的教育程度,资格证书等。若广告中提到需要应聘者具备某些素质,如可以使用最新版本的软件系统,良好的人际关系,团队精神,沟通能力,解决问题的能力等,避免简单陈述自己具备此类能力,而是用具体的事例来说明。避免使用概括性的词语,如:I am an advanced skilled sales person 而要说:Last winter I made a ＄20000 sales in the company. 具体的时间地点及数字更加有说服力。同时要做到实事求是。在当今世界,信息发达,许多公司在招聘过程中会对应聘人做出实地调查,来保证获得信息的可靠。

(8)在求职信的结尾部分,提醒收信人如需更多信息可参看附加的简历或与本人联系,而且要努力争取面试的机会,并最大程度地考虑到雇佣者在时间和地点等方面上的方便。

(9)求职信避免使用复印版。对于每个招聘广告,求职信都会有所侧重,每封求职信都不同。从清晰度上来看,打印版更加可取。

概括来讲,求职信主要分为两大类,一类为 the invited or solicited letter,即针对招聘广告而写出的求职信;另一类为 uninvited, prospecting or query letter,即毛遂自荐向雇佣单位推荐自己的求职信。对于收阅人来说,第一类为好消息信件。公司投入资金招聘人才期待收到回信。因此,写第一类的求职信可以开门见山,说明自己要应聘该职位,解释为什么对该职位感兴趣,自己的资质如何胜任该职位,提供简历及其他相关推荐材料并争取面试机会。而对于第二类的求职信,首先要询问该公司是否有空缺的职位,如果目前没有,什么时候会有,然后和第一类相同,解释应聘的原因,自己的资质等。第二类求职信不是被期待的信件,所以建议发信后可致电相关人士,确定该信被阅读。具体实例如下:

招聘广告回复型求职信例1:

写明收信的具体个人。	Dear Madam Jane:
此信开门见山,交代获得招聘信息的方式并对自己的基本情况作出简要的解释。	Your advertisement in the Kent News for a Senior Environmental Officer caught my attention, since my qulifications match those you are seeking. As a student graduating with a B. Eng in Environmental Engineering from the University of Washington, I would like to apply for the position.
进一步陈述自己与该职位要求有关的经历及能力。	Beyond my specialist academic program, I have has relevant environmental field experience. As my resume indicats, I have spent two summers working with Professor Sonia Leachc in the laboratory and in the wetlands. I also enjoy and am used to the kind of outdoor work you require. In my frst summer as a university student, I worked as a tree planter in harsh conditions in northern British Columbia. If there is work available in Italian, I am able to speak Italian well enough to converse with your Italian-speaking clients.

最后争取面试的机会,也是本封信的目的所在。	I would appreciate the chance to discuss with you how I could contribute to Outlands Developments. Please call or e-mail me to arrange an interview at your convenience. I look forward to hearing from you. Sincerely, Momah Kinson (signature)

招聘广告回复型求职信例2:

	2010 7th Park Street, Boise City, ID 84700 February 2, 2010
发信具体到个人。	Ms. Lexin Fommer MoonSpheer Laboratories, Inc. 11100 Goldengiven Avenue Houston, TX 39099
如实在不知道收信人的姓名,在此例中也可用"Dear MoonSpheer"来代替。	Dear Ms. Fommer:
第一段,清楚地陈述发信目的即应聘经理的职位职位及获得此信息的途径。有时一个公司发出的招聘广告会提供很多招聘岗位,因此具体说明很有必要。	I am applying for the positon of Manager, Chemical Marketing in your office, which was listed on your Web site.
第二段,描述自己目前的情况,确保毕业时间与工作要求的时间相符。	I will graduate from Kent Technical University on 20 June with a Bachelor of Chemical Engineering degree and an overal GPA of 3.4 on a 4.0 scale. My GPA in chemical engineering and supporting course work in chemistry is 3.55.

第三段,说明此职位对自己有吸引力的原因。此例中,发文人不但说明了这一点还让雇主看出该应聘者对于该公司的关注程度,做足了功课。同时说明自己可以胜任该职位的资质。此段为整封信的核心部分。介绍教育背景及工作经历。需要注意的是简历只是一些关键信息的简单的概括,而在求职信中可以就各信息进行具体详细的说明。	After visiting your website and reading an article about Moonspheer in a recent issue of Fortune, I am eager to join your new marketing team. Your company's plan to expand by promoting new fire-suppressant chemical products is particularly interesting to me. My formal educaion in chemistry and chemical engineering, my training in the U. S. Army, and my three years of experience working for the Boise City Fire Department with fire suppressant chemicals should give me the specializations you call for in this position. As a graduate of the Teamwork Leadership School in Kent, Washington, and as a unit supervisor for the BAFG, I believe I have both the training and hands-on experience to provide leadership for sales and service representatives and to work with other marketing staff. Fluent in Germany, I believe I can be very effective in developing and maintaining corporate-client relationshps in German. I am quite familiar with the culture in most parts of the world. The travel requirements are no obstacle for me.
第四段,提醒可参阅其他相关材料。在欧美国家中很流行使用 portfolio,即所做工作的作品集,这最能体现出某人的工作成绩。	Please see my enclosed resume for additional information about my qualificationsand the names of persons who are willing to provide recommendations for me. If interviewed, I can also bring a portfolio of my major school projects, including a marketing research paper that reports the results of my research on how Luke's Condiments Company of Atlanta, Georgia, introduced a new line of Germany goods, including Luke's Mixings and Luke's Seasoned Salt. Part of the background reserch also involved researching the impact of the growing Germany population on the U. S. economy.
第五段,以申请面试作为信的结尾。在此封信中,为了回应招聘广告中提到的要应征者说明对酬薪的要求,发文人灵活得体地做出回答,值得借鉴。	I am fairly flexible on beginning salary, although I expect compensation in line with wht others in similar positons are paid. Given that, I will be happy to discuss my salary requirements with you during an interview. I am, quite frankly, more interested in discussing the opportunity to contribute to Moonspheer's future. I look forward to meeting with you to discuss this opportunity.

	Sincerely,
	Benny Monnet
	Benny Monnet
提醒发文人此信包含附件。	Enclosure：resume and list of references

非招聘广告回复型求职信范例：

写清发信人地址。	887 Burkin Avenue Lubbock，TX 83567
书写日期是，月日年或日月年的顺序均可。	21 April，2009
对于不是针对招聘广告而发出的求职信，十分容易被收阅人忽略或是被当成垃圾邮件删除，因此应确保获得收信人的明确信息。	Charry Beston，Executive Manager Greentree Tourism Company 3456 Mississp Avenue Bishopsville，ME 34212 Dear Mrs. Beston
第一段，陈述此封信的目的。虽然此封信是在毛遂自荐，但应避免过于谦卑，如开篇就道歉，I apologize for taking your valuable time…因为如果这样开头会更让人反感。	I am writing to inquire about available full-time positions with the Greentree Tourism Company. I will be graduating in July with a degree in English，specializing in technical communication and supporting course work in museum studies. After graduation I plan to return to Ponk，and I am interested in pursuing a carreer in which I can use my research，writing，and design skills and my experience as a museum technician.
第二段，表达出自己对此公司的了解和关注，与收阅人拉近距离。	In visiting the Company's Web site，I was impressed by the broad array of functions covered by the Company. Many of its new initiatives involving displays and interpreting art works，cultural objects，and other artifacts of Native American Merican Indians，the American Revolutionary War，and the early year years of maritime commerce appeal to my interests in working as an exhibit specialist，museum technician，and technical communicator.

第三段,用具体的实例来说明胜任此职位。要找到恰当的实例,首先要对应聘的公司有充分的了解。此例中,可以看出发信人事先做了详尽的调查。	My experience as a volunteer docent at the Flains Museum of Texas in Luxas, ranges from working on grant proposals to procure external funding for expanding the pioneer ranch section to preparing informational signs for museum visitors to leading tours and classes for public-school children. The grant proposal led to a $10,000 grant from the Client Traval Foundation of Fort Worth, Texas to purchase and relocate two large windmills to the museum's external exhibition area.
第四段,描述自己早期的受教育经历。里面的地点,机构名称都很具体,供收信人考证。	Although my university education and training have been in Texas, I spent two summers during my high-school years working on research projects for the Kenndy Foundation in Luukport and was an associate member of the Mine Historical Society. My reseach on the illustraions of Newexell in Kenndy's novels culminated in a presentation to the City Council of Luukport, which particallly funded a research trip for me to Chillis Ford, Pennsylvania-Wyeth's home and the location of the Wyeth Gallery-to work further on the topic.
第五段,进一步用实例说明自己的工作能力。	In the course of my education and experience, I have developed a portfolio of documents and presentations, which includes grant proposals, style sheets, guidelines for visitors to the Luukport, an article based on my interview with the chief editor the Travel magazine, and a MS PowerPoint presentation on onlie editing. This material may be accessed by going to my Web site, www. applicant. edu. Doing volunteer work and major class projects, I have learned to work within guidelines and also to work independently on projects. I can work under tight deadlines and with limited resources to accomplish goals.
第六段,与第一段进行呼应,期待回复。	I would welcome the opportunity to contribute to the work of the Greentree Tourist Company and will call you during the first week of March to discuss that possibility. If you would like to contact me sooner, you can reach me at 253.777.999 or benterry@mail.com. Sincerely, **Tonny Benteery** Tonny Benteery
建议使用功能简历,更加强调相关的工作能力。	Enclosure: Resume and List of References

5. 面试后续信及感谢信

在面试后可立即发出面试后续信来表达感谢,在众多应征者中脱颖而出,也可显示出专业素质,抓住最后的机会说服雇主聘用自己。

面试后续信范例:

	676 5th Street, Puyallup, WA 98400 February 2, 2010 Ms. Linnet Breton Sunbright Labratories Company 567 Mountain Raineer Avenue Kent, WA 98778 Dear Ms. Breton:
第一段,开篇感谢对方提供面试机会。再次提到应聘的具体岗位及自己对该岗位的无限向往。	Thank you for the opportunity to interview with Sunbright for the assistant manager, chemical marketing position. My visit with you and Foss Glan and Rachel Pernol has increased my interest in becoming part of the Sunbright marketing team.
第二段,再次提到面试过程中涉及的关键点及相关事项,包括在面试过程中遇到的工作人员及具体的谈论内容。	I enjoyed the tour of Sunbright's headquarters building and the opportunity to talk with Foss Glan and Rache Pernol about the new fire-suppressant chemical products. If I am hired, I would like to follow up on Rachel Pernol's suggestion that I consider enrolling in ground school for polots at the Qwest Flying Service. I can seehowflying rental aircraft to visit the many clients throughout the Southwest is a real time- and money-saver. A few years ago I thought seriously about taking flying lessons aspart of my emergency responder training for the Puyallup City Fire Department. I would welcome the chance to take them now.
第三段,介绍面试对自己的影响及自己在此过程中的受益。如果面试官或相关人员提供了关于工作的重要信息或关于应聘单位的介绍及见解,在这个部分就要表达出自己的欣赏之情。整封信的目的就是要让雇主加深印象,让其了解对于其说的话,都很用心听用心记。	You comments about building a new network of knowledge culture in which evertbody in the organization, not just the R&D people, would be expected to contribute ideas were especially exciting to me. I have reaad about, but I have never visited an organization where all exployees were introduced to all the different areas of the organization where all exployees wereintroduced to all the different areas of the organization-unitil my visit to Sunbright. And I appreciate your suggestion that I read Ron's The Modern Times of Technology. I have already checked out a copy from our library and have begun reading it.

第四段,给出关于发信人日程安排及联系方式的更多细节。	I am in classes until 10 May. After that I will be taking exams through 20 May. I am scheduled to go backpacking on 21 and 22 May and beback for graduation on May 23. On May 21 and 22, I can be reached by cell phone, 253-788-0988. I look forward to hearing from you. Sincerely, **Pheoben Buffett** Pheoben Buffett

6. 推荐信请求信

在找工作的过程中,如果求职信中附上学校或工作单位领导的推荐信会很有说服力,以下所示即一名学生向曾经工作的博物院发出的推荐信请求信。

明确具体收信人。	890 Lonkon Avenue Lubbock, TX 79809 March 10, 2010 Mr. Jason Morthen, Assistant Director Knowledge Museun of West Taxas 4533 North 32th Street Lubbock, TX 79823
第一段,说明此封信的主要内容和目的。	Dear Mr. Morthen: I am writing to request permission to use you as a reference during my current job search.
第二段,用具体的陈述帮助收阅人回忆自己曾经的工作经历。	I have served as a volunteer docent at the Knowledge Museum since August 2008, leading tours and classes for public-school children. In addition, during the school year 2008~2009, I edited a grant proposal that was successful in procuring $20,000 for the purchase and relocation of two windmills from the old Merchant Lanch to the museum's external exhibition area. I also developed a slide show presentation on the Knowledge Museum of West Texas and created many of the informational signs used throughout the museum.
第三段,提供自己应聘的具体信息。有时也可提及需要推荐信的具体时间,建议对方尽快答复。	I will graduate from Texas College with a B. A. in English in Ma. I hope to find a position in a museum or state or national recreation area or park where I can design and write descriptions for the displays.

第四段,提醒对方此信附上简历,加强可信度。 因为此信需要对方帮忙,所以不用 Sincerely 而用 Thank you,更加恰当。	I have enclosed a copy of my resume to bring you up to date on my activities. I will call you next week to confirm that I may use you as a reference, or if you want me tosend you an e-mail before then I can be reached at Donglucy@ texasuinversity. edu. Thank you, **Lucy Dong** Lucy Dong Enclosure: Resume

若得到对方的帮助,如为自己提供推荐信等,应回信表示感谢。
感谢信范例:

	890 Lonkon Avenue Lubbock, TX 79809 March 10, 2010 Mr. Jason Morthen, Assistant Director Knowledge Museun of West Taxas 4533 North 32th Street Lubbock, TX 79823 Dear Mr. Morthen:
第一段,感谢对方提供的帮助。	Thank you so much for providing letters of recommendation for mw.
第二和第三段,告诉对方通过有效的竞聘和对方的帮助自己最新的情况。	I have accepted a position as Communication Specialist with the Greentree Tourism Company in Bishopsville, Maine. I will be working with the Company's Display Coordinator in designing and writing the information boards for all the displays at historical sites in the State Recreation Areas in Maine. I begin work next week, and I am looking forward to relocating back to my home state.
第四段,再次表达感谢。感谢信不需要很长,充分表达出诚意和感谢即可。	Again, thank you for the recommendation.

	Sincerely,
	Lucy Dong
	Lucy Dong

7. 接受信

当收到回复获知得到所申请的工作时,应立刻给予回复并打电话致谢确认表示接受所提供的机会。具体来讲,首先要表示十分荣幸被给予该工作机会,确认接受的具体工作并恰当地提及报酬避免在关键问题上产生误解。接着,具体地讨论到新的岗位报到及开始工作的时间,相关细节可结合面试时双方的谈话内容。最后表达出十分期待在新的岗位工作。以下为一实例:

工作机会接受信范例:

	2345 Canyon Street Beechwood, OH 45480 March 20, 2010
通过努力最后获得工作计划十分不容易,因此,接受工作机会的接受信其目的就是进一步确认被聘用的事实,保证获得此职位。	Mr. E. F. Brown Personnel Manager Taxtile Industries, Inc. 3322 Garfield Parke Drive Bintonville, MI 49888 Dear Mr. Brown:
首先,表达自己的兴奋之情及确认所得岗位的相关重要信息。	I am pleased to accept your offer of a position as assistant personnel manager at a salary of $3,000 per month.
接着,就接手相关工作的时间等信息做具体讨论。	Since graduation is August 10, I plan to leave Dayton on Monday, August 26. I should be able to locate suitable living accommodations within a few days and be ready to report for work on the following Monday, September 2. Please let me know if this date is satisfactory to you.
最后,再次表示期待早日获得进一步的信息以开始工作。	I look forward to a rewarding future with Textile. Sincerely, **Simon Smith** Simon Smith

8. 确认信

当收到了某文件或是其他邮寄物品,写一封确认信有时是十分必要并具专业性的做法。确认信要短小注意礼节表达感谢。如下所示:

确认信范例:

信头	Power Saving System 209 Springriver Street Phoenix, AZ 85300
日期	March 1, 2010
信内地址	Ms. Roger Smith, Associate Consultant 878 Northface Road Phoenix, AZ 85320
第一段,表示收到了相关文件,文件保持完好,并表达感谢。 第二段,交代进一步的收发计划。 此封信短小精悍,作用却十分重要。	Dear Ms. Smith: I received your document today; it appears to be complete and well done. Thank you for sending it so promptly. When I finish studying the document, I will send you our cost estimate for the installation of the Pattern I Power-Saving System. Sincerely, **Robert Warner** Robert Warner Sales Manager

9. 推荐信

在日常生活中时常会受同事或朋友所托写封推荐信。推荐信的用途十分广泛,从帮助某人成功录取入学到详细描述某人的专业成就及个人性格以帮助其找到合适的工作。

要想写出有效的推荐信,首先要对申请人的能力和表现有足够的了解,才能客观而真实地给出评价。推荐信可以作为有效的选拔工具,因此必须要写清申请人的与申请职位有关的技术、能力、知识水平及性格特点等,有时也要包含申请人的工作情况,历史记录如当兵记录等。

在推荐信中,往往有具体的问题需要直接回答,并要包括发信人的各种信息,如:姓名、职务、头衔、雇主、联系方式等以加强此封信的可信程度。在信中要写清认识申请人的时间长短及原因,能够表明申请人才干的具体实例,把最重要的最打动人的写在最前面。最后做出一个对于申请人资质的概括。如下所示:

推荐信范例：

	SEATTLE COLLEGE DEPARTMENT OF BUSINESS SEATTLE, WA 98400 January 20, 2010 Mr. Roger Smith Personnel Director Japson Enterprises 502 Street Tacoma, WA 98444
首先，交代发信人身份，认识该申请人的时间以及原因。	Dear Mr. Smith: As her employer and her former professor, I am happy to have the opportunity to recommend Vivian Brown. I've known Vivian for the last four years, first as a student in my class and for the last year as a research assistant.
接着，详细介绍该申请人的具体情况。在此例中是为一名学生写推荐信，故说明该学生的具体学习成绩，课业表现等相关方面的具体情况。	Vivian is an excellent student, with above average grades in our program. On the basis of a CPA of 5.5 (A=6), Vivian was offered a research assistantship to work on a grant under my supervision. In every instance, Vivian completed her library search assignment within the time agreed upon. The material provided in the reports Vivian submitted met the requirements for my work and more. These reports were always well written. While working 15 hours a week on this project, Vivia has maintained a class load of 12 hours per semester.
最后，对该个人给出客观的评价，说服收阅人相信该个人能够胜任其所申请的工作。	I strongly recommend Vivian for her ability to work independently, to organize her time efficiently, and for her ability to write clearly and articulately. Please let me know if I can be of further service.
信尾部分和开头日期对齐。	Sincerely yours, Michael King **Michael King** Professor of Business

10. 技术信息信

技术信息信实际上是小的技术报告,可用备忘录的形式在公司内部使用,或以信件的形式发给另外的公司或机构以介绍某种技术或信息。

技术信息信范例:

	Sparkside Machines Co. 567 Oceanside Drive Tacoma, WA 98666 February 12, 2010 Ms. Linda Gibson Technical Director Components Division Sparkside Machines Co. Pines, NJ 04222 Dear Gibson:
首先,交代此信的中心问题,即有关电脑区块大小限制的技术问题。	We've discovered a problem with our current block size restriction for the Decade 2010 computer.
以下两段进一步说明该问题产生的背景等相关情况并试图给出解决问题的方式。	Many of our internal and customer publications on utility routines state that the Decade 2010 computer is normally restricted to a maximum block length of 4,025 characters, but that this restriction can be lifted by setting Flag 23. This statement is misleading, and I am beginning to wonder if we should take a different approach. As I understand it, the problem is a hardware restriction in that the processor was wired to accommodate a maximum block length of 4,025 characters. This restriction created a problem for FRA users because a FRA track could accept a block of 4,500 characters. The solution was to make a wiring change to make use of the first bit in the second "TA" character of control words, thereby doubling the maximum block length to 4,809. This change was made about two years ago, but existing systems were not modified. Consequently, if a user who has one of the old systems sets Flag 23, the restriction is not going to be lifted as we say it will. A couple of solutions quickly come to mind. We could instruct the user to set the Flag only if his system can accommodate an 2,034-character block (if we assume that he has this information). We could give him the change number of the update to the processor and instruct him to use Flag 29 only if his processor has that number or greater. I propose that we use the second solution because the user is more likely to know his change number than whether he can accommodate an 8,097-character block.

最后,希望收阅人对此情况尽快给予回复。	Since the customer is directly involved, the solution to the problem should probably be approved by your department. Please let me know as quickly as possible whether you approve of this solution because some of our customer manuals are presently being revised. Sincerely yours, **Paul Gleen** Paul Gleen

11. 邀请函

在日常工作中,邀请函十分常见,邀请相关个人参加某个会议或其他活动等。邀请函要包括以下内容:

(1)邀请人的身份。

(2)邀请的事由,如邀请参加某会议、讲座或是座谈会等。

(3)参加活动的简单介绍,包括时间、地点、主题、活动流程及参加人员等,必要时也要对活动费用进行说明。

(4)提供与活动组织者有效的联系方式。

(5)表达希望对方接受邀请的强烈愿望。

邀请函范例:

	Namina Noble 5678 Garfield, Tacoma Paula Leits Chairman B1 Motors Plc Wookland Business Park Birmingland B345ZA March 11, 2010 Dear Leits:
首先介绍邀请人的身份背景及主要事宜。	I heard you speak at this year's BAC conference and I resolved there and then to try to persuade you to address the Workster Round Table. Now the opportunity has arrived.

第二段,表达对收阅人的了解及敬仰,说服对方接受邀请。	Your name is top of our list for one simple reason: I don't believe anyone knows so much about the car industry in the West Woodland. Among our members we have several men and women whose companies supply goods or services to the major vehicle manufacturers in this area, and I know they would be fascinated to hear your views about the future of the indstry, and have the opportunity to ask a few questions.
介绍活动的报酬安排。	As you may know, the Round Table is not in a position to pay guest speakers. Nonetheless, our annual dinners have attracted some notable guests in recent years, including Sir Linson Edward and Roger Hoton.
介绍活动的住宿安排。	We offer a truly excellent dinner-the Walgreen Oak Restaurant being a new entry in this year's Good Food Guide-and a double room for you and your wife if you would like to stay the night. We would be honored if you would both come.
对活动流程进行介绍让收阅人有更多的了解。	We usually hold our annual dinners in the middle of the week, in early Summer, so if you are able to accept, please let me know as soon as possible and we will fix a date. Finally, the timing of your address would be entirely up to you. Most of your guests opt to speak after th main course, but more than one has opted to speak before dinner, on the grounds that this makes the meal more enjoyable. The choice is yours.
最后再次发出诚挚邀请。	I hope you can make space in your diary for the Woodland Round Table. I know that you will rarely find a more appreciative audience. Yours sincerely, Namina Noble Co-ordinator

另外,在日常工作中,接到邀请函后不管是否接受需尽快回复,这是基本的工作礼节。书写邀请函复函要注意以下几点:

(1)对邀请表达感谢。

(2)明确答复对方是否接受邀请。若接受,对对方的具体要求给出明确答复;若不接受,提供可以让对方接受的理由并表示以后若有此机会必将努力参加给予支持。

接受邀请的复函范例:

首先,表达感谢。接着,对于邀请函的各个事宜进行具体回复并提出合理请求。	Dear Breton: It is with the greatest pleasure that I accept your kind invitation to speak at the Round Table. If it s convenient for you, I would prefer to have my talk scheduled in the early July. My topic is the Relationship between automobile and life style and I wish to speak for about forty minutes before the dinner. I will see to it that the hard copy of my paper, the pdf file of the paper as well as the abstract reach you by June 1. My wife would like to take part in it, too.

最后,表示期待早日参加此活动。	If you have any further requirements, please let me know. I am looking forward to seeing you. Yours sincerely, **Paula Leits** Paula Leits

拒绝邀请函的复函范例：

首先表达感谢。 接着给出拒绝邀请的合理理由并提出可能给予的支持。 期待今后再有机会参加此类活动。 最后,预祝该活动圆满成功。	Dear Breton: Thank you very much for your kind invitation to present a talk at the Round Table. But I regret to say that heavy official duties prevent me from having the pleasure to attend the meeting. Anyhow I still wish to have my paper included in the conference proceedings, and please let me know whether it is possible. I do very much hope that I will be able to attend the next conference. I wish the conference a great success. Yours sincerely, **Paula Leits** Paula Leits

第十四章 报 告

第一节 报告的定义

报告就是为了满足某种需要或要求,把一系列信息进行合理组织和编排而成的文体,在工作和学习中十分常见。报告的目的性十分明确。没有人要自己写一篇报告,而都是在别人的要求下才会写。报告是为了明确的目的,为了明确的读者而呈现明确的信息。

写一篇报告之前首先需要明确的是:读者需要什么样的信息,信息的用途是什么,信息怎样排列效果最好等。信息类报告(Informational Report)要说明一项发现,也包括小部分评论及解释;分析类报告(Analytical Report)需呈现事实及分析;劝说类报告(Persuasive Report)要影响读者的看法或行动。而大多数的报告通常包含这三方面目的。

接着,需要仔细考虑到报告的读者。报告对读者的有益程度取决于报告作者满足其兴趣、目的、需求、及对读者理解能力的准确判断程度。若对读者了解深入,往往收到令人满意的效果。通常对于报告会有明确详细的要求,规定了涉及的信息及步骤,在这种情况下书写报告相对简单,按要求即可。对于没有具体要求的报告,仍有原则和规律可以遵循,以下将进行详细说明。

第二节 报告的分类

报告大致分为正式报告(长报告)和非正式报告(短报告)两大类。两类报告的区别并不在长度上,非正式报告也可能会比正式报告长,而是在结构上,正式报告比较规范统一,涉及比较复杂的问题,非正式报告形式比较灵活多变,内容也比较简单。在这里将主要讨论正式报告。

从内容上讲,正式报告主要分为实验报告(Experiment Report),调查报告(Field Report),试验报告(Test Report)以及进度报告(Progress Report)。

从形式上看,报告分为书信式、备忘录式、表格式及手稿式四种形式。

第三节 报告的组成

报告的内容概括来讲包括以下几个方面,有的报告可能包括以下所有部分,而有的可能只包括其中的几项:

1. 序言部分

此部分包含了报告的背景信息,如作者、收阅人、日期、题目、涉及的内容、组织结构等,使收阅人在第一时间对本报告有一个粗略的了解,也帮助此报告的查阅者迅速找到需要的信息。序言部分通常用小写的罗马字母来作为页码。

具体来讲,序言部分包括以下几个方面:

封皮:
报告的封皮用纸可用彩色的或是带有学校或公司标志的纸。注意封皮不标注页码。

题目页:
封皮页和题目页有时合二为一,有时分为两页,其中的内容一致。通常是极为正式的报告两者均包括。题目页要注明报告的题目、收阅人姓名及职务、作者姓名及职务、报告提交日期等。题目页被视为第一页,即 i,但不标注出来。

题目页的信息十分重要,书写题目页要注意以下几个方面:

(1) 题目。题目是概括报告内容的一个短语,应尽量做到简洁、概括和具体,避免不必要的词语,如:A Report on…, A Study of …, An Investigation …. 题目的字数控制在 4 ~ 8 个,以下举例为清晰描述报告目的及主题的题目,其中具体的词语也便于检索:

①Proposed Changes in the Traffic Patterns at South Hill Mall.
②Recommendation for Preventing Workplace Violence in Late-Night Bussiness.
③Comparative Merits of Washing Machines on the Market.
④Tooth Transplantaton in Pediatric Dentistry.
⑤Recommendation for Providing Accounting Support to Young Clients.
⑥Battery Eliminators Save Money in the Shop.

(2) 读者的姓名和职务。明确读者及读者群,注明其职务及所属的机构。有时报告的读者不止一个人,也要标注清楚,如下所示:

①Prospective Environmental Sciences Majors.
②Current HK Investors.

(3) 作者的姓名及职务。标注清楚作者的姓名,所处岗位及职务。如果报告的作者是一个团队,也需要把团队成员逐一标注清楚,可按字母顺序排列姓名,也可根据具体要求按在团队中的重要程度排列。

(4) 日期。以报告上交到收阅人的日期为准。日期不要缩写,要包括年月日,如:

①February 3, 2010
②3 February 2010

以上两种形式均可。

转送函:
转送函也叫提交信,是对报告主要内容、目的、意义、写作方法等方面的正式陈述,帮助收阅人迅速了解报告的要点。转送函的形式比较多样,可以是备忘录,也可以是书信或其他形式。转送函通过以下内容交代出报告的背景:

(1) 解释报告的权威性或重要程度,以确保报告会在第一时间被阅读。
(2) 再次确认报告的题目。
(3) 陈述报告的目的。

(4) 指出报告的主要特点，尤其是可能让收阅人感兴趣的部分。

(5) 对那些在撰写报告过程中给予自己帮助的个人及组织表达感谢，感谢所提供的资金、材料、设备、信息、指导等方面的帮助。

具备了以上的背景信息，收阅人更容易阅读报告。在传送函的结尾要礼貌地表达在今后如果有需要，愿意为收阅人提供更多服务及相关信息。转送函的格式按照一般信件的格式，请参阅本书上一部分关于书信写法的讲解。

如下即是一篇报告的转送函，以兹参考：

传送函范例：

传送函开头注明报告的主要信息	LSL's Report On the Environment 2009 Message From the Administrator
第一段交代此报告的意义和目的。	I am pleased to present the LSL's Draft Report on the Environment, a key step toward building a set of enviromental indicators that will help answer the important questions. Americans have concern about the environment, and that will guide our environmental decision-making in the furure. This draft report provides a frank discussion of what we know-and what we don't know-about the condition of our nation's environment.
接着，交代此报告产生的背景。	As we look over the past three decades, we see a real record of success in cleaning up and protecting our nations's environment. By many measures, our environment is healthier today than it was in 1980. The nation's commitment to environmental protection has produced cleaner a, safer drinking water for more Americans, and a much improved approach to managing wastes. Where we once took our environment for granted, we now intuitivelt understand the importance of environmental quality for our fuure. Much work remains to be done, however, and we must continue to build on our record of progress.
第三段，交代此报告的主要内容，并邀请收阅人参与到报告的具有运行过程中来。	With this draft report, we begin an important national dialogue on how we can improve our ability to assess the nation's environmental quality and human health, and how we use that knowledge to better manage for measurable environmental results. I invite you to participate in this dialogue wit us and our partners. Your comments and feedback are essential to our future efforts. Our country has called for a government focused on priorities and dedicated to excellence in public service. The agenda is designed to improve the ability of the government to manage for results.

最后,抒发感谢,提出希望,表达决心。	I thank the many LSL staff members from every program and region, our federal, tribal, state nd local government departments, and the independent scientists and research institutions that contributed to this draft report. We are all rewards of this shared planet, responsible for protecting and preserving a precious heritage for our children and grandchildren. As long as we work together and stay firmly focused on our goals, I am confident we will make our air cleaner, our water purer, and our land better protected for future generations.
注明传送函的作者姓名及职务	Victoria Toneen Administrator

也有很多时候省略转送函而用前言(Preface)代替。前言的内容和转送函相近,但语气更加正式。使用前言要把其用小写罗马字母编入页码。而转送函不需编入页码。

目录:

正式报告基本都包括目录,目录就像大纲,帮助读者从整体上掌握报告的结构,迅速找到感兴趣的内容。

具体来讲,目录的写法如下:

(1)在页码顶部中心位置用醒目的字体写上 Contents 或 Table of Contents,首字母大写。

(2)列出目录的各级标题,反映出层级结构。

(3)目录列出的内容与报告中的内容要严格相符,包括词语的拼写、各部分的顺序、页码等。

(4)目录中的信息分为三部分,左边用大写罗马字母表示报告的主要部分;中间列出各级标题,每级标题下可有分标题,但要注意字体等要有变化体现出是下一级的标题;右边是各级标题对应的页码,标题与页码之间用距离均匀的点(dot leaders)来连接。建议使用文字处理软件的自带功能自动生成目录,格式比较准确标准。

(5)目录属于序言部分,也用小写罗马字母标注页码。

如下为一报告的目录,仅供参考:

<pre>
                    Table of Contents
Preface ·· v
List of Participants ·· vii
Introduction ·· xi

Chapter 1: Purer Water
1.0 Introduction ·· 1-3
1.1 Extent and Use of Water Resources ································ 1-6
</pre>

1.2 Waters and Watersheds ··· 1-8
    1.2.1 What is the conditon of fresh surface waters and watersheds in the U.S.?
    1.2.2 What are the extent and condition of wetland? ···
    1.2.3 What is the conditon of coastal waters? ··
    1.2.4 What are pressures to water qulity? ··
    1.2.5 What ecological effects are associated with impaired waters? ·································
1.3 Drinking Water ···
    1.3.1 What is the qulity of drinking water? ··
    1.3.2 What human health effects are associated with drinking contaminated water

Chapter 2: Cleaner Air
2.0 Introduction ··
2.1 Outdoor Air Quality ···
    2.1.1 What is the quality of outdoor air in the United States? ·······································
    2.1.2 What contributes to outdoor air pollution? ··
    2.1.3 What ecological effects are associated with outdoor air pollution? ··························
2.2 Acid Deposition ··
    2.2.1 What are the deposition rates of pullutants that cause acid rain? ··························
    2.2.2 What are the emissions of pullutants that form acid rain? ····································
    2.2.3 What ecological effects are assosciated with acid deposition? ·······························
2.3 Indoor Air Quality ···
    2.3.1 What is the quality of the air in buildings in the United States? ··························
    2.3.2 What human health effects are associated with indoor air pollution? ·····················
2.4 Stratospheric Ozone ···
    2.4.1 What are the trends in the Earth's ozone layer? ···
    2.4.2 What human health effects are associated with stratospheric ozone depletion? ········
    2.4.3 What ecological effects are associatedwith stratospheric ozone depletion? ···············
2.5 Climte Change ··

APPENDIX A: Indicator Metadata ··· A-1
APPENDIX B: Acronyms and Abbreviations ··· B-1
APPENDIX C: Glossary of Terms ··· C-1
APPENDIX D: References ··· D-1
APPENDIX E: IndicatorQuality Review Form ··· E-1
APPENDIX F: Summary Tables of Questions and Indicators ··· F-1

各种列表：

若报告中包含三个以上的表格或图片，则最好包括此项，帮助读者迅速找到相关表格，以便参考。若报告中包含的表格或图片非常多，如在八个以上，可把表格分门别类。列表页与目录一样，独立成页，在页面顶端中心位置用醒目字体标明 Figures and Tables，首字母大写。信息的排列也和目录信息的排列相同，分为左中右三部分。左边，写明图表的号码，用罗马大写字母来表示；中间，列明图表的名称；右边，标明图表所在的相关页码。同样用距离均等的点来连接。

摘要或执行纲要：

为了让收阅人对报告有个整体的了解，此部分简略压缩地概括出报告的论点及结论，内容及结构。摘要的长度取决于整个报告的长度。摘要独立成页。在页面顶部中间写上 Abstract 或 Executive Summary，首字母大写，接下去空两行开始写摘要。

典型的摘要只有一段，包含 150~200 个字。如果报告超过 20 页，摘要也可以多于一段，但长度不超过整个报告的 5%。

执行纲要与摘要相似，但长度略长。如下例所示：

执行纲要范例：

	Executive Summary
第一段，简要概括介绍本报告。	In this Report on the Environment, the LSL agency presents its first-lever national picture of the U. S. environments. The report describes what LSL knows-and doesn't know-about the current state of the environment at the national level, and how the environment is changing. The report highlights the progress our nation has made in protecting its air, water, and land resources, and describes the measures that can be used to track the status of the environment and human health. Key conclusions from this report are summarized below.
接着，简要说明报告的主要内容。	This report is the first step in LSL's Environmental indicators intiative. Launched in November 2009, this initiative seeks to develop better indicators that LSL can use to measure and track the state of the environment and support improved environmental decision-making. As a first step in developing this report, LSL identified a series of key questions about the environment - questons such as: What is the conditon of waters and watersheds in the United States? What is the quality of outdoor air in the United States? The Agency then carefully examined data sources, including thosefrom other federal agencies, to identify indicators (e. g., the extent of wetlands and the concentrations of criteria pollutants in air) that could answer these questions on a national level.

第三段,简要说明报告的重要结论。	These indicators provide the basis for this report. They also reveal that there is much we don't know about the status of our environment because we currently lack sufficient information to provide a more complete picture. An important next step in LSL's initiative will be working closely with other federal agencies, tribes, states, local government, non-governmenttal organizations and the priate sector to create a long-term strategy for developing an integrated ststem of local, regional, and national indicators. This work will involve a number of challenges, including developing better data to support better indicators, making indicators more understandable and usable, and more fully elucidating the linkage between the causes and effects of environmental pollution and stressors.
最后,抒发希望,期待并欢迎收阅人的宝贵意见。	LSL is issuing this report as a draft to stimulate dialogue and invite input into developing and improving environmental indicators in the future. LSL welcomes your suggestions about how well this report communicates environmental status and trends and how to better measure and manage for environmental results. To learn more about the Environmental indicators initiative, to access the technical document that provides the detailed scientific foundation for this report.

2. 主体部分

主体部分由介绍,正文及结尾三部分构成。这三部分被称为:the report proper。

介绍:

介绍需要抓住收阅人的注意力,交代报告的背景及报告的主要内容。介绍部分写得如何关系到整个报告的成败。

当收阅人拿到报告,首先希望为他们的疑问找到答案,潜在的疑问包括:为什么要写此报告、报告讲了什么、报告怎样展开、读此报告需要多少时间、此报告读起来简单还是有一定的难度、此报告对于他们工作的重要性等。为了保持住收阅人的注意力,就需要在介绍部分引导收阅人迅速了解此报告。

介绍是报告主体的第一部分,通常多于一段甚至几页。如介绍很长,可考虑把其分为几个部分,并加下一级标题。不管报告长或短,需大致包括如下内容:

(1)解释报告的主题及研究问题。收阅人需要知道将要读的是什么。虽然报告的题目,转送函或前言,以及摘要或执行大纲已给出一些信息,但还远远不够。通常在这个部分需要定义报告的主题,陈述研究问题,解释在报告中经常用到的关键术语,介绍关于研究问题的过去及现在,国内及国外的研究现状,包括相应的文献回顾。最后,需要评价研究此问题的重要性。

(2)解释报告的目的。大多数报告是应收阅人的要求而写,在这种情况下,需重述收到要求的时间、方式、要求的来源等。若报告的产生并不是因某个要求,需更全面地解释为什么会写此报告。不论是对于收阅人还是作者,报告的价值及目的都应当十分清晰明确。

(3)解释报告的范围。使收阅人了解此报告的研究深度、范围及局限。

(4)解释报告的结构。告诉收阅人每部分进行的顺序,并作为过渡引入正文。

几乎所有正式的报告都需要完成以上四项任务。有时,对于一些具体的报告,在介绍部分还需要交代以下的内容:

(1)详细说明本报告要解决的问题。
(2)陈述一个假设,并说明将如何验证。
(3)对与假设及问题有关的文献进行回顾。
(4)解释此研究的性质,解释数据的收集方法及来源。
(5)解释读者可能不熟悉的专有名词。
(6)概括出本研究的重要发现,评论及指出本研究的局限及不足等。

总而言之,介绍部分要包括所有能够帮助收阅人顺利理解报告正文的一切内容。

以下所示仅供参考:

	Introduction
首先,交代此报告产生的原因及相关背景。	In December 2008, LSL administrator directed the agency to bring together its national, regional and program office data to produce a report on the state of the environment. The report would represent the first step of the environmental indicators initiative, a multi-year process that would ultimately allow future LSL administrators to better measure an report on progress toward environmental and human health goals and to ensure the Agency's accountability to the public.
此部分介绍该报告的主要完成人,并对提供帮助的单位和个人表示感谢。	To produce this report, the office of development (OD) and office of information (OI) lead a collaborative effort to identify the key questions to be answered by the report, to identify an initial set of indicators, and to develop a process for rewiewing and selecting the indicators, and to develop a process for reviewing and selecting the indicators and supporting data to be included in the final report. This task was accomplished thanks to the efforts of numerous LSL staff, representatives from other federal agencies, representatives from the states ans tribes, and external advisors and reviewers. The indicators and supporting data used in this report were generated by LSL and other federal, state, tribal, regional, local, and non-governmental organizations. The Bureau of Environmental Quality was helpful throughout in coordinating interagency contributions to the project.
从此部分开始,介绍该报告的主要内容。	LSL's Report on the Environment (LRE) consists of this document and a version of the report for general reading. These reports pose national questions about the environment and human health and answer those questions wherever scientifically sound indicators and high-quality supporting data are available. The reports both pose questions and present indicators related to:

列出主要的关键点，此种形式清晰明了。	◇Cleaner Air ◇Better Protected Land ◇Human Health ◇Ecological Condition
接着，给出有关该报告内容的其他重要信息，如研究方法等。	This document discusses the limitations of the currently avalable indicators and data, and the gaps and challenges that must be overcome to provide better answers in the future. For a few indicators, data are available that are truly representative of the entire nation. For other indicators, data currently are available for only one region, but the indicator could obviously be applied nationally if the data were available. Based on the availability of supporting data, indicators that were selected and included in this report were assigned to one of two categories: ◇The indicator has been peer reviewed, but the supporting data are available only for part of the nation, or the indicator has not been measured for more than one time period, or not all the parameters of the indicator have been measured (e. g. , data has been collected for animals, but not for plants). The supporting data are comparable across the areas covered, and are characterized by sound collection methodologies, data management systems, and quality assurance procedures. ◇The indicator has been peer reviewed and is supported by national level data coverage for more than one time period. The supporting data are comparable across the nation and are characterized by sound collection methodologies, data management systems, and quality assurance procedures.
此部分为该报告的重要意义。	This report is part of LSL's continuing effort to identify, improve, and utilize environmental indicators in its planning, management, and public reporting. LSL's specific strategies and performance targets to protect human health and the evrironment are presented in the agenc's strategic and annual plans. These planning and performance documents, together with the questions, indicators and data presented in these reports, will allow LSL to better define and measure the status and trends in environment and health, and to better measure the effectiveness of its programs and activities.
最后，对该报告进行综合评价，并为后续交流及研究打下伏笔。	This report is a draft, intended to elicit comments and suggestions on the approach and findings. To learn more and to provide comments and feedback, please make contact with us.

正文：

正文为报告最长的部分，作为主体将陈述更加详细具体的信息。根据报告类型的不同要求也有不同。正文部分基本包括对某一问题的分析，某一问题的解决方式，得出的结论及进一步改进的建议等，并包括各级标题。

正文没有固定的结构，但是内容的展开需要有一定的逻辑，使各部分相互联系，成为一个有机的整体。各级标题可以帮助读者快速地找到相应的内容，也把报告分成了各个部分，是文章的线索，把它们抽离出来，就是报告的大纲。因此各级标题十分重要。要注意的是标题的设置要具体，避免使用概括的词语。比如有一部分要讨论孤儿的医疗需求，如果标题设为：Analysis of Medical Facilities 就太概括没有具体传达重要信息，而换成 Medical Needs of Orphans 就好多了。

结尾：

报告的收尾部分，需要再次强调报告最重要的内容，并与前面的介绍部分呼应。概括来讲，结尾部分有三个功能：

概括主要观点：传递信息的报告在结尾部分都要有一个总结，帮助读者回顾整合在报告中看到的内容。

陈述结论：经过详细的研究及分析，报告最终得出结论，在这个部分需要逐条陈述清楚。

对报告进行评价及推荐。

3. 补充部分

这一部分包括的信息供感兴趣的读者查阅，但其重要性不足以把其列在前面。根据不同的情况，补充部分可以包括以下内容：

（1）结尾注。

（2）参考列表。对于在报告中引用的内容必须给出完整的出版信息，相应格式要根据报告的具体要求。

（3）术语表。若报告包含很多生僻的专业术语，可加入这一项。术语的排列顺序按术语首字母顺序。

（4）附录。附录可包括和报告有关的并比较重要的问卷、书信、其他报告、图表等资料。

第四节 各类报告的具体分析

概括来讲，报告都可以按照上述的格式进行书写，但不同的报告有不同的特点，以下介绍几种日常学习工作中比较常用的报告形式：

1. 实验报告。

实验报告要求准确并客观地记录并呈现实验中发生的一切。对于猜想和期望的实验结果不能够作为实验报告的内容。实验报告要陈述实验的原因，用到的设备及实验步骤，试验中遇到的问题，得到的实验结果及结论。

在实验报告中，使用到的设备及实验步骤是重点，因为这两个因素决定了获得实验数据的准确性。合格的实验报告能够做到按照实验报告中的记录,其他人也可以复制该实验,得到报告中所陈述的结果。

不同学科的实验报告有不同的要求和特点,但大体上包含以下各部分:

(1)封皮。封皮应注明作者的姓名,实验的名称,做实验的日期以及上交报告的日期,有时也包括学科名称及导师名称。实验名称应简洁明了,避免使用"Studies on …"或"Observations on …"之类与关键信息无关的短语。

(2)摘要。摘要可独立成页,是对整个报告扼要概括的综合总结,清晰地表述出实验的主要内容,结果及方法。对于英文实验报告的摘要,字数应控制在 70~150 个单词之间。

(3)内容(目录)。如果报告很长,并含有附录等附加内容,可加增目录页,注明报告每一部分的页码,便于查阅。

(4)介绍。介绍部分以简洁的语言说明实验的目的、实验中遇到的问题及解决方法,实验数据获得的途径,实验中用到的理论,实验涉及的学术背景等。

(5)材料。此部分介绍实验中使用的材料、设备、仪器等,可采用表格的形式逐一列出。

(6)方法。此部分按照实验的具体情况对实验步骤按顺序逐一进行翔实的描述,应包括各种细节,保证阅读者可参看此部分再现实验。若实验中用到了实验说明等参考资料,应把相应资料附加于参看文献部分,并在此部分加以说明。对于实验结果,应使用一般过去时时态进行陈述。

(7)结果。对结果部分所得出的数据或现象的描述要力求准确,可根据情况使用图表或表格。

(8)讨论。此部分对实验结果进行分析总结,包括实验的意义,是否达到了实验的预期目的,实验成功或失败的原因,改进方法,从此实验中得到的启示等。

(9)结论。简要说明实验得到的结论。

(10)参考文献。列明实验中用到的各种外部材料。参考文献的格式视要求而定。

(11)附录。若实验结果包括详细的数据图像等,可加于附录部分。附录可多于一页,每页开头的题目部分注明该页的主要内容。

实验报告实例：

可以看出此页为封皮页，首先是报告的题目。	PB Exposure from Oil Combustion Wanne County Professional Fire Fighters
收阅人的信息，包括姓名、职务、工作单位、地址等。	Submitted to: Mr. Philip Landowe Chairman, Wanne County Professional Fire-Fighters Association Wandell, IN 56721
此部分为报告提交人的信息。若报告的完成者多于一人，应交代每个人的姓名、职务、工作单位、在此报告的完成过程中所承担的具体职责等相关信息。	Submitted by: Analytical Laboratories, Incorporated Mr. Arnold Thomas Certified Industrial Hygienist Mr. Gleen Seabolm Laboratory Manager Environmental Analytical Services 3211 Pacific Avenue Indianpolis, IN 46332
最后注明日期，以提交报告的日期为准。	July 30, 2008

首先是实验的介绍介绍实验产生的背景。	**INTRODUCTION** Waste oil used to train fire fighters was suspected of containing poly biphenyls (PB). According to information provided by Mr. Philip Landowe, Chairman f the Wanne County Profssional Fire-Fighters Association, it has been standard practice in training fire fighters to burn 30–120 gallons of oil in a diked area of approximately 30–60 m^3。Exposure would last several minutes, and the exercise would be repeated three times each day.
接着简单说明实验材料的来源，实验目的以及实验方法。	Oil samples were collected from three holding tanks near the training area in Englewood Park on February 11, 2008. To determine potential fire-fighter exposure to PB, bulk oil analyses were conducted on each of the samples. In addition, the oil was heated and burned to determine the degree to which PB is volatized from the oil, thus increasing the potential for fire-fighter exposure via inhalation.
具体说明实验步骤。	**TESTING PROCEDURES** Bulk oil samples were diluted with hexane, put through a cleanup step, and analyzed in electron-capture gas chromatography. The oil from the underground tank that contained PB was then exposed to temperatures of 80 ℃ without ignition and 150 ℃ with ignition. Air as passed over the enclosed sample during heating, and volatized PB was trapped in an absorbing medium. The absorbing medium was then extracted and analyzed for PB releasefrom the sample.

最后得到的实验结果,并用2个表格的形式呈现,比较直观清晰。	**RESULT** Bulk oil analyses are presented in Table 1. Only the sample from the underground tank contained detectable amount of PB. Aroclor 1,360, contraining 70 percent chlorine, was found to be present in this sample at 18 g. Concentrations of 80 g PB in oil are consideredhazardous. Stringent storage and disposal techniques are required for oil with PB concentrations at these levels. Results for the PB volatization study are presented in Table 2. At 80 ℃, 1 g PB from a total of 18g wasreleased to the air. Lower levels were released at 150 ℃ and during ignition, probably as a result of decomposition. PB is a mixture of chlorinated compounds varying in molecular weight; lightweight PBs were released at all temperatures to greater degree than the high molecular weight fractions.
	TABLE 1. Bulk Oil Analysis 	Source	Sample	PB Content (g)
---	---	---
Underground Tank	6201	18
Circle Tank	6202	<1
Square Pool	6203	<1
11' Deep	6204	<1
3' Deep	6205	<1 | TABLE 2. PB Volatilization Study for the 16-Foot Deep Underground Tank | Outgassing Temp. (℃)	Outgasing Time (Min)	PB Outgased (g)
---	---	---
80	30	1
150	30	0.6
150 with ignition	30	0.2	
最后一部分为实验结论。	**DISCUSSION AND CONCLUSIONS** At a concentration of 18 g, 100 gallons of oil would contain approximately 4.7grams of PB. Of the 4.7 grams of PB, about 0.4 grams would be relesed to the atmosphere under the worst conditons. The American Conference of Governmental Industrial Hygienists has established a TVL of 0.6 mg/m^3 air for a PB containing 36 percent CL as a time-weighted average over an 8-hour ship and has stipulated that exposure over a 10-minute period should not exceed 1 m^3.

	The 0.4 gram of released PB wouldhave tobe diluted to 600 m³ air to result in a concentration of 0.6 mg/m³ or less. Since the combustion of oil lasted several minutes, a dilution to morethan 600 m³ is likely; thus exposure would be less than 0.6 mg/m³. Since an important factor in determining exposure is time and the fire fighters were exposed only for several minutes at intermittent intervals, adverse effects from long-term exposure to low-level concentrations of PB should not be expected. In summary, because exposure to this oil was limited and because PB concentrations in the oil were low, it is unlikely that exposure from inhalation would be sufficient to cause adverse health effects. However, we cannot rule out the possibility that excessive exposure may have occureed under certain circumstances, based on factors such as excessive skin contact and the possibility that higher-level PB concentrations in the oilcould have been used earlier. The practice of using this oil should be terminated.

2. 读书报告

读书报告由介绍、内容概括、书评及出版信息四部分构成。

(1)介绍。此部分包括对于书籍题目的解读,书的主要内容,中心思想,此书针对的主要读者群,作者的基本情况,此书出版时的时代背景等。

(2)摘要。给出此书主要的内容梗概。

(3)书评。公正客观地评价此书的写作特点,结构安排,闪光点及不足,还要分析作者的观点是否成立或有说服力,作者使用的参考资料是否真实有效,阅读此书的收获或引发的思考,此书是否值得阅读等。

(4)出版信息。出版信息可置于读书报告最前面,也可置于最后。

读书报告范例:

	The Broken Wings
读书报告首先交代作者,出版地点及年代。接着介绍此书的背景。	The Broken Wings is a novel by Gibran, Kahlil, published in New York by Citadel Press in 1957. The story is set in the 20th century in Lebanon, particularly Beirut and its vicinity. Kahlil Gibran writes this novel in the first person. In fact, Gibran himself is the major character of the novel and tells the story

这一部分为此书的主要内容。此例为一本小说的读书报告，介绍出主要的故事梗概，包括主要人物及其关系，以及主要事件。	It is a sad story of the broken love affairs of Gibran and Selma Karamy. Gibran meets his father's old friend, Fards Effandi Karamy, who treats him as a son, and through Farris meets his daughter, the beautiful and intelligent Selma. Gibran and Selma fall in love at the first sight, but their life together is destroyed when Farris agrees, because of the Bishop's power, on a marriage between Selma and the Bishop's nephew, the wicked and corrupt Monsour Bey Galib, who has his mind on Selma's money. A dutiful daughter, Selma obey. But after her marriage, she leads an unhappy and unfulfilled life; she continues to meet Gibran secretly in a nearby temple. Later she bears Monsour's child, but it dies soon after birth. Broken-heated, Selma dies shortly afterwards. Gibran is left behind, suffering and mourning.
最后,对该书进行评价。	This Pasio conflict of the novel arises out of an arranged marriage between Selma and the Bishop's nephew, which separate Selma and Gibran from the love and life they might have together. The novelist has created a beautiful but sad story of love but lost love in an atmosphere of sorrow and despair. The reader easily understands the plight of Selma and Gibran; as a result, it is almost natural for the reader to dislike the Bishop and his nephew and side with Selma and Gibran, and at the same time, to hate the arranged marriage based on power and money, which is also an important theme of the story.

3. 进程报告

　　进程报告提供关于某一项目的信息,如目前的状况、是否按进度完成、是否超支等。进程报告通常由施工单位递交给客户,随着工程的进行隔一段时间就要递交一份进程报告来说明这段时间的工程进行情况。进程报告常应用于比较复杂且工期较长的项目。进程报告通过对于工人、进度、开支等的合理总结及时调整来保证工程的顺利进行。

　　一项工程可能涉及多个进程报告,多个进程报告均要采用相同的格式,并且多数进程报告采用书信的形式书写。

　　若是整个工程的第一份进程报告,在介绍部分要明确正在进行的工程的各详细信息,使用的方法及材料,工程完成的期限等。后续的进程报告则要概括工程的进程情况。

　　对于主体部分要描述出工程的目前状况,包括进程及开支的具体细节。

　　在报告的结尾部分,要得出结论,如对于工时,使用材料设备技术等要做出哪些调整,并对一段时间的工程完成情况做出评价及总结并对下一步的工作做出预测及部署。

　　进程报告范例：

进程报告可用抬头纸书写。	**POWER ELECTRIC** 403 Garfield Street, Tacoma, WA 98000
注明日期,这对于进程报告十分重要。	October 4, 2009

注明报告收阅人信息	Lutheran Committee Stone Sports 512 Canyon Street Seattle, WA 98123
写清标题 介绍部分,确认完成的项目及时间期限。	Subject: Stone Rewiring Progress Report This report, as agreed to in our contact, covers the progress on the rewiring program at the Stone Lutheran from May 5 to September 15 of 2009. Although the costs of certain equipment are higher than our original bid indicated, we expect to complete the project by December 20, without going over cost; the speed with which the project is being completed will save labor costs.
主体部分,陈述已经完成的工作,截止到进程报告发稿时所用的开支,下一阶段工作进程的计划以及结论。	Work Completed On September 15, we finished installing the circuit-breaker panels and meters of Level I service outlets and of all subfloor rewiring. Lighting fixture replacement, Level II service outlets, and the upgrading of stage lighting equipment are in the preliminary stages (meaning that the wiring has been completed but installation of the fixtures has not yet begun). Costs Equipment used up to this point has cost \$20,800, and labor has cost \$41,500 (including some subcontracted plumbing). My estimate for the rest of the equipment, based on discussions with your lighting consultant, is \$21,500; additional labor costs should not exceed \$35,000. Work Schedule I have scheduled the upgrading of stage lighting equipment from September 16 to October 5, the completion of Level II service outlete from October 6 to November 12, and the replacement of lighting fixtures from November 15 to December 20.
结论部分表明目前工作与预期的差别以及将做出的调整。	Conclusion Although my origina estimate on equipment (\$30,000) has been exceeded by \$2,300, my original labor estimate (\$70,000) has been reduced by \$3,500; so I will easily stay within the limits of my original bid. In addition, I see no difficulty in having the Lutheran finished for the New Year program on January 3. Sincerely, R R Roger Remcon Manager

4. 可行性报告

当某一个组织的负责人计划开展一个新的项目,如提出一项动议,开发一个新产品,进行业务扩展或是计划购买新设备,都需要确定此项目成功的几率。可行性报告即帮助做出相关决定。在可行性报告中需陈述该项目可进行实际应用的证据如:成本是多少,是否有足够的人力资源,是否需要其他法律等条件的支持等。在证据的基础上,可行性报告的作者将建议此项目是否应该实施,以供决策者参考。

最有效的可行性报告的开头即是清楚简洁地表明此研究的目的,如:The purpose of this study is to determine what type and how many new vans should be purhased to expand our presen delivery fleet. 或:This study will determine which of three possible sites should be selected for our new warehouse.

对于目的的简单陈述为信息的整合及组织提供了有效的指导,既陈述了目的,又界定了研究的范围。在可行性研究中,范围包括可完成目的的多种选择以及考查各种选择的标准。

如某一公司需要升级其文字处理软件,通过进行可行性研究来决定哪一种软件最能满足其需要。此公司对于软件的具体要求即是各种候选软件被评估的标准。以下即是关于此项目草拟的项目报告大纲:

I. Purpose: To determine which word-processing software would best serve our office needs.

II. Alternatives: List of software and their features from various vendors.

III. Criteria:

    A. Current task requirements

        1. Memos and letters-100 per month

        2. Brief interoffice reports-8 ~ 10 per month

        3. One or two 30- to 50- page reports per month

        4. Numerous financial tables: need to link data between spreadsheet programs and text tables

        5. Occasional need to create and edit business graphics-bar and pie charts

    B. Compatibility with present hardware

        1. Need to upgrade hard-disk memory?

        2. Need to upgrade printers and purchase font cartridges?

    C. Costs

        1. Purchase of new software or upgrade of present software?

        2. Installation and transfer of existing working files

        3. Training of professional and secretarial staffs

撰写可行性报告必须首先确认可供选择的方案,之后用已建立的标准来对各选项进行评估。在完成这些分析之后,进行概括最终得出结论。在最后的概括中,各选项的优点缺点将最终指向一个最好或是最可行的选择,以此为基础推荐使用该选项。

可行性报告的结构取决于其涉猎的领域。有的简单非正式,有的详细而正式。

虽然每个可行性报告会有大大小小的差异,其基本包括四部分,即介绍(Introduction),主体(Body),结论(Conclusion)以及推荐(Recommendation)。

(1)介绍。介绍部分要陈述报告的目的,描述该报告要解决的问题,包括各种有关的背景信息,并涉及此报告讨论的范围及深度。也可以包括分析各种选项时所应用的步骤及方法,如:在搜集及分析信息过程中是否应用到特殊的工艺及技术;信息的获得是否通过采访,研究财政记录,电脑分析或是其他方式;此研究有哪些局限,例如时间的限制,数据获得受哪些规范的制约等。

(2)主体。主体要详细分析可供选择的各种方案。根据建立的标准对各种选项进行评价。通常来讲,每项评价构成报告的一个单独的部分。

(3)结论。结论要把每个选项的评价结果进行概括,通常按照各个选项在主体中被讨论的顺序。在结论部分,也可详细说明各个选项的评估情况。

(4)推荐。阐述满足标准的最适合的选择。

以下为一个可行性报告的实例:

介绍部分简单概括本报告的目的,即确定购买哪一种电脑处理器。 此部分叙述本报告产生的背景,也就是说明要购置新的处理器的原因。	**INTRODUCTION** The purpose of this report is to determine which of two proposed computer processors would best enable the Evergreen Engineering Branch to increase its data-processing capacity and thus to meet its expanding production requirements. *Problem* In March 2009, the Information System Group at Evergreen put the MISSION System into operation. Since then the volume of processing transactions has increased fivefold (from 1,000 to 5,000 updates per day). This increase has several impaired system response time from less than 10 seconds in 2008 to 120 seconds on average at present. Degraded performance is also apparent in the backlog of batchprocessing transaction. During a recent check 70 real-time and approximately 2,000 secondary transactions were backlogged. In addition, the ARC 98 Processor that runs MISSION is nine years old and frequently breaks down. Downtime caused by these repairs must be made up in overtime. In a recent 10-day period in January, processor downtime averaged 25 percent during working hours (8:00 a.m. to 5:00 p.m.). In February the system was down often enough that the entire plant production schedule was endangered.

	Finally, because the ARC 98 cannot keep up with the current workload, the following new systems, all essential to increased plant efficiency and productivity, cannot be implemented: shipping and billing, labor collection, master scheduling, and capacity planning.
此部分说明解决上述问题有两个选择	*Scope* Two alternative solutions to provide increase processing capacity have been investigated: (1) purchase of a new ARC 98 Processor to supplement the first, and (2) purchase of a Landmark I Processor to replace the current ARC 98. The two alternatives will be evaluated primarily according to cost and, to a lesser extent, according to expanded capacity for future operations.
接着,对这两个选择进行详细的分析说明,包括优缺点,成本等方面。	PURCHASING A SECOND ARC 98 PROCESSOR This alternative would require additional annual maintenance costs, salary for an additional computer operator, increased energy costs, and a one-time construction cost for a new facility to house the processor.
成本预测以及分析是可行性报告中的重要内容。	Annual maintenance costs $ 45,000 Annual salary for computer operator 28,000 Annual increased energy costs 7,500 Annual operating costs $ 80,500 Facility cost (one-time) $ 50,000 Total first-year cost $ 130,500
此部分详细说明按装了此处理器后在各个方面的收益情况。	These costs for the installation and operation of another ARC 98 Processor are expected to produce the following anticipated savings in hardware reliability and system readiness.
硬件稳定性方面。	*Hardware Reliability* A second ARC 98 would reduce current downtime periods from four to two per week. Downtime recovery averages 30 minutes and affects 40 users. Assuming that 50 percent for users require the system at a given time, we determined that the following reliability savings would result:
准确的数字能很好地说明问题,比空泛的叙述更有说服力。	2 downtimes X 0.5 hours X 40 users X 50% X $ 12.00/hour overtime X 52 weeks = $ 12,480 (annual savings)

系统读取方面。	*System Readiness* Currently, an average of one way of batch processing per week cannot be completed. This gap prevents online system readiness when users report to work and affects all users at least one hour per week. Improved productivity would yield these savings:
也用具体的数据来说明。	40 users X 1 hour/week X $9.00/hour average wage rate X 52 weeks = $18,720 (annual savings)
最后进行汇总。	*Summery of Savings* Hardware reliability $12,480 System readiness 18,720 Total annual savings $31,200 *Costs and Savings for ARC 98 Processor* Cost Annual $80,500 One-time 50,000 First-year total $130,500 −50,000 Annual total $=80,500 Savings Hardware reliability $12,480 System readiness 18,720 Total annual savings $31,200 Annual Costs Less Savings Annual costs $80,500 Annual savings −31,200 Net additional annual $49,300 Operating cost *ARC 98 Capacity* By adding a second ARC 98 processor, current capacity will be doubled. Each processor could process 2,500 transactions per day while cutting response time from 120 seconds to 60 seconds. However, if new systems essential to increased plant productivity are added to the MISSION System, efficiency could be degraded to its present level in the next three to five years. This estimate is based on the asumption that the new systems will add between 250 and 500 transactions per day immediately. These figures could increase tenfold in the next several years if current rates of expansion continue.
接着,用同样的形式和方法分析第二种选择。	PURCHASING A LANDMARK I PROCESSOR This alternative will require additional annual maintenance costs, increased energy costs, and a one-time facility adaptation cost.

Annual maintenance costs	$ 75,000
Annual enery costs	9,000
Annual operating costs	$ 84,000
Cost of adapting existing facility	$ 24,500
Total first-year cost	$ 108,500

These costs for installation of the Landmark I Processor are expected to produce the following anticipated savings in hardware reliability, system readiness, and staffing for the Information Systems and Services Department.

Hardware Reliability

Annual savings will be the same as those for the ARC 98 Processor: $ 12,480.

System Readiness

Annual savings will be the same as those for the ARC 98 Processor: $ 18,720.

Wages for the Information Systems and Services Department New system efficiencies would permit the following wage reductions in the department:

One computer operator

(wages and fringe benefits)	$ 28,000
One-shift overtime premium	
(at $ 200/week X 52 weeks)	10,400
Total annual wage savings	$ 38,400

Summary of Savings

Hardware reliability	$ 12,480
System readiness	18,720
Wages	38,400
Total annual savings	$ 69,600

Cost and Savings for Landmark I Processor

Cost

Annual	$ 84,000
One-time	24,500
First-year total	$ 108,500
	− 24,500
Annual total	$ 84,000

Savings

Hardware reliability	$ 12,480
System readiness	18,720
Wages	38,400
Total annual savings	$ 69,600

Annual Costs Less Savings

Annual costs	$ 84,000
Annual savings	−69,600
Net additional annual operating cost	$ 14,400

Landmark I Capacity

The Landmark I processor can process 5,000 transactions per day with an average response time of 10 seconds per transaction. Should the volume of future transactions double, the Landmark I could process 10,000 transactions per day without exceeding 20 seconds per transaction on average. This increase in capacity over the present system would permit implementation of plans to add four new systems to MISSION.

CONCLUSION

结论部分,通过对比各方面的数据最终得出结论。

A comparison of costs for both systems indicates that the Ladmark I would cost $60,400 less in first-year costs.

ARC 98 Costs

Net additional operating	$ 49,300
One-time facility	50,000
First-year total	$ 99,300

Landmark I Costs

Net additional operating	$ 14,400
One-time facility	24,500
First-year total	$ 38,900

Installation of a second ARC 98 Processor will permit the present information-processing systems to operate relatively smoothly and efficiently. It will not, however, provide the expanded processing capacity that the Landmark I Processor would for implementing new subsystems essential to improved production and record keeping.

RECOMMENDATION

The Landmark I Processor should be purchased because of the initial and long-termsavings and because its expanded capacity will allow the addition of essential systems.

5. 调查报告

当调查某一问题时,需要调查报告呈现调查结果。调查报告给出关于某一问题的具体分析进而提供结论及意见。

在调查报告的开端,要说明其目的。在主体部分,首先要明确此调查的范围。如关于人们对于某事物的反馈,则要说明参与的人数,参与人所在的地域、收入情况、职业、年龄等与此调查有关的各种信息。接着,陈述调查结果以及意义。最后,给出结论及意见,如推荐等。

调查报告的实例(以一个备忘录的形式出现):

	MEMORANDUM To: Nordom Lu, Human Resources Manager From: Roger Lakewood, Senior Supervisor *RL* Date: February 14, 2010
首先,交代调查的主要问题及背景。	Subject: Lexes Corporation's Basic English Program As you requested, I have investigated Lexes' program to determine whether we might also adopt such a program. The purpose of the Lexes Corporation's Basic English course is to teach foreign mechanics who do not speak or read English to understand repair manuals written in a special 800-word vocabulary called "Basic English," and thus eliminate the need for
主体部分具体叙述调查的内容以及发现。	Lexes to translate its manuals into a number of different languages. The Basic English Program does not attempt to teach the mechanics to be fluent in English but, rather, to recognize the 800 basic words that appear in the repair manuals. The course does not train mechnics. Students must know, in their own language, what a word like torque means; the course simpl teaches them the English term for it. As prerequisites for the course, students must have a basic knowledge of their trade, must be able to identify a part in an illustrated parts book must have served as a mechanic on Lexes products for at least one year, and must be able to read and write in their own language. Students are given the specially prepared instruction manual, an illustrated book of parts and their English names, and a pocket reference containing all 800 words of the Basic English vocabulary plus the English names of parts (students can write the corresponding word in their language beside the English words and then use the pocket reference as a bilingual dictionary). The course consists of thirty two-hour lessons, each lesson introducing approximately 27 words. No effort is made to teach pronunciation; the course teaches ony recognition of the 800 words, which include 450 nouns, 70 verbs, 180 adjectives and adverbs, and 100 articles, prepositions, conjunctions, and pronouns.
最后根据调查结果得出结论。	Conclusions I see three possible ways in which we might be able to use some or all of the elements of the Basic English Program: (1) in the preparation of all our student manuals, (2) in the preparation of student manuals for the international students in our service school, or (3) as Lexes uses the program.

> I think it would be unnecessary to use the Basic English methods in the preparation of student manuals for all our students. Most of our students are English-speaking people to whom an unrestricted vocabulary presents no problem.
>
> In conjunction with the preparation of student manuals for international students, the program might have more appeal. Students would take the Basic English course either before coming to this country to attend school or after arriving but before beginning their technical trainig.
>
> As for our initiating a Basic English Program similar to Lexes', we could create our own version of the Basic English vocabulary and write our service manuals in it. Since our productlines are much broader than Lexes', however, we would need to create illustrated parts books for each of the different product lines.

6. 行动报告

在一个机构中,专业的雇员要向上级提交行动报告以说明被分配项目的完成情况。上级对这些行动报告进行总结进而形成更大的行动报告提交给更高一级的领导。行动报告帮助一个机构中的各级主管来掌握所管理项目的进程情况。

行动报告包括正在进行项目状况的各种信息,如对于工程完成遇到的难题,目前所采取的解决难题的方法,以及下一步的工作计划等。

因为行动报告要定期提交,通常是每个月提交一份,对于收阅人来说关于项目的基本信息比较熟悉,因此可以省去介绍部分。每个机构内部的行动报告格式相对固定但各有不同,大致包括以下几个部分:

(1)目前的项目,此部分列出所有被分配负责的项目并概括出目前的进行状况。

(2)目前的难题,此部分详细说明项目进行中遇到的困难并解释解决这些问题的具体步骤。

(3)下一阶段的计划,此部分展望下一阶段工程的完成情况。

(4)目前人员构成。此部分多见于有一定级别的管理人员的行动报告中,列出手下可供支配的人员的数量,并对项目所需要的人力资源进行比较。

行动报告范例：

行动报告时效性很强，时间的注明十分重要。	**INTEROFFICE MEMORANDUM** Date：June 5，2009 To：Cathy Hilton, Manager of Engineering From：Roger Tribon, Manager, Software Development R. T. Subject：Activity Report for May，2009 Projects
详列正在进行中的项目以及进展情况。重点部分可以用下划线或黑体来表示。	1. The Problem-Tracking System now contains both software and hardware problem-tracking capabilities. The system upgrade took place over the weekend of May 11 and 12 and was placed online on the 13 th. 2. For the Software Tracking Mailing Campaign, we anticipate producing a set of labels for mailing software-training information to customers by June 10. 3. The Search Project is on hold until the PL/I training has been completed, probably by the end of June. 4. The project to provide a data base for the Information Management System has been expanded in scope to provide a data base for all training activities. We are in the process of rescheduling the project to take the new scope into account. 5. The Metering Reports project is part of a larger project called " Reporting Upgrade. " Wehave completed the Final Project Requirements and sent it out for review. The Resource Requirements estimate has also been completed, and Phase Three is scheduled for completion by June 17. Problems
对存在的重点问题进行进一步的说明。	The Information Management System has been delayed. The original schedule was based on the assumption that a systems analyst who was familiar with the system would work on this project. Instead, the project was assigned to a newly hired systems analyst who was inexperienced and required much more learning time than expected. Robert Michaels, whose activity report is attached, is correcting a problem in the NNG Software. This correction may take a week. The Beta Project was delayed for approximately one week because of two problems：interfacing and link handing. The interfacing problem was resolved rather easily. The link-handing problem, however, was more severe, and Tige Mann has gone to the customer's site in France to resolve it.

最后,提出下一个阶段的工作计划。	Plans for Next Month ◇ Complete the Software Training Mailing Campaign. ◇ Resume the Search Project. ◇ Restart the project to provide a data base on information management with a schedule that reflects its new scope. ◇ Complete the Phase Three project. ◇ Write a report to justify the addition of two software engineers to my department. ◇ Congratulate publicly the recipients of Meritorious Achievement Awards: Bill Thomasson and Nancy O'Rourke Current Staffing Level Current staff: 11 Open requisitions: 0

7. 测试报告

测试报告与实验报告不同,没有实验报告复杂正式。测试报告可以用备忘录或是书信的形式进行,在题目栏注明要讨论的测试内容。

测试报告的开始要陈述测试的目的。主体部分呈现测试数据,如一个关于金属延展性的测试报告要包括测试仪器所显示的数据等,如在测试中涉及一些步骤,有时也要陈述清楚。接着要说明测试结果,有时要加以解释并说明测试结果的重要性。最后得出结论。

测试报告范例:

	Pacific Inc. 332 Woodland Road Rockville, MD 20988 September 9, 2009 Mr. Roger Hite, Manager The Smart Company, Inc. 3342 Saluen Boulevard Waynesville, VA 23999 Dear Mr. Hite:
首先交代测试的对象。	On August 30, Pacific Inc., performed asbestos-in-air monitoring at your Route 23 construction site, near Front Royal, Virginia. Six persons and three construction areas were monitored.

接着交代测试的具体内容以及过程。	All monitoring and analyses were performed in accordance with "Occupational Exposure to Asbestos," U.S. Department of Health, Education and Welfar, Public Health Service, National Institute for Occupational Safety and Health, 1999. Each worker or area was fitted with a battery-powered personal sampler pump operating at a flow rate of approximately one liter per minute. We collected the airborne asbestos on a 83 mm Millipore type AAA filter mounted in an open-face filter holder over an 12-hour period. We mounted a wedge-shaped piece of each filter on a microscope slide with a drop of 1:3 solution of dimethyle phthalate and diethy1 oalate and then covered it with a cover clip. We counted samples within 48 hours after mounting, using a microscope with phase contrast option.

最后交代测试结果并得出结论。	In all cases, the workers and areas monitored were exposed to levels of asbestos fibers well below the NIOSHINE standard. The highest exposure we found was that of a driller who was exposed to 0.81 fibers per cubic centimeter. We analyzed the driller's sample by scanning electron microscopy followed by energy dispersive X-ray techniques which identify the chemical nature of each fiber, thereby, verifying the fibers as asbestos or identifying them as other fiber types. Results from these analyses show that the fibers present are tremolit asbestos. We found no nonasbestos fibers.
	
	If you have any questions about the tests, please call or write me.
	
	              Yours truly,
	
	              Gallen Williams
	
	              Gallen Williams
	              Chemistry Professor

第十五章　项目申请

社会进步的一个重要标志是资源不断优化，即最好的资源流向最适合的人及项目。某些机构设立的基金提供资金等支持鼓励在该领域的优秀人士不断进行深入的研究以促进其蓬勃发展。要获得相应的资金支持，首先要递交项目申请，或叫项目申请书、项目申请报告，来说明此项目的价值，说服相关人士把有限的资源投向此项目。为了申请境外的项目资金，或是到国外留学或进行研究，也要首先写出符合要求的英文项目申请。

1. 注意事项

总体来讲要写出成功的项目申请需注意以下几个方面：

(1) 项目申请具有时效。世界发展日新月异，几个月或几年前很有突破性的创新方法可能在今天看来稀松平常，因此项目申请要快而及时，具有时效性，能解决当下问题的项目申请更容易成功。

(2) 学会开发新想法。很多项目的想法直接来自报刊、杂志、电视或网络，而这种想法既不是项目申请人首创的也不是新的，因此这样的项目很难成功。另一方面，新想法新主意不会凭空浮现于脑海，需要大量的阅读和研究，对本领域有深入的了解，从而试图从已有的观点或想法联系、结合或引发出新的观点。

(3) 确认并利用已有的资源。成功的项目申请人要在尊重知识产权的前提下创造性地利用已经掌握的知识，而不是从零开始。

(4) 搜集必要的材料。撰写项目申请最好从搜集必要的材料开始。首先要明确本学科所提供的各种项目基金，很多项目注明了具体的研究性质、方向及写作要求，这种资料在图书馆通常可以找到。

(5) 选择符合自己能力的项目。了解了可供选择的项目后，项目申请人可以选择短期的小项目，也可以选择长期的大项目，而选择的标准如下所示：

①项目的性质和要求，如项目的类型，项目提供的资金数额，项目中涉及的注意事项等；

②申请人的能力，如具备的专业素质水平，现有各方面条件的限制，以及申请人性格；

③申请人所在机构的要求和能力，如所在机构可以提供的支持，该项目对于所在机构发展的贡献程度。

(6) 期限。所有提案申请 (Request for Proposal) 都注明最后提交的期限，如准备时间不够建议第二年再申请相关项目。很多项目具有稳定性，每年的要求变化不大。准备不充足，提交的项目申请质量不高很难在众多候选者中脱颖而出。不同的项目需要准备的时间也有不同。建议经常关注有意申请的项目的相关信息。

2. 项目申请的构成

不同的项目对其成分的组成有不同的要求,但大致包括以下几个方面:

(1)题目页:包括项目的名称,项目主持者的姓名,完整的联系方式,提供基金的机构名称,项目的日期,预算请求以及项目申请人的签名。通常要整个项目申请完成后最后填写题目页,因为有的信息如预算等要最后才能确定。不同项目的题目页会有不同,按要求准确填写。如下例所示:

不同的项目封皮信息会有不同。项目名称及呈交日期,有时也涉及项目编号。申请单位名称:主办机构的名称及地点。具体项目题目:预算部分,开始时间及所需时间。在项目封皮中均包括签名部分	**Proposal to the Department of Education** **Mathematics & Science Improvement Program** *Closing Date*: *March* 16, 2010 NAME OF APPLICANT INSTITUTION: University of ---- NAME AND ADDRESS OF OPERATING UNIT | TITLE OF PROPOSED PROJECT Education for Teachers of Physics	SUBJECT AREA Classroom Education | |---|---|
BUDGET TOTAL	DESIRED STARTING DATE	DURATION
$50,245.00	January 1, 2010	10 weeks | The application institution has a state-approved teacher education program in the subject area of the proposed project. The person whose signature appears as project director is authorized by the applicant institution to make this proposal. Endorsements for the applicant institution: *Signature*: _____ *Name and Title*: _____ SECOND SIGNATURE, IF APPLICABLE: *Signature*: _____ *Name and Title*: _____

在题目页后有时可以加入一个目录,使整个项目清晰易读。

	Education for Teachers of Physics Proposal Table of Contents		
目录页可由办公软件自动生成。如项目很小,有时该项也可省略。	I. PROJECT SUMMARY	Page	1
	II. PROJECT DESCRIPTION		2
	A. Objectives		2
	B. Participant Selection		4
	1. Number of participants		4
	2. Policy for admission		4
	3. Selection procedure		5
	C. Program Content		6
	1. Physics 110		6
	2. Physics electives		7
	3. Integrated laboratory		8
	4. Seminar		9
	D. Additional Components		9
	1. Follow-up activities		9
	2. Evaluation		9
	III. SFAFF		10
	IV. FACILITIES		11
	A. Instructional Facilities		
	B. Housing Facilities		12
	V. INSTITUTION SUPPORT		12
	VI. BUDGET		14

(2)行动纲要:对项目的目的、目标、需要、完成的衡量标准及结果进行清楚的概括。若项目最后得以采用出版,此部分则是出版的可以代表整个项目的简短描述,要清楚简洁并包含所有重要的观点。行动纲要十分重要,其包括了该项目最重要的信息,像广告一样推销该项目,说服收阅人支持该项目。基本上行动纲要包括以下几个部分:

①要解决的问题:简单陈述申请人发现的问题,可由一至两段构成;

②解决方法:简单描述该项目,包括该项目的具体措施以及实施后的影响,花费时间及项目实施的人员,可由一至两段构成;

③经费要求:对该项目所需资金进行说明,可由一段构成;

④机构及专业素质:简单介绍所在机构或个人的名称、历史、性质、活动以及开展并完成该项目的能力,可由一段构成。

撰写成功的行动纲要的诀窍是在整个项目申请准备完毕后再撰写。所有关键的重点都将熟捻于心。通常,行动纲要控制在300个英文单词之内。

以下三个行动纲要因项目的复杂程度差异而长短不同,但均成功地呈现给读者该项目的重点部分,并十分有说服力。

示例1:

这是计划在校园中实施的项目。虽然只有一段,但涵盖了该项目最关键的方面,即该项目实施的原因、依据、需要的经费、所用时间及起始时间、实施的人员以及评估的方式,让收阅人迅速了解该项目的主要内容。	**Proposal Summary** An investigation shows that students and faculty in Department of Criminal Justice Studies (DCJS) like the concept of peer advising. Peer advising is being successfully used in other colleges in the United States. This proposal reqests $5,926 to set up a pilot program in peer advising in DCJS. The pilot program would run for 13 months from April 2010 through April 2011. The pilot program will be monitored by DCJS faculty. Evaluative reports will be written an dissemination at the end of the pilot program.

示例2:

Project Renewal 是项目的名称,此项目需要50,000美元来为纽约城的流动诊所增加一名工作人员。第一段交代了该项目的主要内容及经费要求。 第二段,介绍纽约流动诊所的相关背景。 第三段,解释说明当前流动诊所工作中遇到的困难及增加工作人员的必要性。	**Executive Summary** Project Renewal requests from the Memorial Fund a grand of $50,000 to support the addition of a Social Worker to our Mobile Medical Outreach Clinic-or MedVan, as it is known on te streets of New York. Launched in 1986, MedVan was the nation's first mobile medical clinic to serve homeless people, providing primary care and referrals to thousands of indigent NewYorkers on the street, and in the shelters, soup kitchens, and drop-in centers where they congregate. Two critical factors make it urgently necessary to break more new ground by adding a Social Worker to MedVan's professional team: first, MedVan's patients are displaying ever more complex suites of medical problems, often requiring multiple visits and long term care to arrive at a complete diagnosis and treatment-a situation that has severely stretched the capacity of MedVan's medical professionals; second, though MedVan patients often qualify for medical entitlements and other public services, they frequently need help in obtaining them-a need that MedVan's medical team has valiantly tried to satisfy, while also trying to meet an ever more demanding patient load.

第四段,详细而又具体地列出增加的工作人员将如何解决流动诊所工作中存在的问题。	Adding a Social Worker to MedVan will solve these problems by: ◇ Helping significantly more patients to obtain entitlements and other services; ◇ Tracking patients through referrals, which will encourage them to take full advantage of available services; ◇ Freeing the MedVan team to treat more patients; ◇ Resulting in more repeat patients, which will enable the MedVan team to perform more complete diagnoses and treatment.
最后一段,简洁地说明此项目成功实施的重要意义。	The ultimate benefit of this initiative will be improved health among MedVan's homeless patients. This is an absolutely essential step in the process of helping homeless people to rehabilitate themselves-which is Project Renewal's mission.

示例3:

这是一个社区公益服务的项目。第一段,简单介绍此项目的历史及产生的背景。	**Executive Summary** At Mind-Builders, we believe that family is our community's most precious resource. In 2002, in response to the needs of the growing numbers of young girls and women in our community faced with the breakup of their families and removal of their youngsters to foster care, Mind-Builders initiated the Family Services Center.
第二段,简单地介绍实施该项目的机构信息以及该项目的作用。	The Family Service Center provides intensive counseling, education and support services to young girls and women who are parents, many of whom have a history of substance abuse. The Program helps women to remian drug free; develop appropriate parenting and other life skills; and to become regularly engaged in constructive activities that promote positive family and community lifestyles.
第三段,说明该项目要解决的问题和解决方式。	Many of the women and young girls who are served by the Family Services Center have a background of public assistance. Some are single parents, some are married, and some have steady work histories. What all of these women have in common is that they have been overwhelmed by the pressures and destructive influences of an environment and culture where substance abuse and crime run rampant, and poverty and dependence are a way of life. Mind-Builders Family Services Center offers at-risk families a real alternative with practical help available 24 hours a day.
第四段,进一步说明项目可以有效成功地实施。	Mind-Builders has a continuous record of honest and effective service based on the premise that communities can best respond to the urban crisis by drawing upon their own traditions, talents and determination to create positive altrnatives for families. With the Family Services Center, Mind-Builders further enhances a community movement, thus enabling a neighborhood to achieve empowerment and act as a positive force for change.

最后,说明该项目的预算以及需要得到的经济支持。	Our project budget for this year is $558,281. To date, we have secured a $500,000 lead grant from the Child Welfare Administration and have received one generous commitment of $25,000 for this project from the Alternative Trust. To met our budget, we must raise $33,281 from the private sector We request a grant of $10,000 from the Works Fund to help maintain the Family Service Center's counseling and support services offered to at-risk women and girls.

(3) 目的陈述:清楚地描述项目要达到的目标及目的以及预期要达到的结果,并说明此项目的深远意义。确认此项目的目的与基金提供方的要求吻合。

(4) 项目展望与任务:项目展望指若从宏观上看,该项目顺利进行,将产生怎样深远的影响;任务描述则指从微观上看该项目如何进行。有时,部分(3)与部分(4)可以结合在一起。如下所示:

清楚地叙述此项目的相关背景及重要意义。	Physics is the study of the laws of nature at the most fundamental level. As a result, all of modern science and technology derives much of its success from physics. It is because of scientific discoveries and applications that we live in such a technologically advanced world. For decades, our nation has been the leader in science and technology. These past developments are strongly tied to the successful education of our citizenry, and education wil continue to be the key in the development of our nation. Education in the sciences and mathematics is not only important in terms of training future scientists, engineers, and technicians, it is equally important for those who opt for other careers. We live in a highly complex country in which the results of science and technology affect us on a daily basis. We benefit from advances in communications, entertainment, and medicine, and at the same time, we must contend with unwanted results such as pollution and the danger of nuclear annihilation. As consumers and as citizens, both scientists and nonscientists must be prepared to make intelligent decisions regarding science and technology. Recent studies have shown that our nation has fallen behind many other industrialized ountries in educating its citizens. In addressing the reasons for this decline, someone has poointed out a severe shortage of qualified science and mathematics teachers almost everywhere in the country. A recent survey of all the school superintendents in this country has documented the shortage of qualfied physics teacher (see Attachment). While this study clearly identified secondary schools where inadequately prepared teachers are teaching physics, it did not include the many small, rural secondary schools throughout the state which do not offer physics at all because of the lack of a properly trained teacher. Both of these situationsare of major concern.

项目展望与任务。	Of the many alternatives which could prove to be effective solutions to this dilemma, the most immediate would seem to be to retrain secondary teachers who are already certified in other fields. It is for this reason that the university enthusiastically accepts the state department of education's call for proposals. The university proposes an institute which is planned to meet the following objectives. The program will provide 15 teachers from throughout the nation opportunities to: 1. Develop the understandings and skills needed to effectively teach the most commonly used physics textbook in this nation's schools at this time. An experienced secondar school physics teacher will provide specific training to help participants use this text in the classroom and in the laboratory. 2. Develop the knowledge and understanding which is expected in basic uniersity physics courses. 3. Develop laboratory skills associated with basic physics courses, including the use of computers in the laboratory. Emphasis will be placed on designing low-cost experiments which can be used in all secondary schools, including those with the least facilities, equipment, and supplies. 4. Enable each participant ot earn 12 semester hours of credit toward Clas B certification in physics. It will be communicated, however, in the announcement of this program, that this benefit to the participants is secondary in significance, that the actual number of hours it will reduce certification attainment will vary among the participants, and that neither the university nor the state department of educaion will be obligated to provide futher grants to those students to help them complete their certification requirements. Indeed, the participants, themselves, will be encouraged to assume this responsibility. The program will provide for follow-up reinforcement and evaluation during the coming school year.

(5)需要描述清楚地描述出项目进行中遇到的困难。可使用真实的数据来说明此项目的必要性,紧迫性及重要性。如下所示:

详细说明此项目所针对的特殊问题。	**Statement of Need** 　　Mind-Builders serves the communities of Garfield. Both neighbourhoods are fragile places with unertain futures. Poverty, crime and drug use have increased at an alarming rate in this area over the past 20 years. Working class families struggle to maintain a good quality of life within this economically mixed area set against a backdrop of major areas of poverty and significant crime. Because of their critical importance, Tocoma has designated these neighborhoods as Special Neighborhood Stabilization Areas and targeted them as a priority for human service resources. Mind-Builers is the only organization of its kind in an area underserved by social programs and youth services. 　　The young women and girls of our community face an enormous uphill struggle to make a safe passage through adolescence into adulthood. As teenagers, they are often overwhelmed by the difficulties of living in a hostile environment where widespread drug use and street violence and crime put personal safety at constant risk.
运用具体的数字更有说服力。	The very common occurrence of teenage pregnancy, combined with a lack of economic resources and employable skills have put many young women on a fast track to welfare dependency before they have even left thir teens. Most recent statistics for our community show that 41.5% of our young people 18 years and under reside in households dependent on public assistance. 　　Young women too often adopt behavior patterned on a cycle of poverty and dependence. These women grow up resisting and fearing chage from the habits they have picked up on the streets, which often includes alcohol and / or substance abuse. 　　The economic and social pressures faced by young women and girls who have children stretches families to the breaking point. When mothers trun to alcohol and / or substance abuse, or succumb to other pressures, the family falls apart, and the children are placed in foster care. The costs to society, in both human and monetary terms, resulting from the separation of children from their families are tremendous. To avoid these devastating lossed we must respond by empowering, not punishing young girls and women and helping them to build positive lifestyles andto maintain their families

(6)项目设计。包括项目进行的方法,步骤及行动方案。行动方案包括要进行的所有步骤以及各项步骤进行的顺序,具体到时间、地点及执行的人员,确保项目的进行符合项目的总体目标。项目设计部分要展示出申请人对整个项目深思熟虑。设计中具体的要素在项目执行过程中可能会有变动,但首先要有一个清晰的计划。可加入有关此方面的文献作为参考资料来支持此项目设计。如下所示:

示例1:

| 注意每部分的名称并不是固定的。详细说明该项目的组成部分及具体的实施步骤,包括时间安排和具体的内容。 | **Program Design and Implementation**
　　The Family Services Center establishes a supportive, task-centered and goal oriented partnership with the families. The Center combines intensive counseling, 24-hour crisis intervention by beeper, and the development of life and arenting skills. The Center arranges for training, advocacy, supplemental child care, nutrition and health cre education and transportation and／or escort services that enable families to stay together in their communities.

　　Within 48 hours of referral from a Child Welfare Administration worker, a Family Center Counselor completes a joint visit with the CWA worker to the family's home for a formal introduction to the family. The Family Services Center Staff are expected to perform whatever tasks are reasonable and necessary to ensure the safety of the mothers and children in their own home, while exhausting every effort to prevent the children's foster care placement. Staff Counselors develop trusting and supportive relationships with the women and girls and their children. Counselors assess, identify and reassess family problems; develop prioritized strategies for the problems' resolution; and structure plans to accomplish their goals.

　　In addition, a series of Family Education Workshops presents speakers who discuss issues and topics of relevance to women. Presentations sheduled for this year include; "Family Conflicts-Problem Resolution and Effective Communication," "Parenting Skills-Discipline and Praise／Constructive Criticism and Building Self-Esteem in Children," and "Job Readiness and Family Budgeting － Earning an Income and Making the Most of it." |

示例2：

可以从格式中看出在此项目中共有4个重要的步骤。	**Program Content** 　　The major components of this program are as follows: 1. PHYSICS 110-Secondary School Physics for Teachers. The most immediate impact the proposed program can have on the teaching of high school physics is to improve the effectiveness and confidence of the participating techers in the use of a text and related materials in their classrooms in the coming year. This course wll concentrate mostly on the content of the text; laboratory work will be covered in a separate phase of the institute. Although all the institute staff will particpate in this course in appropriate ways, the lead instructor will be an experienced high school teacher. The survey of the text will be intensive and detailed. The rationale for the course is that the most important prerequisite for effective use of the text is a teacher who has a thorough competence in all the subject matter of the text and confidence in the ability to explin that subject material to students. Each concept in the text will be examined and developed to whatever depth is necessary in order to achieve that competence on the part of all participants. 　　This course will also cover methods for supplementing the high school physics text. Demonstrations will be used as an aid in teaching the textbook material, with an emphasis on the use of low-cost demonstrations for high school courses. Computer-aided instruction will also be covered. Many high schools are acquiring microcomputers which can be used as a tool to help teach physics, if adequate software is avalable. A part of the course will emphasize selecting and using software for computer-aided physics instruction. 2. Physics Electives 　　Each participant will select one appropriate undergraduate physics course during each sesion of the summer term. The course selected by the participant will depend upon the prior experience. Participants who have not taken a physics course in recent years will be advised to enroll in PH101. Because of the special needs of the participants, a special section of PH101 will be offered during the first summer session which will be open only to the institute participants. In addition to regular class attendance, each participant will be scheduled for tree hours per week of tutorial meetings with the class instructor. The purpose of the tutorial meetings is to provide the extra in-depth explanations of course material that may be useful to participants who have been away from undergraduate study in the sciences for an extended period. Participants will be evaluated on their work in regular classroom activities as well as tutorial sessions.

	3. Integrated Laboratory for Physics Elective and for Physics 101

	Laboratory experiences are important both for the physics elective and the survey of a secondary scool physics text. In the proposed program, these laboratory experiences will be integrated into a single laboratory organized for the institute participants. The laboratory will meet for thirteen three-hour sessions each term. Experiments will be selected from the regular lab of the physics elective and, wherever possible, will be conducted in parallel with similar experiments scaled for use in a high school laboratory. The purpose of this approach is to give participants two types of experiences. First, they need knowledge of the type of experiments currently conducted in undergraduate college level courses. More importantly, however, they need practical experience in setting up laboratory experiments appropriate for the high school physicslaboratory. The content of the integrated lab will be planned on an individual basis by the insructor of the physics elective and the consulting high school teacher. A graduate student will assist in the laboratoy.
	
	    Some of the laboratory meetings will also be devoted to using microcomputers in the physics laboratory. Some experiments will be performed in which the computer is used to assist with taking and analyzing data.
	4. Seminar for Teachers.
	    In order that the separate components of the program may be brought together to form a more unified experience, a weekly seminar for participants in the institute will be held. The content of the seminar will, in part, be developed based on the perceived needs of participants. In part, however, the seminar will be derected toward suupplemental material and other sources of information on opics of current interest, puzzles, and games that stimulate interest in physics.

    (7)管理方案:包括项目设计的时间表,可用表格的形式来说明项目中涉及的个人及其具体职责的关系。要努力说服项目收阅人此项目安排有序,时间利用有效,并说明项目执行过程中的决策方法。

良好的执行是项目完成的关键。此部分介绍项目的管理,包括项目的负责人员及具体职责,工作范围等。	**Management** William Monica will supervise the entire peer advising experiment as part of her duties as Coordinator of Advisers for the DCJS program. He will be readily accessible to the peer advisers. He will monitor their procedures and provide advice and counsel when needed. Throughout the year she will provide informal reports to Mr. Mont. At the end of the experiment she will provide an evaluation of the peer advising.

(8)评估方案:描述将怎样评价及衡量项目的进程以及成果;对需要收集的数据类型,使用到的工具,数据分析的过程以及结果的使用和记录做出计划。此部分计划最好包括定性数据收集方法(侧重于数据的性质)及定量数据收集方法(侧着于数据的数量)。确保评估方案与项目的目标紧密相连。评价既要有完整性又要有概括性。

示例1:

在此项目中共提供了两种评估方式。第一种为由参与者进行评估。	**Evaluation** 　　The proposed program will be subjected to two types of ealuation. (a) Evaluation by participants. 　　Participants will be asked to evaluate the program at two stages. The initial evaluation wil be made by a questionnaire administered near the end of the summer session. The effectiveness of each conmponent of the institute will be evaluated. A second evaluation will be conducted near the end of the school year after participants have had classroom experience in using skills developed in the institute.
第二种为由非项目参与者进行评估。评估方式要避免单一,做到公正客观。	(b) Evaluation by an outside observer. 　　At an appropriate point in the institute an evaluation will be sought from one or more outside observers. For this evaluation an effort will be made to obtain the services of an individual with supervisory experience and special knowledge in secodary level science education, in a national school system, the state department of education, and/or another institution of higher education in the nation.

示例2:

对于项目的评估,很多时候也可采取报告或论文的形式。	*Evaluation*. April 1~30, 2011. During April 2011, the two peer advisers will consolidate the information they have gathered throughout the year and write their evaluation report. A total of 18 hours is scheduled for this task.

示例3:

该项目采用定期座谈、发放问卷、提交报告、实地采访等形式评估推进项目的进行。问卷的写法参看本书的下一节。	**EVALUATION** 　　The Family Service Center staff meet weekly to discuss and evaluate individual cases and share ideas to develop and execute plans to serve the program participants' needs. A Staff Survey and a Family Interview Questionnaire are completed after the six month interval of each family's involvement in the program. Pursuant to a CWA mandate the program must provide monthly statistical reports and schedule periodic on-site visits.

需要注意的是项目的评估不是孤立的元素,而是整个项目的有机组成部分。	Mind-Builders is in the process of structuring a formal Family Services Center evaluation component for integration into routine service operation. The new evaluation component will consist of an evaluation by an independent source, program audits and / or review of program planning and management systems.

（9）宣传方案:描述怎样应用并促进此方案的进行。包括详细描述将提交的报告类型,在相关会议上的讲演,怎样利用各种方法来使项目顺利进行,如网络、刊物或其他多媒体。

（10）项目人员资质:展示项目执行者的能力来表明其整个团体可以成功完成该项目;列出项目重要执行人员以及其职责并附加相关人员的简历。尤其需要强调项目主持人的资质。

对于此项目,在这一部分首先概述说明项目参与人员的数量以及构成。 接着说明人员选拔的原则和标准。	**Participant** 1. Number of participants. Fifteen participants will be provided total support. Up to three additional certified secondary teachers who wish to gain certification in the area of physics will be allowed to participate in the program without support. The university will provide tuition grants for these teachers. 2. Policy for admission. Of particular concern is that some teachers are now teaching physics in the nation's secondary schools without having been certified. Hence, the selection of participants for this institute will give first priority to noncertified teachers who are already teaching physis in our secondary schools. Other secondary teachers who teach sourses in other fields have been offered opportunities to teach physics as replacements for retiring teachers and noncertified teachers. These teachers who also have positions awaiting them next fall will receive secondary priority in the screening of applicants for this institute. If there are other teachers who hold secondary teaching ertificates who wish to achieve certification in the area of physics, they will receive the next priority in the selection process. Candidates within each of these groups will be rated on the basis of letters from their employers, previous scholarships as evidenced by their academic records, and their personal commitment to teaching physcs as expressed in a letter which they will be required to write. An attempt will be made to select applicants from small rural high schools over a broad geographic area.

然后说明人员选拔的具体步骤，包括时间安排等。	3. Selection procedure a. All teachers holding temporary certification in physics will be identified through department of education records. Each will receive a notice of this institute. All superintendents and curriculum supervisorswill also receive a copy of the announcement. An announcement will also be sent to the department of education with a request for inclusion in the local newsletter. b. To be considered for this institute, applications must include a participant information form, a letter of testimony from an appropriate school administrator which specifies the candidate's expected teaching assignment, an academic transcript, and when available, test scores. Applications must be received by March 17, 2010. c. The selection will be completedand notification will be sent by May 10. Participants will be asked to respond by May 22.
最后，作为补充，说明该项目涉及的其他工作人员。	**STAFF** Professional staff for the proposed institute will be composed of one coordinator, two assistant coordinators, a consulting high school teacher, the instructors of the physics elective, and the lab instructor. Resume of principal participating staff are included as an appendix. A physics graduate student with experience in physics laboratories will supervise the integrated laboratory. The content of the laboratory will be a joint responsibility of the consulting high school physics teacher and the instructors for the physics electives.

（11）预算：描述项目的成本，并详细说明项目进行中需要的各种支持。预算必须以项目的需要以及设计为基础，确保列出的预算项目合理，有时要对各项预算进行简单说明。

示例1：

在此项目中预算分为两个大部分，一部分是自身可以解决的，另一部分则需要项目基金的支持。	**INSTITUTIONAL SUPPORT** The university is able to commit support to the proposed program in the following ways: Released time for co-ordinators and secretarial staff Head 25% for 12 weeks $ 3,000 Teacher of Physics 15% for 12 weeks 2,000 Secretary 10% for 14 weeks 300 Supplies for curriculum development projects, Correspondence, etc. 200 Travel for follow-up activities 300 Tuition grants will be provided by the university 3,000 TOTAL IN-KIND CONTRIBUTION $ 8,800

| 用大写字母来表示预算构成的几大方面。 | **BUDGET**
TUITION AND FEES:
Tuition
University Fees
Lab Fees

FIRST-TIME APPLICANTS:
PARTICIPANT SUPPORT:
Commuters
Mileage
Meal
Lab kids/ materials
Textbooks

Residents
Room
Mileage
Meals
Lab kids/materials
Textbooks

TOTAL PARTICIPANT SUPPORT
TRAVEL FOR FOLLOW-UP ACTIVITIES
INDIRECT COST REIMBURSEMENT
PROJECT BUDGET TOTAL for 15 | $ 500
150
$\underline{100}$
750 X 15 = 11,250
100

$ 700
200
50
$\underline{30}$
800
X 4 = 3200

$ 500
60
600
40
$\underline{30}$
1230
X 11 = 13,530
$ 28,080
500
2,000
30,580 |

示例2:

预算部分用图表形式表现比较清晰明了。不要遗漏任何细节上的花销。合理的预算是提案被采用的关键。	**Budget** 　　Because DCJS is furnishing office space, office supplies, and clerical help, the entire budget needed is for salary for the two peer advisers. The normal student hourly wage of $7.50 is requested. The budget breaks down in the following manner:

Training Time	Salary for 2 peer advisers	20 hours	$ 130.00
Office Hours	Salary for 3 hours of advising a day for 176 days	528 hours	3432.00
	Salary for additional advising time in September Advising time in september	40 hours	260.00
Evaluation Time	Salary	16 hours	104.00
	Total	604 hours	$ 3,926.00

(12)持续性计划:表明从长远来看将进一步进行研究,即若得到基金的支持将以此作为开始,使今后的研究与此项目成为一个有机的整体。持续性是对一个项目的基本要求,若一个项目有很广阔的发展前景将提高其申请成功的几率。

此部分表明在此项目中,在项目结束后还会有相关的跟踪调查,修正项目中出现的问题,更为今后进一步研究提供思路。	Follow-Up Activities During the second half of the fall semester the co-directors will make an on-site visit to each participants's school. This follow-up visit will serve two purposes: (1) it will provide an opportunity to assess the value of the institute and (2) it will provide each participant opportunities to clarify any misunderstandings and to fill in any knowledge gaps about the content or skills set forth in the objectives of this institute.

(13)附件:根据不同项目的性质以及要求此部分可附加不同的必要的文件,如包括佐证书(Letter of Support)、审计书(Audit)、项目执行人员的个人简历等。在项目最开始阶段列出详细的所需要的文件的清单并分配相关人员对此文件进行收集整理。只附加对整个项目起到重要作用的文件。

第十六章 问 卷

　　问卷即是发给一定数量人的关于某个主题的一系列问题,是一种书面采访。和面对面的采访相比,问卷可以收集到更多人的观点,不受时间和地域的限制,发一封邮件就可完成。被采访的人也不必忍受面对面被提问的压力,可以轻松作答,并有充足的时间思考,使答案更加准确而富有逻辑。被访问者只需面对书面问卷,不受提问人语气及表情的影响,可以更加客观地回答问题。相比之下,问卷采访的成本也远远低于现场采访。另一方面,问卷调查也有自身的缺点。如只有对问卷感兴趣的人才会认真地填写问卷,这一点将影响问卷的准确性;现场采访的可控性更强,可根据被采访的回答进一步地提出问题,而这是问卷无法企及的;收回问卷整理信息需要大量的时间和精力等。

　　一份问卷只有认真合理地设计才会收到预期的效果,以便用最少的投入搜集到最多的有用信息。

　　成功的问卷要遵循以下原则:

　　◇简洁。通常来讲,问卷越长,被采访者完成或返回问卷的可能性就越小。

　　◇易于理解。让人迷惑的问题会得到让人迷惑的答案,问卷的用词要准确简单。为了减少后续汇总答案的工作量及被采访者的负担,最好用"Yes"或"No"就可以回答问题,如:

Would you be willing to work a four-day work week, ten hours a day, with every Friday off?

Yes _____

No _____

No opinion _____

　　如果不能简单地用"Yes"或"No"来回答问题,可把可能的答案按照一定的标准划分为几个区间。答案的划分必须要客观,用词必须要中性,避免有所倾向的答案项。如下例:

How many hours of overtime would you be willing to work each work?

4 hours _____   10 hours _____

6 hours _____   More than 10 hours _____

8 hours _____   No overtime _____

　　在这则问题中,已经预设了采访者愿意超长工作,最好把这个问题改成:

Would you be willing to work overtime?

Yes _____   No _____

If yes, how many hours of overtime would you be willing to work each week?

4 hours _____   10 hours _____

6 hours _____   12 hours _____

8 hours _____   More than 12 hours _____

　　这样一来提问更加科学,收到的信息反馈也会更加地准确。

　　在设计问题时,必须时刻铭记最后要汇总所有的答案,所以确保答案易于统计,而符合这样答案的问题通常不需要被访者自己写出具体的答案,避免让被访者自由发表观点的开放式问题。如有必要,问卷可以包括一个部分供被访者就问卷的主题发表观点以供参考。

通过邮件发放的问卷要附加一封说明目的来由的书信，其中包括问卷的发放者信息，问卷的目的，问卷的使用方式以及期待的问卷返回时间。如果所提供的信息需要保密或是被访者的身份不会被公开，也要在此信中说明。

◇科学选择被访者。根据问卷的目的，制定选择被访者的标准，有的需要多而全，而有的只需发放给有代表性的被访者。

如下的问卷为一个大公司发放给其参加为期 6 个月的灵活工作时间项目的雇员，根据这个项目，雇员每周工作 5 天共计 40 小时，其开始工作及结束工作的时间都比较灵活。仅供参考：

此问卷以备忘录形式呈现。	**MEMORANDUM** 　　　　　　　　　　　　　　　　　　　　March 5, 2010 To: All Company Staff From: Nickson Bannett, Manager of Human Resources *NB* Subject: Review of Flexible Working Hours Program Please complete this questionnaire regarding Lexes Corporation's trial program of flexible working hours. Your answers will help us to decide whether the program should continue. Return the questionnaire to the Human Resources by March 29. If you want to discuss any item in morre detail, call Tina Petterson in Human Resources at extension 5678. 1. What kind of position do you hold? 　　_____　　　　_____ 　　　supervisory　　　　　　nonsupervisory 2. Indicate your exact starting time under flexitime. 3. Where do you live? 　　Lakewood County _____ 　　Greene County _____ 　　Montgomery County _____ 　　Other, specify _____
	4. How do you usually travel to work? 　　Walk _____ 　　Drive alone _____ 　　Car pool _____ 　　Bus _____ 　　Bicycle _____ 　　Motorcycle _____ 　　Train _____ 　　Other, specify _____

5. Has flexitime affected your commuting time? If so, please indicate the approximate number of minutes.

    _____   _____   _____
       increase   decrease   no change

6. If you drive, has flexitime affected the amount of time it takes to find a parking space?

    _____   _____   _____
       increase   decrease   no change

7. Do you think that flexitime has affected your productivity?

    _____   _____   _____
       increase   decrease   no change

8. Have you had difficulty getting in touch with colleagues whose work schedules are different from yours?

    _____   _____
         Yes   No

9. Have you had trouble scheduling meetings?

    _____   _____
         Yes   No

10. Has flexitime affected the way you feel about your job?

    _____   _____   _____
     feel better   feel worse   no change

11. How important is it for you to have flexibility in your working hours?
    Very _____   Not very _____
    Somewhat _____   Not at all _____

12. If you have children, has flexitime made it easier or more difficult for you to obtain babysitting or day-care services?

    _____   _____   _____
       easier   more difficult   no change

13. Do you recommend that the flexitime program be made permanent?
    Yes _____   No _____

14. Do you have suggestions for any changes in the program? If so, please specify.
    _____

参考文献

[1] 秦狄辉. 科技英语写作[M]. 北京:外语教学与研究出版社,2007.
[2] 俞炳丰. 科技英语论文实用写作指南[M]. 西安:西安交通大学出版社,2003.
[3] 李旭,张志宏,陈大中,等. 英语科技论文写作指南[M]. 北京:国防工业出版社,2005.
[4] 魏汝尧,董益坤. 科技英语教程[M]. 北京:北京大学出版社,2005.
[5] 张道珍. 实用英语语法[M]. 北京:外语教学与研究出版社,1995.
[6] 辜嘉铭. 英语论文写作精要[M]. 武汉:武汉大学出版社,2006.
[7] 黄欣. 科技英语写作教程[M]. 北京:化学工业出版社,2009.
[8] 金坤林. 如何撰写和发表SCI期刊论文[M]. 北京:机械工业出版社,2011.
[9] 孔庆炎. 英语科技论文和科技文摘写作精解[M]. 武汉:华中理工大学出版社,1997.
[10] 李晓文,刘晓辉. 英语学术写作:传播科学的媒介[M]. 北京:机械工业出版社,2011.
[11] 任胜利. 英语科技论文撰写与投稿[M]. 北京:科学出版社,2009.
[12] 唐国全,何小玲. 科技英语论文报告写作[M]. 北京:北京航空航天大学出版社,2004.
[13] 王建武,李民权,曾小珊. 科技英语写作:理论·技巧·范例[M]. 西安:西北工业大学,2008.
[14] 郑福裕. 科技论文英文摘要编写指南[M]. 北京:清华大学出版社,2008.
[15] CHARLES T. BRUSAW, GERALD J. ALRED, WALTER E. OLIU. Handbook of Technical Writing [M]. 4th ed. New York:St. Martin's Press,1993.
[16] Donald H. Cunningham,Elizabeth O. Smith,Thomas E. Pearsall, Thomson Wadsworth. How to Write for the World of Work [M]. 7th ed. US:Wa dsworth Publishing,2005.
[17] Northey, Margot & Jewinski, Judi. Making Sense-A student's Guide to Research and Writing [M]. 2nd ed. Canada:Oxford University Press,2007.
[18] Richard Worth. Webster's New World Business Writing Handbook. [M]. Indiana:Wiley Publishing, Inc. ,2002.